CHRISTOLOGY IN CONTEXT

THE CHRISTIAN STORY

A Pastoral Systematics

CHRISTOLOGY IN CONTEXT

THE CHRISTIAN STORY

A Pastoral Systematics

VOLUME 4

Gabriel Fackre

WILLIAM B. EERDMANS PUBLISHING COMPANY
GRAND RAPIDS, MICHIGAN / CAMBRIDGE, U.K.

© 2006 Gabriel Fackre

All rights reserved

Published 2006 by

Wm. B. Eerdmans Publishing Co.

255 Jefferson Ave. S.E., Grand Rapids, Michigan 49503 /

P.O. Box 163, Cambridge CB3 9PU U.K.

Printed in the United States of America

11 10 09 08 07 06   7 6 5 4 3 2 1

Library of Congress Cataloging-in-Publication Data

Fackre, Gabriel J.

Christology in context / Gabriel Fackre.

p.   cm. — (The Christian story, a pastoral systematics; v. 4)

ISBN-10: 0-8028-6314-0 / ISBN-13: 978-0-8028-6314-0 (pbk.: alk. paper)

1. Jesus Christ — Person and offices. 2. Pastoral theology.   I. Title.   II. Series.

BT205.F33   2006

232 — dc22

2006009367

www.eerdmans.com

Contents

Acknowledgments

A s befits a pastoral systematics, the christological themes in this work have been tried out over the years at pastors' conferences and seminary lectureships — United Church of Christ; Evangelical Lutheran Church in America; Presbyterian Church, USA; Episcopal Church, USA; Reformed Church in America; United Methodist; Moravian; American Baptist; Southern Baptist; and Roman Catholic — as well as in ecumenical and evangelical venues. Of course, students in systematics classes at Andover Newton over a quarter century have had to put up with their professor's ruminations and formulations on this subject and, in turn, have had their say and effect. Then too, as mentioned in the Introduction, colleagues during a stint at the Princeton Center of Theological Inquiry gave me some important feedback. In an era of the Internet, a whole new testing ground for theological proposals has emerged, so twelve years of back-and-forth with numerous pastors (and some relentless lay theologians) on a "Confessing Christ" site have had their impact on what appears here. Most of all, thirty years of a weekly "Theological Tabletalk" group of pastors and faculty begun at Lancaster Theological Seminary, continued at Andover Newton Theological School, and currently conducted on Cape Cod have meant hearing a constant kindly yes and no to one or another of the ideas here presented. I acknowledge my deep debt to all.

Thanks go to publications that have given me permission to reprint the substance of articles in their journals or books:

"Claiming Jesus as Savior in a Pluralist World" in the on-line *Journal of Christian Theological Education* (2003)

"Christology in Evangelical Perspective" in *Evangelical Theology in Transition: Theologians in Dialogue with Donald Bloesch,* 1999, Elmer Colyer, copyright holder for InterVarsity Press

"Christ and Those Who Have Never Heard," as "Divine Perseverance" in *What about Those Who Have Never Heard?* John Sanders, editor, copyright 1995, InterVarsity Press, PO Box 1400, Downers Grove, IL 60615

"Christology in Ecumenical Perspective" as "The Joint Declaration and the Reformed Tradition," in *Justification and the Future of the Ecumenical Movement: The Joint Declaration on the Doctrine of Justification,* William G. Rusch, editor (Collegeville, MN: Liturgical Press, 2003)

"Christ in Chiaroscuro" in *Theology Today* 33 (1976)

"Christ and the Angels" from "Angels Heard and Demons Seen" in *Theology Today* 51 (1994)

"The Galilean Christ," as "Bones Strong and Weak in the Skeletal Structure of Schillebeeckx's Christology" in *Journal of Ecumenical Studies* Vol. XXX, No. 2 (Spring 1984)

"The Risen Christ" as "The Resurrection and the Uniqueness of Christ" in *Christ the One and Only,* Sung Wook Chung, editor and copyright holder (Baker Academic, 2005)

"Addendum on 'The Passion of the Christ'" in *Lectionary Homiletics,* Vol. XV, No. 4 (June-July 2004)

"The Person of Christ and the Being of the Church" in *Tradition and Trajectory,* Theodore Louis Trost, editor (forthcoming).

Other chapters have appeared in out-of-print journals or publications: portions of "The Crucified Christ" as "A Theology of the Cross" (November 1975) and "Christ and the People of Israel" as "Perspectives on the Place of Israel in Christian Faith" in the former *Andover Newton Review* (Winter 1990), and "The Work of Christ and the Doing of Ministry" as "Christ's Ministry and Ours," in *Laity Project,* Andover Newton Theological School, 1982.

How can I adequately acknowledge my debt to Dorothy Fackre for all she has contributed to my thinking about deep theological things? Often by dedicating a volume to her. That will come again in volume 5 of this series on the doctrine of the church, the fruit of our common labors in the Body of Christ. This time, just a simple, but profound, "Thanks."

Introduction

Dietrich Bonhoeffer bestirred a generation to ask, ever and again, "Who is Jesus Christ for us today?" That question was a constant for me in years of preaching to milltown parishioners, then teaching students preparing for pastoral ministry. It resulted in a mountain of scribbled notes and some random essays.

However, the "today" became "todays" in our era of rapidation when every decade brought new challenges to be addressed by the Word preached and taught.[1] Those contexts proved consuming for this writer. A full-scale answer to Bonhoeffer's question was placed on hold, "Christology" as the doctrine of the Person and Work of Jesus Christ. What seemed more pressing was joining Jesus in the ranks of the civil rights revolutionaries in the 60s and thus Christology cum *The Pastor and the World,* then witnessing to Jesus in movements of *Do and Tell: Engagement Evangelism* in the 70s, then challenging the captivity of Christ to political fundamentalism in *The Religious Right and Christian Faith* in the 80s, then finding common ground in Christ in the 90s in an evangelical exchange of *Ecumenical Faith in Evangelical Perspective* and in an ecumenical dialogue on *Affirmations and Admonitions,* and more.[2]

---

1. So argued in "Theology, Ephemeral, Conjunctural and Perennial," in *Altered Landscapes: Christianity in America, 1935-1985,* a *Festschrift* for Robert Handy, ed. David Lotz with Donald Shriver and John F. Wilson (Grand Rapids: Eerdmans, 1989), pp. 246-67.

2. Books along the way: *The Pastor and the World* (Philadelphia: United Church Press, 1964); *Do and Tell: Engagement Evangelism in the 70s* (Grand Rapids: Eerdmans, 1973); *The*

These decades were not all exercises in *ad hoc* theology. As I served for the last quarter of the twentieth century as a professor of systematic theology, Christology had to be confronted in doctrinal as well as cultural context. That meant locating who Christ was and what Christ did within the biblical trajectory that ran from creation to consummation. So came an early appreciation for a narrative framework for faith and the beginning of the *Christian Story* series in 1978. As it unfolded, the time approached to deal with the chapter on Jesus Christ. The Center of Theological Inquiry in Princeton graciously gave me some months in 2001 to think and write about it.

In the lead-up to that period, I had become immersed in research on fascinating developments in my field, the resurgence of writings in systematic theology and the revival of the discipline itself. I surveyed seminary teachers of doctrine and the outpouring of new systematics projects.[3] Was encounter with this phenomenon a way of approaching the Person and Work of Christ? I gave it a try in a detailed paper on the Christologies of several contemporary systematics, written for scrutiny by Center colleagues. Their response was sobering. Why these theologians and not the giants? How can you possibly cover the multitude of new works? How can you do justice to your own point of view when attempting an ambitious survey of the present scene? And the most telling critique: we thought you were doing a "pastoral systematics," not just fare for the academy.

Right on all counts. Was I being called back to my original intention of a pastorally oriented work? Yes. When so reconceived the involvements of the earlier years began to look different, less diversions from the task and more the tools to undertake it.

The result of this reorientation is the reclaiming of a history of my contextual sorties in Christology. When gathered together, they, in fact, formed a pattern of exploring various dimensions of this systematics locus, now situated in the settings in which pastors have to preach and teach.

Religious Right and Christian Faith (Grand Rapids: Eerdmans, 1982); Fackre with Michael Root, *Affirmations and Admonitions* (Grand Rapids: Eerdmans, 1998); *Ecumenical Faith in Evangelical Perspective* (Grand Rapids: Eerdmans, 1993).

3. As in "The Surge in Systematics," *The Journal of Religion* 73, no. 2 (April 1993): 223-38; "The Revival of Systematic Theology," *Interpretation* 44, no. 3 (July 1995): 242-54; "In Quest of the Comprehensive: The Systematics Revival," *Religious Studies Review* 20, no. 1 (January 1994): 7-12. The survey of courses in systematics done as preparation for an American Theological Society presidential address is summarized in "Reorientation and Retrieval in Seminary Theology," *The Christian Century* 108, no. 20 (June 26-July 3, 1991): 653-56.

"Pastoral systematics" ought to be done in the places where the Person is embedded and the Work is carried out.

As a result, this volume departs from the standard outline of systematics topics. I do not attempt here to enlarge methodically what was already covered at some length in the overview volume of this series, *The Christian Story*, Vol. 1: the Person of Christ as deity, humanity, and unity, with attention to the ancient christological debates and the response to them in the creeds and Chalcedonian formula, and related questions such as the virginal conception and the sinlessness of Jesus; the Work of Christ in its prophetic, priestly, and royal offices and their background metaphors and theories of atonement vis-à-vis reductionist alternatives.[4] Rather, this volume presupposes that examination and draws out the import of these classical topics and sub-topics. Thus, the thread of christological teaching evoked by varied contexts is here followed, with the topics organized into sections that reflect general areas of concentration. While some chapters bear the clear marks of an earlier decade, I have left them largely unaltered to illustrate both the discontinuities, often more semantic than substantive, and continuities in this journey in a contextualized Christology.

Part I provides the general framework of "narrative" that marks this series, demonstrating its bearing on Christology. At the same time, it does so in the setting of issues that press upon the pastor's preaching and teaching. Chapter 1 takes up Christology in the context of religious pluralism. What claims can we make for Christ in a world of surging Islam, the Asian Buddhist neighbors down the street, and New Age devotees in the bookstore around the corner? Chapter 2 addresses the meaning of Christ against the backdrop of the commanding visions and horrifying realities of an earlier decade, but one still much with us, and, arguably, even more so.

Part II deals with the relation of Christology to the arena in which the pastor serves, the church and its ministry. Chapter 3 shows the bearing of the Person of Christ on the nature of the Body of Christ through the eyes of the churchly Mercersburg theologians. Chapter 4 takes the reader into the middle of a congregation, exploring the collegiality of the ministries of clergy and laity as a continuation of the threefold Work of Christ.

Part III confronts questions that parishioners have in these days of religious contention and spiritual quest, as they are addressed by classical

---

4. *The Christian Story: A Narrative Interpretation of Basic Christian Doctrine*, vol. 1, 3rd ed. (Grand Rapids: Eerdmans, 1996), pp. 99-151.

teaching about the Person and Work. Chapter 5 explores angelology from the point of view of the offices of Christ. Chapter 6 examines the destiny of those "who have never heard" about Jesus Christ, an issue posed by both religious pluralism and Christian evangelism. Chapter 7, against the backdrop of waves of anti-Semitism and the inflamed questions of today's Israel/Palestine, takes up the question of the relation of Christian faith to the Jewish people.

Part IV is devoted to dialogue with two formative twentieth- and twenty-first-century movements, evangelicalism and ecumenism. Chapter 8 is an encounter with the Christology found in evangelicalism's most ambitious current systematics, the seven-volume series of Donald Bloesch. Chapter 9 is a plunge into ecumenical dialogue on Christology by way of a Reformed–Lutheran–Roman Catholic interchange.

Part V returns to the narrative framework of this systematics by a focus on the Jesus story within the overarching saga — his life, death, and resurrection. Chapter 10 takes up the Galilean Christ by engaging a contemporary systematic theologian, Edward Schillebeeckx, who, more than most in this discipline, has sought to draw on both critical scholarship and contemporary experience with a focus on the Galilean Jesus. Chapter 11 addresses the theology of the cross with the stark juxtaposition of the visions and realities that mark our time. Chapter 12 attends to the resurrection as a turning point in the macro-story. The book concludes with some observations on the journey ventured as they relate to the church in which today's pastor serves.

In his influential sociological study, *The Transformation of American Religion*, Alan Wolfe devotes a chapter to "doctrine."[5] His data and anecdotal evidence lead him to conclude that it has largely disappeared from the churches. For that matter, he contends that the same fate has overtaken all of the country's religions, molded as we all are by the culture's all-powerful agenda. While questions can be raised about the presuppositions — indeed the shaping secular "doctrine" — that Wolfe himself brings to the study, there is enough truth in his judgments to give us — the teachers and preachers of the churches in question — pause.

With the sociological profile of our churches in mind, we return to Bonhoeffer and some theological counsel he gave to the Christians of his

---

5. Alan Wolfe, *The Transformation of American Religion: How We Actually Live Our Faith* (New York: Free Press, 2003), pp. 67-95.

own time: do not be "servile before the factual." Why not? Because we are dealing with a Reality not discernible by the naked sociological eye. Teach, preach, and be obedient only to "the one Word of God . . . Jesus Christ," as the Barmen Declaration of his Confessing Church had it. He took his own advice and paid dearly with his life. While our todays are more subtle in their seductions than the Nazi juggernaut of his, they are no less demanding of Christians to go right to "Christ the Center."[6]

The Center is the central chapter of the Christian story. The church has meditated on it for two thousand years. Whether our culture is hospitable to it or not, understandings of this chapter constitute the *doctrine* of Christ, "Christology." Teaching and preaching, that, by the grace of God, help to free the church from captivity to the ideologies of the hour cannot be done without this witness to who Christ is and what Christ does. From pulpit, table, lectern, font, and, yes, sidewalk and street, some are specially called to steward these mysteries. This work aims to assist them in telling that story.

6. Dietrich Bonhoeffer, *Christ the Center*, trans. Edwin H. Robertson (San Francisco: HarperCollins, 1991).

PART I

NARRATIVE CHRISTOLOGY

CHAPTER 1

The Story of Christ in Our Pluralist World

We come to the One who is the central chapter of the Grand Narrative. But who is Jesus Christ for us in today's pluralist world?

A working answer was given by more than a few pastors in post-9/11 religious events in America. Characteristic of such religious services, both Christian and interfaith, was the pervasive use of generic prayer. No offense given to fellow-mourners, Muslim, Jewish, or otherwise, as would be the case if we interceded "in Jesus' name." No talk of scandalous particularity, following the advice of *New York Times* columnist Thomas Friedman who asked, "Can Islam, Christianity and Judaism know that God speaks Arabic on Fridays, Hebrew on Saturdays and Latin on Sundays?"[1] If poll results are to be believed, the 2002 *U.S. News*/PBS's *Religion & Ethics Newsweekly* findings confirm this confidence in an indulgent and multilingual deity.[2] Widespread is the "plural shock," kindred to "culture shock," that makes for christological heart failure.

A comment in passing on the irony entailed in this current relativist orthodoxy: Christians whose interfaith sympathies prompt generic prayer,

---

1. Thomas L. Friedman, "The Real War," *New York Times,* November 27, 2001, *New York Times on the Internet.*

2. Detailed in Jeffrey Shetler, "Faith in America," *U.S. News and World Report* 132, no. 14 (May 6, 2002): 40-49.

or alternately, hold that God gives equal linguistic time to the three Near Eastern faiths, actually demean the other religions they are seeking to honor. By disallowing particularity, we deny to them the universal soteriological and epistemological claims that make them what they are.[3] Generosity to the religious "other" has to do with *how* we make such claims, not forgoing them, speaking the truth in love not hate, with a commensurate listening to the prayers and testimonies of alternate faiths.

Important is a commitment to that well-chosen "the" of John 4:42 — Jesus Christ "*the* Savior of *the* world"[4] — "for all," not the "for me" or "for us" of today's modernisms and postmodernisms, but a universal truth claim for Christ's scandalous particularity.[5] But Jesus, the savior of the

3. As in S. Mark Heim's insightful critique of a pluralist threesome — Wilfred Cantwell Smith, John Hick, and Paul Knitter — in *Salvations: Truth and Difference in Religion* (Maryknoll, N.Y.: Orbis Books, 1995), pp. 13-126.

4. The issue of "the" was noted by Al Krass in earlier debates on religious pluralism, as in his comment, "In the minds of the early Christians there was no doubt but that *their* Lord was *the* Lord," in "Accounting for the Hope That Is in Me," *Christian Faith in a Religiously Plural World,* ed. Donald G. Dawe and John B. Carman (Maryknoll, N.Y.: Orbis Books, 1978), p. 158. See also Russell F. Aldwinkle, *Jesus — A Savior or the Savior?* (Macon, Ga.: Mercer University Press, 1982). Diane Eck's recent work, *A New Religious America: How a Christian Country Has Now Become the World's Most Religiously Diverse Nation* (San Francisco: Harper, 2001), is an argument for removing the "the," indeed, from all the claims of the Johannine text to be discussed. Her evidence for the extensiveness of the change in the new America in terms of the number of adherents of other religions is directly challenged by the recent detailed study by Tom W. Smith, "Religious Diversity in America: The Emergence of Muslims, Buddhists, Hindus and Others," National Opinion Research Center, University of Chicago, Internet available. Generalizing from a multitude of recent surveys and studies, Smith concludes: "This indicates that non-Judeo-Christian religions are much smaller than frequently cited high-end estimates and have hardly transformed the religious landscape as much as often portrayed. . . . Non-Judeo-Christian religions make up a small, but growing share of America's religious mosaic. In 1973-1980 the General Social Survey (GSS) indicated that they accounted for 0.8% of the adult population. This grew to 1.3% in 1981-1990 and 2.6% in 1990-2000. . . . The Muslim population is commonly overestimated by a factor of 3-4. . . . Impressive as the actual changes in non-traditional religions have been, they can not match these and many related claims about the growth and size of these religions" (pp. 5, 1, 4).

5. Kathryn Tanner notes the transformation in contemporary theology of Luther's *pro me* from its focus on "a dimension of the reality of Christ's working" to the "modern penchant for making questions of human subjectivity paramount." Kathryn Tanner, "Jesus Christ," *The Cambridge Companion to Christian Doctrine,* ed. Colin Gunton (Cambridge: Cambridge University Press, 1999), pp. 253, 264. In the case being given here, the subjectivity

world from what? The answer is suggestively stated in another Johannine text, "I am the way, and the truth, and the life. No one comes to the Father except through me" (John 14:6). This remarkable verse is the claim that Jesus is the *way/hodos/path* that God makes into the world to rescue it from sin, thereby bringing *reconciliation;* saving us from error, bringing the *truth* of the knowledge of God, *revelation;* delivering us from death, bringing the fullness of *life* in all its aspects, *redemption.*[6] Of such are the three dimensions of salvation, the last two derivative from the first, following theologically the epexegetical role of *alētheia* and *zōē* vis-à-vis the primary predicate, *hodos,* in the text.[7]

What happens when this threefold claim is set down in the midst of today's religiously plural world? It provides us with an illuminating framework for interpreting a range of current perspectives on this matter. Each, in its own way, takes a position on how Jesus Christ is reconciler, revealer, and redeemer — where the *deed* is done, where the *disclosure* is made, where the *deliverance* happens. The diversity goes well beyond the familiar but inadequate typology of exclusivism, inclusivism, and pluralism. After a thumbnail sketch of a wide spectrum of views, with some documentation, the last perspective will be developed, a "narrative" view of the Person and Work of Christ. In what follows, the appearance of "ideal types" in relation to the threefold claim, and the use of a chart, pictorials, typology, alliteration, metaphor, and the master metaphor — story — reflect this effort in pastoral systematics, striving to make the complexities of the discipline accessible to working clergy.[8]

---

is given a postmodern turn expressed in its pop phrase, "it works for me" (while something very different may "work for you").

6. The distinction between "reconciliation" and "redemption" follows, roughly, that made by Barth in his *Church Dogmatics.* A detailed exegesis of this verse is found in Fackre, *The Christian Story,* vol. 2, *Scripture in the Church for the World* (Grand Rapids: Eerdmans, 1987), pp. 254-341.

7. The case made by Raymond Brown and others. See *The Christian Story,* vol 2, p. 262.

8. A chart appears on p. 6.

A Range of Current Views[9]

Pluralist Perspectives

The first five perspectives are "pluralist," in that they put to the fore a commonality shared by Christianity with other religions.

1. Common Core

At the center of all the great religions of humankind is to be found a common core of divine (however conceived) doing, disclosing, and delivering. Each faith approaches it through its own heroes, expresses it in its own language, celebrates it in its own rituals, formulates it in its own rules of behavior, and passes it on in its own communal forms. While the rhetoric of each religion may claim that its way, truth, and life are for all, these absolutist professions are, in fact, "love talk," the metaphors of commitment, not the metaphysics of reality. Jesus is, therefore, "*my* savior," not "*the* savior." In pop idiom, "you do your thing and I'll do mine." Christian faith and other religions are different routes to the same core Reality. Often added is that the test of their validity is a universally discernible norm of ethical fruitfulness. Thus a "C" assigned to each of the three claims in the following chart:[10]

	Way	Truth	Life			Way	Truth	Life
1.	C	C	C		6.	P	PC	CP
2.	C?	C?	C?		7.	P	P	CP?
3.	C	CP	C		8.	PC	PC	PC
4.	C?	P?	C?		9.	P	PC	P
5.	C	PC	C		10.	P	PC	PC?

9. This more complex spectrum of views began with an early sifting and sorting in "The Scandals of Particularity and Universality" in *Midstream* 22, no. 1 (January 1983): 32-52, and runs to a recent version in "Christ and Religious Pluralism: The Current Debate," *Pro Ecclesia* 7, no. 4 (Fall 1998): 389-95.

10. The "love talk" characterization is that of Krister Stendahl in "Notes from Three Biblical Studies," in *Christ's Lordship and Religious Pluralism*, ed. Gerald H. Anderson and Thomas F. Stransky (Maryknoll, N.Y.: Orbis Books, 1981), pp. 13-15. A terse formulation of the core as the "pattern of the new being encoded 'in the name of Jesus' for Christians, but in other names for other religions" appears in Donald G. Dawe's essay, "Christian Faith in a Religiously Plural World," in Dawe and Carman, eds., *Christian Faith in a Religiously Plural World*, pp. 13-33. John Hick, Wilfred Cantwell Smith, and Paul Knitter probably are the best-known twentieth-century exponents of this view; they and others express it in one form or

2. Common Quest

Perspective 2 makes no claim for a reachable core, as perspective 1 does. Postmodern ambiguity rather than modern foundational certainty is the order of the day. Religions are quests for self-understanding, not paths to Reality. Like the relativism of the common core view, this too is describable in popular idiom as "different strokes for different folks." Unlike it, View 2 judges that the common quest provides no way to an ultimate truth and life. Rather, "my savior" is the profession and practice of "what works for me" in the midst of my day-to-day penultimacies, a pragmatic test in a postmodern world for what is self-referentially adequate. Thus all the "C's" are followed by question marks.[11]

3. Common Pool

Like its predecessors, View 3 gives pride of place to religious commonalities, but seeks to respect the uniqueness of a religion and not dissolve it into a common core, contra View 1, and insists that such is in touch with Reality, not just involved in a quest for it as in View 2. It does this by maintaining that each is a reconciling way to a needed aspect of the truth, delivering some feature of a saving life. The way of Christ into Reality grants to Christians one illuminating take on the truth, and offers one dimension of life. Other religions have different deeds, disclosures, and deliverances. The challenge is to pool the best from each with the goal of a "world faith." Thus a "C" is assigned to each, but with an add-on revelatory "P" of particularity in revelation, recognizing the contribution Christ makes to a fuller disclosure.[12]

4. Common Community

Challenging the individualism of the foregoing options, the common community view sees us as creatures of formative cultures. Our communal

---

another in John Hick and Paul Knitter, eds., *The Myth of Christian Uniqueness* (Maryknoll, N.Y.: Orbis Books, 1987).

11. See Richard Rorty, *Objectivism, Relativism and Truth: Philosophical Papers,* vol. 1 (Cambridge: Cambridge University Press, 1991), for the philosophical underpinnings of this view.

12. Although John Hick's writings can be associated with variations on View 1, his argument in *Death and Eternal Life* (New York: Harper & Row, 1976) falls into this category. Gavin D'Costa has traced Hick's developing point(s) of view in *John Hick's Theology of Religions* (Lanham, Md.: University Press of America, 1987).

destiny is normative for us as well as descriptive of us, a call to know who we are, and live out of the traditions in which we are immersed. For Christians, this means clarity about our defining characteristics, knowing our ecclesial language and lore and respecting its rules of believing and behaving. Christ can be no other than the way, truth, and life *for us*. Given our postmodern circumstances, we can lay no claim to reaching ultimate reality through our way, or assert such to be true and saving for everyone. Hence, Christians are to "keep the faith," but share with others the common condition of ambiguity, a question mark after each CP.[13]

5. Common Range

The fifth perspective shares the pluralist premise of the former options. The religions are on common ground in matters of way, truth, and life, all providing reconciliation, revelation, and redemption. However, when it comes to disclosure of the Really Real — accessible here too, as in Views 1 and 3 — Jesus' light is the brightest and best. To change the figure, Jesus is on the same mountain range as Mohammad, Buddha, Moses — or for that matter other great prophets from Socrates to Gandhi and Martin Luther King, Jr. — but is the Mt. Everest among the peaks of human experience. The difference is in degree, not kind, for Christ offers the same saving benefits as other high religions. A higher degree of truth is signified by placing a P before the C of the revelatory category.[14]

13. Another "narrative" view, associated with Hans Frei and George Lindbeck and a notable company of their students, is regularly under discussion as in the critique by I. M. Wallace, "The New Yale Theology," *Christian Scholars Review* 17, no. 2 (December 1987): 154-70. However, Bruce Marshall has shown that Lindbeck's communal narrativity does include a claim of "correspondence to the real order." "Aquinas as Postliberal Theologian," *The Thomist* 53, no. 3 (July 1989): 353-402. For the struggle of postliberal theologians to come clear on this issue, see Garrett Green, ed., *Scriptural Authority and Narrative Interpretation* (Philadelphia: Fortress Press, 1987).

14. See W. Norman Pittinger's oft-referenced development of "degree Christology" in *The Word Incarnate* (New York: Harper and Brothers, 1959) and his later development of this view vis-à-vis the specifics of religious pluralism in "Can a Christian Be a Buddhist Too?" and "Can a Buddhist Be a Christian Too?" in *Japanese Religions* 11, nos. 2 and 3 (September 1980): 35-55.

Particularist Perspectives

The next five declare for the definitive singularity of the deed God does in Jesus Christ to reconcile the world. How that impacts disclosure and deliverance distinguishes the perspectives from one another.

6. Anonymous Particularity

Only at one point in human history does God come among us to do the necessary deed of reconciliation. Jesus is *the* "absolute savior" not *a* relative one, the singular incarnate Word, reconciler of God and the world. However, this particularity has a universal scope. The power from the christological center of history radiates everywhere in incognito fashion, giving all humans and their diverse religious traditions a sense, to one degree or another, of the divine purposes, the option of responding aright and the offer of grace to do so. With that right response, they become "anonymous Christians." While so granting the universal possibilities of both revelation and redemption, only in the privileged church of Christians is there the clear knowledge of the divine and assurance of the path to salvation.[15] Thus a P for reconciliation, a PC for revelation, and a PC for redemption.

7. Revelatory Particularity

God comes to reconcile the alienated world in only one way, and gives ultimate truth only in one place, in Jesus Christ. This divine deed is so radical that all human beings are delivered by Christ from the divine judgment, as they die with Christ in his humiliation and rise with him in his exaltation. The church is uniquely given the revelation of this truth, and called to get this Word out to the human race of "virtual believers" so reconciled. Are all then finally redeemed by the reconciling way of God in Christ? We have a right to *hope* that is so based on the deed done, but not to assert universal

---

15. Expounded in Karl Rahner, *Theological Investigations,* vol. 17, trans. Margaret Kohl (New York: Crossroads 1981), pp. 24-50, and his *Foundations of Christian Faith: An Introduction to the Idea of Christianity,* trans. William V. Dych (New York: Seabury Press, 1978), pp. 138-321. A variation on this theme is developed in evangelical idiom by John Sanders in his sections of *What about Those Who Have Never Heard? Three Views on the Destiny of the Unevangelized,* ed. John Sanders (Downers Grove, Ill.: InterVarsity Press, 1995).

salvation as an article of faith. Only the sovereign God decides the final outcome. Hence a solitary P at both way and truth and a CP? at life.[16]

8. Pluralist Particularity

Christ is the particular way the triune God of Christian faith makes into the world, giving a unique truth and saving life. Yet the generosity of God provides in different religions other ways, truths, and life (variously described as "salvations," or "religious fulfillments"). Christians believe that the one to which they testify is the supreme deed, disclosure, and deliverance and seek to witness that superiority to all, while acknowledging that other religions have their own reachable goals. A primary P is placed under the way, but also a secondary C alongside it, and similar PCs under truth and life.[17]

9. Imperial Particularity

Christ is the particular way God came into the world to bring the only truth and only saving life to be had. The elect and/or those who decide for Christ during their time on earth, know the truth and are saved. Those who are passed over and/or do not decide for Christ perish eternally. Christians are charged to preach the saving gospel so that those called to salvation may respond in saving faith. Therefore a singular P as deed, a primal P under truth with a C that recognizes non-salvific general revelation, and a solitary P under deliverance.[18]

16. Karl Barth's *Church Dogmatics*, IV/1-4, is the most detailed outworking of this view, with *apokatastasis* as an "article of hope" described in *Church Dogmatics*, IV/3, first part, trans. G. W. Bromiley (Edinburgh: T. & T. Clark, 1961), pp. 477-78. Whether Barth departs significantly from his revelatory exclusivity with his discussion of "free communications" and "parables of the Kingdom" in *Church Dogmatics*, IV/3, first part, is a matter of continued debate. For a discussion of this see Fackre, *The Doctrine of Revelation: A Narrative Interpretation of Revelation* (Grand Rapids: Eerdmans, 1997), pp. 136-37, 143-45.

17. A view given prominence initially by Joseph DiNoia in "The Universality of Salvation and the Diversity of Religious Aims," *World Mission*, Winter 1981-1982, pp. 4-15, but developed in detail by S. Mark Heim in his two works, *Salvations* and *Depths of the Riches: A Trinitarian Theology of Religious Ends* (Grand Rapids: Eerdmans, 2001).

18. With a qualification here and there, but substantially a detailed exposition of the imperial views, is Ronald H. Nash's *Is Jesus the Only Savior?* (Grand Rapids: Zondervan, 1984), and his sections in John Sanders, ed., *What about Those Who Have Never Heard?*

10. Narrative Particularity[19]

A narrative is "an account of characters and events in a plot moving over time and space through conflict toward resolution."[20] The defining deed, disclosure, and deliverance take place in the central chapter of a Grand Narrative that runs from creation to consummation. But as the Story of God, the chapters that lead up to and away from the Center play their role in the plot of reconciliation, revelation, and redemption, as reflected in a P for way, a PC for truth, and a PC? for life. To that centerpoint — described in traditional terms as the Person and Work of Jesus Christ — we now turn, situating its exposition narratively, with a comparison of the views just canvassed.

Narrative Particularity: The Person and Work of Christ

Locating who Christ is (the Person) and what Christ does (the Work) in the setting of the biblical macro-story provides a framework for grappling with the concerns of the pluralist options without eroding the scandalous particularity of John 14:6. Jesus Christ is *the* Savior of *the* world. At the same time, the Story requires both a width and length to the divine mercy that make for a "generous orthodoxy" in a religiously plural world.

The Christian story begins with a prologue, the eternal being of the tri-personal God.

The loving life together of Father, Son, and Holy Spirit — the immanent Trinity — sets the stage for a journey toward a comparable end *ad extra* — the unfolding of the drama of the economic Trinity. Who God is as *Agapē* cum *Shalom* is what God wills.[21] Regarding the Person of the Son,

19. The postmodern veto of meta-narratives of the sort to be discussed is rejected for these reasons: (1) Postmodernity as an intellectual construct is itself a meta-narrative. What is sauce for the goose is sauce for the gander. (2) The imperiousness and violence attributed to meta-narratives depend on the contents of same, not their character as cosmic story. Postmodern ideology has its own history of imperialism when it achieves power, as in sections of academia. J. Richardson Middleton and Brian J. Walsh, *Truth Is Stranger Than It Used to Be: Biblical Faith in a Postmodern Age* ((Downers Grove, Ill.: InterVarsity Press, 1995), pp. 75-79 and *passim*, take up some of these matters.

20. Gabriel Fackre, "Narrative Theology: An Overview," *Interpretation* 37, no. 4 (October 1983): 341.

21. Fackre, *The Christian Story*, vol. 2, pp. 245-46.

Theophilus of Antioch speaks of this inner Word of who God is as the *Logos endiathetos.*[22]

Reflecting the divine Life Together, God wills the coming to be of a covenant partner, this outgoing work being that of the *Logos prophorikos,* sourced by the Father and empowered by the Spirit. Thus the world is called out of nothing into created being for a life together with God, and within itself. Chapter 1 is the creation of this other, beckoned into relationship with its Creator, an invitation to respond in kind to God's loving reach. (So God and Adam as portrayed on the ceiling of the Sistine Chapel.) The creature with the human face is in special relationship and responsibility to God (Gen. 1:26; 2:15-17), and derivatively to one another (Gen. 1:27; 2:18), the double meaning of the *imago Dei.*[23] As such, humanity is called to be, and capacitated to be, a creature of God, not to "play God" (Gen. 3:5). Whatever an atom, an animal, an angel, or other created beings are given and charged to be, as in Barth's wise agnosticism, we can only guess.[24]

As the story unfolds, what God wills for us, and what we will toward God, go on collision course. So comes "sin," the self's idolatrous curve inward (Luther) rather than outward toward God, the human other, and creation itself. The result is a life *alone,* not a life together (Gen. 3:6-13). Chapter 2 is about the stumble and fall of the world, our alienation from God and its derivative estrangements from truth and life (Gen. 3:14-24). Thus the Christian problematic: our breach of the intended relationship between God and the world and the loss of its accompanying light and life.

---

22. See Theophilus of Antioch, *Ad Autolycum* 2 for the journey of the *Logos* to be tracked here. William Placher notes, however, that "'Wisdom' . . . has some claim to be the earliest term Christians used for the relation of Jesus Christ to the one he called 'Father'" and that "in a number of texts from shortly before the time of Jesus, 'Word' and 'Wisdom' are used more or less interchangeably." William C. Placher, *Jesus the Savior: The Meaning of Jesus Christ for Christian Faith* (Louisville: Westminster John Knox, 2001), pp. 22, 25. Given the feminine gender of Wisdom and thus its deconstruction of a too-simple masculine characterization of the triune God, and the precedent of interchangeability with Word, there is no reason to deny the journey of the second Person as describable also as that made by Wisdom. It may have special resonance when considering the work of common grace. For all that, we honor the insight of Theophilus by using his own language.

23. Fackre, *The Christian Story,* vol. 2, pp. 68-71.

24. Karl Barth, *Church Dogmatics,* III/2, ed. and trans. G. W. Bromiley and T. F. Torrance (Edinburgh: T. & T. Clark, 1960), pp. 78, 374, 395, 521.

To turn the world around requires a saving way of reconciliation with God with its derivative revelation and redemption.

The purposes of God are stronger than our perverse powers. So chapter 3 in the Story, the renewal of God's bonding with the world. Its first phase is the covenant with Noah, the pledge of the Creator to stay with creation even in its rebel state, signaled by the rainbow promise of divine perseverance (Gen. 9:12).[25] With it is given sufficient light and power to keep the Grand Narrative going forward.[26] Christologically viewed, this is the sustaining largesse of the *Logos spermatikos* with a variety of gifts to know and do things true, good, beautiful, and holy, a "common grace" that discloses something of the path ahead and delivers its receivers from impediments on that journey (Gen. 9:1-7; 14:18-20; Heb. 7:1-17).[27] It whets the world's appetite for a More, and amidst the distorting effects of the fall on our efforts to pursue that goal, genuine evidences of its presence are manifest. To anticipate, why would this common grace not be at work in many and diverse ways where world religions cohere with the divine purposes?

Chapter 3, Part II in the narrative can be pictorially described as an end point of the rainbow that settles among a particular people. God makes a special covenant of grace with Abraham, whose faith makes him the veritable "father of us all" (Rom. 4:17). This singular covenant includes its Mosaic form of law grounded in faith and its Exodus deliverance of the chosen people, embodying the ministries of prophets, priests, and kings, and the dream of a *shalom* to be. In Pauline retrospect, this people with its special graces of revelatory disclosure as well as covenantal deed and deliverance

---

25. See David Novak, *Image of the Non-Jew in Judaism: An Historical and Constructive Study of the Noahide Laws* (Lewiston, N.Y.: Mellen, 1984). C. H. Dodd's durable study of "the Noachian covenant" is in "Natural Law and the Bible," *Theology*, May and June 1946, reprint. A recent review of Reformation thought on the natural law aspects of the Noachic covenant vis-à-vis aspects of the theology of Thomas Hooker is found in the monograph by W. J. Torrance Kirby, *The Theology of Richard Hooker in the Context of the Magisterial Reformation*, Studies in Reformed History and Theology New Series, Number 5 (Princeton: Princeton Theological Seminary, 2000). For an extended discussion of covenant with Noah as it relates to contemporary theologies, see Fackre, *The Doctrine of Revelation*, pp. 61-102.

26. Anticipated in the time between the fall and Noachic covenant by the sustenance of the world to that point, interpretable as the broken but not destroyed *imago*, now confirmed and extended to the End by the covenant with Noah.

27. For an interesting discussion of "common grace" and the "Melchizedek factor," see Gordon Spykman, *Reformational Theology: A New Paradigm for Doing Dogmatics* (Grand Rapids: Eerdmans, 1992), pp. 320-21, 424-27.

participates proleptically in the central scandal of particularity to come, warranting an anti-supersessionist understanding of the place of the Jewish people in Christian faith.[28] Indeed the opened book of this people gives us the story we are telling, pointing — again in Christian retrospect — toward chapters yet to be.

In one Jew, a Galilean carpenter, the rainbow end becomes an intersection, a cruciform representation of the doctrine of the Person and Work of Christ: *incarnation* as the deep drive of God into our world, and *atonement* — at-one-ment — as the bringing together of the alienated parties to God's purposes.

Incarnation

A narrative interpretation of the Incarnation is given in patristic formulations of the journey we are following, culminating in the *Logos ensarkos,* the enfleshed Word. Theophilus' trajectory throughout is based on the Johannine narrativity, as in the prologue's "In the beginning was the Word, and the Word was with God, and the Word was God. . . . All things came into being through him. . . . in him was life, and the life was the light of all people. . . . And the Word became flesh and lived among us. . . ." Missing in classical and creedal constructs is the Story's chapter on Israel (as in the prologue's references to Moses and the prophet John),[29] but otherwise, the path of the *Logos* is that traversed in the Story we are here following. Its contribution to a narrative interpretation of the Person of Christ is its trinitarian refinement of the Who of the incarnation. Not the Father, not the Spirit, but the Son becomes flesh. The intersection of God with the world is the Word incarnate. For all that particularity, the Word is the Word of

28. For commentary on the state of the question see "A Symposium on *Dabru Emet: A Jewish Statement on Christians and Christianity*," *Pro Ecclesia* 11, no. 1 (Winter 2002): 5-19. For a review of current supersessionist and anti-supersessionist views, and my own position, see Gabriel Fackre, "The Place of Israel in Christian Faith," in *Gott lieben und seine Gebote halten,* In memoriam Klaus Bockmuehl, ed. Markus Bockmuehl and Helmut Burkhardt (Basel: Brunnen Verlag Giessen, 1991), pp. 21-38. A portion of this essay appears in this volume as Chapter 7.

29. The chapter missing in too much traditional Christian teaching has contributed to the terrible legacy of anti-Judaism. Interesting, however, Theophilus did see the *Logos* at work in the Old Testament theophanies.

the Father, enfleshed by the power of the Spirit, and thus, the issue of the Father of the Son by the Holy Spirit.

By dint of the divine action Jesus Christ is "true God from true God" (Nicene Creed). The second Person of the Trinity "became" Jesus of Nazareth (John 1:14). No qualified or compromised entry of deity here.[30] Keeping in mind the multiple meanings of *logos* in the ancient world, we can say the eternal word, purpose, plan, reason, vision . . . came to dwell among us. The divine Intention for creation's "life together" lived and breathed in this Nazarene. His words and deeds embodied the *agapē* and *shalom* that God is and wills. Nothing less than God among us can deal with the alienations to which we are heir.

As important as the divine initiative, no less consequential is the reality of the being "among" us, the "becoming" one of us. There is no illusory flesh here diminished or dissolved by deity, as the church's credos and definitions of the first four centuries of christological debate were at pains to assert.[31] The Word-in-the-flesh meant God's taking on our finitude, in matters of the mind not being a "know-it-all" but rather learning to "grow in wisdom"; in matters of the body, urinating and defecating, sweating in a carpenter shop and bleeding on a cross; in matters of the soul, wrestling with doubt on that same tree. The Person of Christ is truly human as well as truly God, yet truly one, "without confusion, without change, without distinction, without separation."[32]

When lodged in a narrative framework these standard assertions of classical Christian teachings have implications for our spectrum of options on the issues of religious pluralism. For one, the narrative reading is placed among the particularist views regarding the first rubric, "way." As the once-happened incarnate Word, Jesus Christ is the singular way God makes into our world to reconcile it to its Creator. Here is the decisive turning point in the Story, God among us first-hand.

The Word made flesh, however, is no bolt from the blue. The *Logos* is the architect of creation. The Word that "was God . . . was in the beginning with God [and] all things came into being through him" (John 1:1-3). The same Word, after the fall, graces the world with Noah's rainbow. Wherever

---

30. Contra the Ebionisms, Adoptionisms, Arianisms, and Nestorianisms of the christological controversies.

31. Contra the Docetisms, Modalisms, Apollinarianisms, and Monophysitisms of the same controversies.

32. Formula of Chalcedon.

creation displays marks of its Creator, visible by the preserving light of common grace, the second Person of the Trinity is the mediator of that disclosure. So too, wherever deliverance from death to life takes place, the hidden Christ is present. As these gifts are given from the Work that Christ performs, we postpone the discussion of the effects of common grace in the world religions.

The rainbow of universality touches down at a point of particularity. Two-thirds of Christian Scripture witness to the special graces of disclosure and deliverance given to a chosen people. Who Christ is and what Christ does cannot be understood or come to be without this trajectory toward the Story's center, recorded in the Hebrew Scripture with the Christian Bible. Paul's declaration of Abraham as the "father" of faith, and his assertion that "the gifts and the calling" given to this people are irrevocable, place the Jewish people in unique relation to God's saving purposes (Rom. 4:16; 11:29).[33] We shall say more about the final soteriological implications in discussing the atoning Work of Christ. Nevertheless, the accomplishment of the purposes of God happens only when the rainbow arc is driven deep at the particular point of one Jew. What this enfleshment does is the Work of Christ, the reconciliation of the alienated parties to the divine purposes.

Atonement

The Work of the Person is to transform the condition of the world from separation to communion. The central chapter of the Christian story tells us that the at-one-ing charge from the Father to the Son by the Holy Spirit is carried out in the life, death, and resurrection of Jesus Christ. This micro-narrative, set within the context of the macro-narrative we have been tracing, is our framework for interpreting the doctrine of the atonement. That is, traditional concepts associated with the doctrine, such as the threefold office of Christ, redemption accomplished and applied, the finished and continuing Work of Christ, etc., will be construed narratively, constituting a perspective on the issues of religious pluralism posed by John 14:6 that differs from the others, but one that attempts to incorporate their insights while avoiding their missteps.

33. See Chapter 7.

The Threefold Office of Christ

The *munus triplex,* developed in detail by John Calvin but also in wide ecumenical usage,[34] provides a framework for interpreting the Jesus story that addresses the claims of reconciliation, revelation, and redemption in Christ.

The Prophetic Office

The life of the prophet Jesus discloses who God is. His Galilean ministry is a demonstration of the *Agapē/Shalom* of God. His being, his relationship to others, to creation and to the Father, his healings, his preaching and teaching concerning the yet/not yet reign of God, all embody the Life Together that God is.

Prophecy is "forth-telling" the word about God encompassing the "foretelling" of the outcome of the purposes of God in the kingdom to come. As such, the knowledge of the fullness of who God is and what God wills, hidden from view in a fallen world, is revealed in the prophetic ministry of Jesus who as the Word enfleshed makes that ultimate disclosure. The first office, correlated narratively with the Galilean ministry, is the *revelation* of ultimate truth about God and the kingdom of God, obscured elsewhere by the pervasive error of sin (more than the ignorance of finitude) that damages (but does not destroy) our *imago Dei.* Thus the giving of the truth of the knowledge of God in the prophetic office.[35]

The radical nature of the fall is such that the world is enraged by the presence in its midst of a loving Word over against all that the world is in its hates and hurts. Evoking that wrath, absolute love as "burning coals" (Rom. 12:20), the prophetic office *exposes* the depth of human sin and *discloses* the heights of the divine *Agapē.* The life of the prophet ends in crucifixion. Yet the cross opens a new sub-chapter in Jesus' story. With it comes the priestly ministry.

---

34. From John Calvin's *Institutes of the Christian Religion,* Book II, Chapter XV, trans. Henry Beveridge (Grand Rapids: Eerdmans, 1957), vol. 1, pp. 425-32, to the Second Vatican Council's "Decree on the Apostolate of the Laity," in *Documents of Vatican II,* ed. Walter Abbott, S.J. (New York: Guild Press, 1966), p. 491 and *passim.*

35. The three offices are themselves a "life together" reflecting their trinitarian origins. Hence, the priestly and royal ministries of Christ also participate in the prophetic office, and vice-versa, even as each has its distinctive role. See Fackre, *The Christian Story,* vol. 2, pp. 149-50.

The Priestly Office

A priest sacrifices for sin. Jesus, our high priest, sacrifices for the sin of the world.

This priest is like no other for he is the victim that he, the priest, lays on the altar. And, like no finite other, as God enfleshed on that altar, the victim-priest has an infinite capacity to deal with the infinite magnitude of the world's sin. The Person of Christ takes into the divine being the full measure of judgment we are due, and thus "the cross in the heart of God" (Charles Dinsmore), the godly Mercy that overcomes the divine Wrath (Luther). No God "up there" exacting punishment on Jesus "down here," as in pop piety or child-abuse ideology,[36] but the crucified God who takes away the sin of the world. Thus the Johannine assertion that Jesus is "*the way*" that God the Son makes toward us in order to overcome sin and reconcile the world.

We linger a bit longer at this central office in wonder at what happened on the cross to turn the world around. Can a story Jesus tells shed light on the narrative of his own death? The tale of the running father and the returning son hints strongly of what was to come (Luke 15:11-24). Where did the expected Semitic punishment of an ungrateful offspring go? Where else but into the father's own heart? There acceptance absorbed anger in a suffering love that made for that spurt to greet the wayward. And the parental run was on while the son was "far off," an unconditional *(agapē)* welcome innocent of the whys and wherefores of the return.

How can we not have here a portent of the divine mercy that on the cross takes into itself the divine judgment against sin? A Word that God's suffering Love welcomes those who return, in the faith that a sinner can be received? A trust in a spontaneous and unconditional *Agapē?* The tenth view of the saving Work of Christ turns to story to illumine God's own Story, with evocative narration that explores, not a neat theory that explains.

The Royal Office

The accomplishment of the Work of Christ requires dealing with the "last enemy," death. Death is mortality and more, including as it does all the evil and suffering that militates against life. Easter morning announces the de-

---

36. Cf. Placher, *Jesus the Savior,* pp. 112-13.

feat of that final foe. The resurrection confirms the victory of the victim's sacrifice and gives assurance of the things hoped for, the world's future healing.

Regents rule their terrain. The resurrection announces the truth that the kingdom will have its ruler, the divine-human Person. Christ the risen king is the surety that reconciliation has come to be and that redemption, as the "application" of its "benefits" by the Holy Spirit, is assured. Christ is the deed that delivers as well as discloses. Thus the Johannine assertion that Christ is the "life" as well as the way and the truth.

The threefold office makes possible a full-orbed understanding of the Work of Christ as portrayed in the biblical account of this central chapter. It is an ecumenical formula that challenges the reductionisms that tend to be embodied in historic traditions, ones that focus exclusively on the prophetic Jesus who saves from ignorance, the priestly Jesus who saves from sin, and the royal Jesus who saves from death.

The Continuing Work

The Work of Christ as revelation, reconciliation, and redemption is accomplished in the life, death, and resurrection of Jesus Christ. For the Grand Narrative to move toward its conclusion, the world must share in the consequences of the deed done. The "finished work" requires a "continuing work"; atonement accomplished moves to atonement applied. The ascension of Jesus Christ to the right hand of the Father extends the royal reign, stretching it toward the finale when Christ "hands over" his rule to the Father (1 Cor. 15:24).

The ascended Christ continues all three ministries in the time between the times of Easter and Eschaton. Wherever the fruits of reconciliation — revelation and redemption — happen, Christ is present and active. The story of Pentecost is paradigmatic of the giving of his gifts.

On that Day, the ascent of Christ is followed by the descent of the Spirit, the light of the risen Sun issuing in tongues of fire settling upon disciples that, so graced, become apostles (Acts 2:1-4). The gift of *kerygma* given by Christ the prophet opens the mouth of Peter to tell the Story (Acts 2:15-36). The charism of *leitourgia* given by Christ the priest empowers the community to celebrate the Story in baptizing and breaking bread (Acts 2:41-42). The church's means of grace — Word and sacrament — thus work to disclose the truth of the reconciling deed of God in Christ, and to offer life-giving deliverance to those who receive the Word audible and visible in justifying faith.

The gifts of *koinōnia* and *diakonia* join *kerygma* and *leitourgia* in the continuing work of the in-Spirited Son of the Father (Acts 2:42, 44). As the sanctifying power of love that mirrors the Life Together of both God's being and God's doing, the life together of the Christian community and its service to the neighbor in need are charisms of the kingship of Christ that defeat the death-dealing powers of evil inimical to the divine purposes.

The continuing prophetic, priestly, and royal work of Christ ranges over the world beyond the borders of church. Wherever any truth is disclosed and any life is nurtured, the hidden Christ exercises his threefold office incognito (Matt. 25:31-46). The Noachic covenant now is seen to be the gift of a christological common grace. So the New Testament assurance that God has "not left himself without a witness in doing good . . . so that they would search for God and perhaps grope for him and find him . . ." (Acts 14:17; 17:27). Of such are the derivative disclosure and deliverance of the "absolute Savior." These gifts given by the hidden Christ are that measure of the good, true, beautiful, and holy required for the Grand Narrative to go forward to its goal. Common grace does not save the world from sin. Only one incarnate and atoning Way does that. But it does maintain "truth" and "life" in the world, preserving it from untruths, evil, ugliness, and unholiness that would be death to its journey toward its Center and End. Reflecting this distinction, *Cruden's Concordance* lists under "salvation," two meanings in its fifty-eight citations, the former "deliverance from sin and its consequences" and the latter "preservation from trouble or danger."[37] The fullness of salvation as deliverance in Scripture and Christian faith, therefore, includes both vertical and horizontal dimensions, both the forgiveness of sin by grace through faith, and deliverance from error, suffering, sorrow, oppression, and all that militates against the making and keeping of human life human and creation as it is intended to be — redemption of creation in all its aspects as in the vision of the world's eschatological fulfillment.[38]

Christ's Noachic arc over our fallen world, with its universal grace, in-

37. On the various meanings of salvation in Scripture, see Aldwinkle, *Jesus — A Savior or the Savior?*

38. Fackre, *The Christian Story,* vol. 2, pp. 190-207, 227-30.

cludes a rainbow of world religions, instruments of his preserving purposes. Within them, amidst their chapter 2 constraints, are manifest truth and life that enlighten and empower their adherents in the world's journey on its way, so discernible by light from the Center of the Story. In this respect, the narrative view is distinguished from View 7, with its revelatory exclusivity and its delimited concept of what constitutes redemption. "Common" grace, it should be noted, does not mean the sameness of religious truth and life, for a variety of differing charisms are dispersed through this generous universality.[39] Such gifts are saving in the Scripture's second sense, historical and "horizontal," contra View 9, which acknowledges only one kind of deliverance and diminishes accordingly the soteric weight of "general revelation." On the other hand, a narrative view of the gifts of these common and christological graces is tethered to the biblical Storyline and does not make the speculative leap of View 8 that takes the humanly enriching religious insights and experiences (saving "horizontal" graces) into the trans-historical "vertical" and eschatological realms as varied (albeit lesser) religious fulfillments. Nor can it raise the significance of common grace to offer anonymously the eternal deliverance claimed for such by View 6. In all cases, what measure of light and life is granted to any one world religion can only be judged by the defining disclosure at the center of the Story.[40] The wider ministries in the continuing Work of Christ are made possible by the once-happened accomplishment of atonement, the defeat of sin at the center of the Story, in the life, death, and resurrection of Christ.

39. Common grace and general revelation do not require equivalency of disclosure and deliverance as might be concluded from the language of "common" and "general." The latter refer to the universal grace at work beyond the historical particularity of Jesus Christ, and can accommodate the idea of differing dimensions of that grace present in varied religious traditions, "revealed types," as argued by Gerald McDermott in *Can Evangelicals Learn from World Religions?* (Downers Grove, Ill.: InterVarsity Press, 2001), pp. 113-19.

40. So Barth's helpful investigation of the same in *Church Dogmatics*, IV/3, first part, pp. 125-28. Gerald McDermott also deploys this christological norm, while giving attention to the "light" God gives to other religions, one that can even enrich the understanding of the truth in Christian faith itself, drawing out its implications. See *Can Evangelicals Learn from World Religions?* passim. By using the biblical distinction between the two forms of deliverance, this paper speaks of the "life" possible as well in salvation from earthly evil through non-Christian religions.

The Consummating Work of Christ

The continuing Work is consummated by Christ, the Hound of Heaven, who pursues us beyond the gates of death and to the very End. As the whole world has been reconciled by the saving way God has made into our midst, we have a right to hope that the Word of truth with its offer of life will be heard by all. The divine perseverance is such that Christ "descends to the dead" (Apostles Creed) and proclaims the Good News "even to the dead" (1 Peter 4:6), those whose earthly journey has not been graced by the Word.[41]

Trust in the promise of this universal reach, the length to which God's mercy will go, is not universalism's assurances that all will be saved. Both the divine sovereignty to decide such and the freedom granted to resist the divine invitation preclude such human claims to know what is not within our ken.

At the End of the Story, Christ's invitation becomes adjudication. "He will come again to judge the living and the dead" (Apostles Creed). Eschatological consummation is closure, a reminder of the gravity of choices made. Returning to our present post-9/11 context, it is Christ the judge of the quick and the dead whom the suicide bombers will meet at the Great Assize, as will all of us who contributed to the circumstances that brought that day to be. Of course, given the trajectory of the Story, as View 7 argues, we may consider the possibility of a final penitent and believing "Yes" to all who have not heard aright the Word of truth from the all-loving and all-powerful God. But the divine love is tough as well as tender, making such prognostications an article of hope, not an article of faith.

What of Paul's confidence that "all Israel will be saved" (Rom. 11:26)? Such suggests a different destiny for Jewish people of faith. Might it be that the heirs of Abraham, the "father" of faith (Rom. 4), will learn on that Day the identity of the agent of their Abrahamic faith in the Person and Work of Jesus Christ? Not unlike what faithful Jews contend when they hold that Christians saved by their Noachic faith will learn of its source in the God of Abraham, Isaac, and Jacob.[42]

---

41. This "Andover theory" with its roots in patristic thought is developed in Chapter 6 of this volume.

42. I engaged in just this exchange with Jewish philosopher Michael Wyschogrod during a two-year Jewish-Christian Theological Panel sponsored by the United Church of Christ. For a survey of its materials see "God's Unbroken Covenant with the Jews," *New Conversations* 12, no. 3 (Summer 1990).

Conclusion

To affirm Jesus as the Savior of the world entails the telling of the Great Story, a plot with its characters and events moving over time and space through conflict to resolution. Our reading of the sequence of its chapters seeks to honor the wider grace at work without eliminating the offense of the gospel. We need a Christology much sturdier than the weak accommodations current among the pluralists. Yet also needed is a bold particularity ready to acknowledge the wider mercies of Christ's common grace.[43] Of such is this narrative version of evangelical theology that seeks to interpret his claim to be the way, the truth, and the life, in the context of today's religiously plural world.

43. Philip Jenkins in *The Next Christendom: The Growth of Global Christianity* (New York: Oxford University Press, 2001) documents the demographic changes of an eroding Northern Christianity with its strong pluralist strains and an exploding Southern Christianity with its own orthodox but not so generous tendencies.

CHAPTER 2

Christ in Chiaroscuro

A refrain running through recent theological experimentation that both reveals something fundamental about our times and captures an important facet of the gospel is the motif of *vision*. The word itself appears frequently in contemporary theology and has wide currency in our culture. The reason is that the opening years of the second half of the twentieth century were visionary times, and prophets dreamed great dreams. Imaginative, political, social, psychological, ecological, personal, and ecumenical goals were projected and acted upon with high expectation. The motif of vision is also an ocular metaphor expressing the visual as well as the visionary, suggesting the significance of the media that have been so formative in the same epoch.

The biblical tradition is no stranger to the imagery of vision — from the sight of creation beheld with satisfaction by Yahweh, through the temple vision of Isaiah, to the giving of sight to the blind by Jesus, and the Johannine vision of a new heaven and new earth. The time of this imagery

---

This chapter is the first attempt at laying down the lines of a Christology for this systematics series. Its imagery reflects the "today" of the 1970s with its visionary inheritance from the 1960s as it clashed with the counter-realities of that decade. However, the "light-night" juxtaposition is a constant in the writer's own figural bank, no doubt influenced by his father's Eastern Orthodox heritage, and carried forward through a later Calvinist usage.

may well have come, not only in terms of its explicit biblical usage, but more so in illuminating the center of Christian faith. We take this motif-metaphor as a clue for doctrinal reformulation.

But it is an incomplete clue. Our times have been marked by a rising awareness of the clouds that cross the horizon of high expectation. Sanguine forecasts of earlier futurists have given way to nightmare scenarios. Exuberant promises of "coming of age," friendship with the earth, movement toward peace and freedom, etc., have not been kept.

Hopes are constantly shattered by realities. The vision of the late twentieth century and early twenty-first is not a static one but is on pilgrimage, as a pillar of fire that makes its way along a night journey. Our age is characterized by both affirmation and anguish, dreams so compelling, yet reality so intractable. The larger clue to what moves us is vision-and-reality. And it is a perception about which Christian hope and Christian realism have something to say.

Vision-and-reality can serve as an idiom for the restatement of the person of Christ. And with this primary metaphor we make use of a secondary, supporting one that is also widespread in contemporary society and frequently found in the pedagogy and hymnody of the church, namely, light and darkness. *Vision* is the horizon light that lures us forward; yet *night shadows* are everywhere to be seen. Is it dusk or dawn? To struggle with that question is to be contemporary.

Can we make use of the powerful light-and-darkness themes so prevalent in the Scriptures and the Christian tradition, while at the same time affirming that "Black is beautiful"? The use of light imagery assumes that it can be rescued from white racist captivity (viz. the concept of black light, and the interpretation of darkness as the absence of vision, light, and color, rather than as synonymous with the color "black").

In composing a chiaroscuro doctrine of Christ, we can employ other themes that facilitate the connection between Christian faith and contemporary culture. One is drawn from the Old Testament and one from the New Testament. In the early centuries *Logos* provided the church with a vehicle for interpreting its belief about Christ to a society familiar in one form or another (Platonic, Stoic, Gnostic, Philonic) with such a universal principle. While its wide and varied significations (1300 in Philo alone) made for considerable ambiguity, the thread of common meaning was a conviction about the existence of an organizing principle in the cosmos, an "architect's plan." Given the particular philosophical climate, this design was viewed in rational terms, being understood as "reason" or "word." When the *Logos* theologians used the term, they declared that the cosmological ground-plan had appeared in Jesus Christ. The Prologue of John's Gospel explicitly (and other Johannine literature and the Epistle to the Hebrews implicitly) provided a platform within the New Testament for declaring that the *Logos* had become flesh. In this conversation with culture, it became natural to state the concept of divine design in rational and auditory terms as the "Word of God." In subsequent usage, reinforced by the assumptions of print and/or verbally oriented societies and subcommunities, *Logos* continued to be understood as "Word."

The term *Logos* is, of course, for us archaic. Even its cognitive-verbal clothing may be wearing thin. Yet it represents a quest for, and assertion of, "meaning" in the universe that continues to be real and powerful. In the movements and moods of this epoch, there is either a longing for or conviction about a goal worth pursuing in the world, a dynamic that moves it, or a purpose that pervades it. We can translate *Logos* in this contemporary visual and visionary era, therefore, as the "Vision of God." In continuity with, yet distinct from, the ancient tradition of *visio Dei,* this is not *our* vision of God, but *God's* vision of and for us.

In handling this *Logos* tool, we must remember the wounds it has inflicted on its own users. Its danger lies in allowing society to determine its content. The fundamental reference point for its meaning must be the Christian story and its central chapter, Jesus Christ. The person of Christ is not the supreme exemplification of either some transient sensibility or some "eternal truth of reason." The continuities with the human situation that the *Logos* theme provides must be held in tension with the discontinuity of a "Vision of God" that is both finally revealed and finally fulfilled in the incarnation and the atonement. The *Logos,* as interpreted from within faith, helps us to understand and answer culture's questions, yet it must also do its work by questioning culture's answers.

Logos is a formal concept expressing the "thatness" of universal meaning in Jesus Christ. *Shalom* is a biblical tool we can use to shape its "whatness." The *Logos* principle derives mainly from the New Testament; the image of Shalom from the Old Testament.

In fixing upon the *Shalom* reference point within the lore of faith, we seek to be sensitive to two considerations: (1) the Marcionite temptations that attend efforts to be faithful to the Bible and free of cultural accommodation, and thus the alleged christocentric interpretations that not infrequently fail to take into account their Old Testament environment; and (2) the moment of pregnancy for a biblical accent. The word and idea of *Shalom* are meaningful on both counts. There is a ripe time for its appearance and high visibility. It is a biblical theme that connects with the visual and the visionary. Most of all, its vision of fulfillment is the frame of reference in which Jesus understood his own mission; and his life, death, and resurrection embodied and transfigured the concept.

The content that *Shalom* pours into the divine purpose is best captured in the imagery of the prophetic seers of the "Vision." They project on the screen of the future pictures of wolf and lamb together, swords beaten into plowshares, a child with its hand over the asp's nest, each human being under vine and fig tree. It is a portrait of wholeness, of peace, and of freedom involving nature, humanity, and God. This future-oriented vision is caught initially by the people of Israel in their liberation out of Egyptian bondage and movement toward a land of milk and honey. And its contours are marked out by the sharp demands of the "Law" of that land. In Exodus, Law, and Prophet there merges a dream of liberation and reconciliation before and with God, in the midst of neighbor and nature. The power of this vision continues to move those who struggle for wholeness and hope in self and society. And the agonies in the pilgrimage toward that dream are known by prophets — now as then.

With the motifs of vision and reality, light and darkness, and the interpretive tools of *Logos* and *Shalom*, we have the essential ingredients for a restatement of the doctrine of the person of Christ. Or in the language of the Nairobi Assembly of the World Council of Churches: "Jesus Christ Frees and Unites."

"In the beginning was the Vision, and the Vision was with God, and the Vision was God" (John 1:1). The Vision *of Shalom* is the "indwelling *(endiathetos)* Logos," the everlasting counsel of wholeness, freedom, and peace.

As the Word has its origin in the One who speaks it, or Wisdom in the One who knows it, so the Vision has its source in the Envisioner. It is comparable to the most decisive trinitarian analogy. Father and Son, these are attempts to draw parallels from our experience that express the unity and distinctions pointed to in the Johannine text (John 1:1) and developed in the classic Christian teaching about God. As Athanasius observed in the Nicene debates that there can never be a father without an offspring, so in this analogy an envisioner cannot be conceived without a vision. There never was a time when it was not. It is in this sense that the Son eternally pre-exists in the Godhead. He is the content of the divine intentionality. As in the Augustinian thesis that the Son is the knowledge by which God knows "himself," so the Son is the Vision by which God sees himself. He is the "effulgence of the divine splendor, and the stamp of God's very being" (Heb. 1:3), God of God, Light of Light.

The Envisioner is no "pure visionary," able to fantasize but not to facilitate. God is empowerment as well as envisioning. The Holy Spirit is the enabler of the eternal Vision. God is able to bring the dream to reality. Father, Son, and Spirit are Envisioner, Vision, Power.

Because the Spirit is the guarantor of fulfilled dreams, vision is to be understood as the *promise* as well as the possibility of God. Vision is the resolve and covenant of God, the spiration of intent as well as its aspiration. The Spirit is the pledge, the "assurance of things hoped for," and as such distinguishes Christian hope with its promise of fulfillment from other hopes surrounded by their "maybes." It is in this sense that the second person of the Trinity is the Hope of God.

While the divine intention is empowered by the Spirit, it cannot be thought of as a serenely sketched or carefully detailed blueprint of things to come. The Vision of God is fulfilled in a way commensurate with the divine nature. Or, to adapt a phrase used by Emerson in another context, the end pre-exists in the means. The word "vision" and its companion symbol "light" point to the lure of a long-suffering love, not the coercions of a despot. While fruition is assured, how the goal is to be reached is shaped by the covenant partner. God is the Hound of Heaven willing to follow our most devious trail of flight. Thus *time* is integral to the fulfilling of the divine will, for time is the maneuvering room given by the Envisioner of liberation as well as of reconciliation. Our choices must be won if in the end we are to be free to be together. Since God "takes time seriously," the outworking of the hope of God becomes *a story,* the drama of the moves and counter-moves of a stubborn love in quest of its partner.

"The Vision then was with God at the beginning, and through him all things came to be; no single thing was created without him" (John 1:2-3). By the "law of the Trinity" all the subsistences in the Godhead are present in each of the Deity's acts. As the odyssey of Light begins, Envisioner, Vision, and Power are all at work in creation; the Spirit and Son of the Father fashion the world. Thus the universe is formed by the *Logos prophorikos:* it is made for the destiny of *Shalom.* By the power of the Spirit the intention of God is etched on all there is. A reflection of the vision is to be seen in the patterns and rhythms of nature. And the capacity to discern the purpose of creation is given to one creature formed with eyes to see the light, made "in the image of God." "All that came to be was alive with life and that life was the light of men" (John 1:4). The *Logos prophorikos* includes the *Logos spermatikos*, seeding humanity with its percipient graces. The world of humanity and nature is made in order to be drawn toward its luminous goal.

Or so it was in the Edenic purposes of God. How can we express the goodness of this creation and at the same time honor what happened, and happens, when the dream meets the reality of choice by those called to pursue it? For the cosmologies of another age, a paradisiacal before-the-fall is believable. We in turn mumble about the intention before the act, yet wonder if this psychologizing does justice to the opening chapter of the tale once referred to as "original righteousness." Can it be conceived as a good world evolving to the level of a developed freedom, and at this stage of creativity having those gifted with such choice saying a lethal "No!" to the vision? However expressed, the abysmal fact of human malevolence intrudes upon the movement outward of the eternal purpose. A shadow falls across the path of light. Human sin turns upon its heel away from the invitation toward the envisioned future. The Holy Spirit is taken away, and human vision loses its power.

The Christian story tells of a companion to human sin, the Devil. The Evil One accounts for that surd of militancy against the divine intent that cannot be neatly traced to human willfulness, and one asserted to be the occasion for it. While this satanic power was viewed in other times as personal, it comes to us in the impersonal onslaughts of high-technology warfare, systemic oppression, subterranean psychological drive, historical and natural cataclysm. We experience its reality as impersonal force. The ally of sin comes dressed in the mask of Evil rather than Devil. The work of these partners is the demise of the dream. The wages of sin and Evil are death.

Yet the Creator does not give up on creation. The Story's light imagery continues. So comes the rainbow of Noah. Its multi-colors suggest the variety of graces that sustain the world in its ongoing journey to its Easter sunrise Center and meridian End. Historically, the promise to preserve the world on its pilgrimage by giving it a glimpse of the true, the good, the beautiful, and the holy has been called the Noachic covenant, a chapter in its own right. By the muted light of this arc, human sight can see the distant contours of a promised land it cannot reach. Its transcendent unity is intuited in the myths and mysteries of the world's religions, however that unity is relocated from its position out and ahead to one conceived to be in, or down, or back. The mind of the philosopher and scientist, the eye of the artist and reformer — fragments of a universal conscience — darkly perceive the outlines of the end that claims us. God has not left us without a witness to the goal for which we are made. Yet these intimations come as yearnings, elusive imperatives, broken by our untruth, ugliness, and perversity.

How will the promise be kept, the vision penetrate darkened hearts, death turned into life? A patient love signals rebel humanity. Light again arises. So a pillar of fire moves before a people chosen for a special disclosure of light, pointing the way out of slavery into freedom and toward a far country of righteousness and peace. The leadership of this pilgrim band is given sight to see the law of this promised land. And when it is violated, an unswerving Envisioner illuminates the horizon for still other seers, prophets who look toward the future and glimpse the lineaments of *Shalom* in vine and fig tree, leopard and kid, plowshare and pruning hook.

It is the grace of Israel to see more clearly. What is dimly perceived by the common eye through the "common grace" of Noah's rainbow now radiates the horizon of a tiny near-Eastern tribe. This people of God has 20-20 vision of the goal for which we are made, and is, as such, the conscience of humanity. And the human race, comfortable in the illusions of its myopia, pours out its rancor on an Israel that reminds it of what it chooses not to see.

As the covenant people lived with the luminous, its prophets increasingly apprehended the ambiguities in its own history. Thus the "Day of the Lord" threatened to turn into night. It seemed that where *Shalom* became visible it came at the same time under attack from within and without. The visionary people were scattered; their seers and exemplars drank the cup of suffering. Who will deliver *Shalom* from its defeats? Surely the God of Israel will not forsake the promise. Will some empowerment come to the powerless dream? Will a messianic king of glory usher in the day? Is the historical suffering of the vision itself a clue to how victory will come? The unresolved question of the relationship of the divine faithfulness to an ungrateful creation, the determined pursuit by God of the vision and the unremitting assault upon it, sets the stage for the decisive act in the Christian drama.

"The Vision became flesh; he came to dwell among us, and we saw his glory, such glory as befits the Father's only Son, full of grace and truth"

(John 1:14). *The doing of God* in history and nature becomes the *being* of God in our world; *Logos prophorikos* (promised) becomes *Logos ensarkos* (enfleshed). The light that signaled from a distance through the darkness draws near. Upon this man Jesus a spotlight fell, and bathed him in its radiance. He lived and moved and had his being in it, and we "beheld the light in the face of Christ."

"The girl's name was Mary. The angel that went in said to her, 'Greetings most favored one! The Lord is with you'" (Luke 1:27b-28). Where there is gracious *favor toward,* there is also *power in.* In trinitarian terms, where the Envisioner projects the vision, there also is power. Father, Son, and Spirit are together at Incarnation. The "virgin birth" is a traditional way of expressing this empowerment. At the conception of the Holy Spirit something really happens in history evidencing the eternal procession toward and into time. How can this empowerment be stated in an epoch moved by its own kind of miracles? The commanding miracle in a time sensitive to the collision of vision and reality is their friendship, the presence of *Shalom* in a world of hate and hurt. Thus the empowerment of the vision is best communicable as the radiance *in* Christ of the light that shined *upon* him.

The miracle of love must be expressed free of the Docetisms and Monophysitisms that erase the real humanity of Jesus. The very metaphor we are using has lent itself to this dehumanization, with the historical Jesus disappearing in a blaze of light (the patristic figure of a glowing coal). Against this it must be asserted that the one to whom light became proximate was a man of Israel with flesh and history of a piece with ours. This solidarity with us means growth, struggle, temptation. He was "of one substance" with our humanity, sharing our finitude, including that point so gingerly treated by the very Fathers and Councils that made formal declarations of his consubstantiality with us — his perception of the way things were, that finite mind taken from him by the Apollinarians and even imperiled by orthodoxy. He saw the world as a first-century Jew, out of a gestalt of memory and hope that furnished him with the framework for understanding what was happening in his time, and materials for his own self-understanding.

He was what we are in all respects except one. On him shone the full light of the divine glory. Its intensity and omnipresence in his life was so compelling that he could not "take his eyes off of it." An overwhelming vision claimed unswerving attention. He beheld the divine glory with "unclouded vision." This undeviating orientation to the purpose of God was the issue of proximate light. It was constituted by an illumination of the perception of the events of his time, and an empowerment to enact a role in the drama he saw unfolding. This expression in him of the "wisdom of God" and the "power of God" took the form of: (a) his teaching about the in-breaking of the kingdom of God, (b) his self-understanding as a participant in that action of the future, (c) his conduct toward this vision that gripped him.

From the "new quest" among biblical scholars, through the effort to "begin from below" in Christology, to a post-critical tendency in exegesis that seeks to relate but not capitulate to fashions in biblical studies, there is a current determination to root the meaning of Jesus Christ in the data we have about what he said and did.

(1) Jesus pointed to and prayed for the onrushing future. The reign of God was coming toward the world, the rule in which the pure in heart would see God, the peacemaker would be vindicated, the prisoner released, the lame walk, the dead be raised, and the kingdom come. In political, personal, and natural idiom he portrayed Israel's ancient hope of *Shalom*. For him this New Age was at hand, when humanity, nature, and God would be free and peaceful before and with each other.

This pointing was more than the future-orientation of the prophet. "At hand" meant here as well as near. The power of evil was even now under attack and losing ground to the coming King. And this heavenly favor toward us manifests itself as power among us, as the finger of the Regent even now casts out of the world the occupying armies of the Evil One. That is why the sick are healed, sins are forgiven, demons exorcized, temptation overcome, and faith empowered. And we are called to pray that this kingdom finally come on earth in the power of its fulfillment and the glory of its light.

(2) Who is this Jesus who tells this tale? He is the first wave of the in-breaking future. Through him the powers of the New Age find expression. He has authority over the demonic and makes the wounded whole. Through him others are put in touch with the flow toward freedom and reconciliation. He is liberator and peace, the firstfruits of the kingdom that shall be. He is in unity with the new realm and on terms of intimacy with its King. While the debate over the meaning and self-application of the titles of Jesus continues to wax warm, there is an impressive body of scholarship which holds the view that Jesus saw himself to be of a piece with the divine initiative being taken in the kingdom's arrival.

From Jesus' self-understanding it is a short step to the church's declaration that in Christ "dwells the fullness of the Godhead bodily" (Col. 2:9), and the varied expressions of this unity in the names and categories ascribed to him. He is the Son of the Father, the second Adam, Lord, *Logos*. Here is the one in whom vision became reality, in whom light penetrated darkness.

The way of life of this man confirms his pointing and self-understanding. He does what he says and is. His faithfulness to and exemplification of *Shalom* establishes Jesus as "proper man," the prototypal human being whose existence fulfills the hope frustrated by Adam. He is truly human in a normative as well as descriptive sense.

The intention of the traditional concept of the perfect humanity and "sinlessness" of Jesus can be expressed with the help of the imagery of vision and light. Jesus' true and fulfilled humanity was constituted by his clear-sighted perception of, and unswerving obedience to, the vision. He saw the light and lived and moved and had his being in it. Because the light drew near to him, it so captured his gaze and orientation that it possessed him. He followed its path to the end. The tales of temptation at the opening and close of his ministry portray the persisting invitation of the powers of darkness to turn aside from the direction of light. But his commitment was undeviating, the "set" of his will and behavior arrow-straight. The lure of the light *of Shalom* guided the life he lived toward those honored citizens of the kingdom, the wretched of the earth, the despised, the persecuted, the peacemaker, the stranger, the poor, the prisoner, the sick, the sinner. In his love, he was the love announced to be arriving. And his final act, the acceptance of Calvary, crowned his career of suffering servanthood.

In grasping the relation of the historical Jesus to the doctrine of the Person of Christ, we make only passing reference to the current discussion of his political role, as that question is raised both by those who hold him to have affinities with the Zealot tradition and by those who seek accreditation for an apolitical or even anti-liberation understanding of the Christian faith. The portrayal of Jesus as a revolutionary, however well intentioned in its effort to demonstrate the liberation implications of faith, is not supported by the evidence. How could it be otherwise if we are correct in our understanding of Jesus as the one who saw himself, and the one who in fact was, the enfleshment of a *Shalom* in which swords are beaten into plowshares, neighbor does not rise up in anger against neighbor, and all dwell in peace and freedom from hate and hurt? On the other hand, to draw a straight line from this transcendent future unity to a lifestyle of interiorized piety, disdainful of worldly thrust toward political liberation, is faithless to both Bethlehem and Calvary. The impact of Incarnation on ethics is, on the one hand, the definition of the vision that both claims and judges us, without which we would have no ultimate reference point for our conduct. On the other hand, it dignifies that arena in which we grope toward the vision, that grubby world of hard political, economic, and social choices. The crucifixion of the vision both shows us its depths as suffering love and makes clear the terms on which we in this dark valley must pursue it — in brokenness and approximations of the perfection in which it appeared in Christ, in anguish and penitence for actions of lesser evil necessitated by obedience to the vision in a corrupt world, and thus judged by, as well as lured toward, its horizon light.

When we speak about the cross, we have reached the boundary between Incarnation and Atonement. From the side of Incarnation, the cross is seen as the deepest penetration into our history by the light of God. If Bethlehem and Galilee, birth and life, give us the *esse* of enfleshment, then Jerusalem and Golgotha, passion and death, give us its *plene esse*. On Calvary, there is the same selfless love as earlier, but now subjected to its heaviest attacks, and disclosing in its response its profoundest resources and deepest reality. "Greater love has no man than this. . . ." Suffering and dying love is *Shalom* at its fullest. And here, at the same time, the disclosure turns into action; on the cross God *does*, as well as *is:* The Incarnation is crowned and completed by the Atonement, the redemptive suffering, death, and resurrection of *Shalom* that defeat the night powers. The Work of Christ is the issue of the Person who is very God, very human, truly one, the vision enfleshed and empowered.

The doctrine of the Person of Christ can be understood in terms of a God who *is* what is envisioned and *does* what is dreamed. The Incarnation is at the center of a saga of the vision of God and its struggle with a recalcitrant reality. As the drama unfolds, the indwelling purpose moves out in creative and beckoning love, only to be spurned by an abused freedom. In patience, *Shalom* returns to confer special vision on a chosen people, and finally enters a rebel humanity to absorb and overcome its last assaults. This is the story of the God who keeps a promise. At its heart is an event in which vision intersects reality, one that points toward a fulfillment in which vision *becomes* reality.

Part II

CHRISTOLOGY, CHURCH, AND MINISTRY

CHAPTER 3

The Person of Christ and the Being of the Church

T he Person of Christ . . . the Incarnation. We sing about it every Christmas:

> "Joy to the world, the Lord has come!" "O Come, O come, Emmanuel . . ." "Veiled in flesh the Godhead see, hail the incarnate Deity . . ." "Word of the Father, now in flesh appearing. . . ."

The very Lord God comes among us as an infant. The eternal "Word of God," the "Word of the Father" or the "Son of the Father," took our very own flesh and blood. Here is the defining deed of God in the biblical Story.

One of the advances made by the Reformation was its placing at the heart of Christian belief "justification by grace through faith." We are made right with God not by our presumed good works, but by the gracious act of God in Christ! As the liturgy says it:

> "Lamb of God who takes away the sin of the world. . . ."

God, in the Person of Christ, received the judgment you and I deserve for rebellion against our Maker. All the suffering, death, and hell we bring on ourselves by our sin finally does not fall on us but on *God* . . . on the cross, the "crucified God." Jesus Christ, truly God as well as truly human, is sacrificed for our sin. Here, the Reformers said, is the central atoning Work of

Christ — the at-one-ment of God with an alienated world made possible by the death of Christ on the cross.

When this atoning Work is received by sheer faith alone, the drama of "justification" reaches its goal. The divine deed on Calvary of justifying, atoning Love is received by the believer's justifying faith — one made possible again only by God's own initiative — a "grace" that births in us the faith that justifies.

The fundamental Reformation teachings are part and parcel of the theology of the Mercersburg theologians of the nineteenth century, Philip Schaff and John Williamson Nevin. But these men also said to the Reformation churches: while you are stressing the Atonement, don't forget the Incarnation! They saw it — and its implications — getting diminished, and even eliminated, by those caught up in the revivals of their period. What came through in these "awakenings" was an Atonement available to those who had a fervent conversion experience, often induced by firebrand preachers — a practice symbolized by a convert's trip down the aisle to the "anxious bench." So the emphasis in revivalist religion turned more and more to what *we* do, rather than what God has done in Christ.

As a result of the preoccupation with one's own interiority, "church" became an association of individuals who laid claim to the approved experience. With it came a "sect spirit," a splitting off from other Christians, with the declaration that only those so experientially accredited constituted the true church. As part of this "sect plague" came a disdain of, and departure from, the historic church that had originally birthed and nurtured them.

What is missing in all this is *the Incarnation.* Yes, said the Mercersburg folk, the sectarians are right about some things: the world is fallen and needs to be redeemed; Christ came to give life to the dead, to atone for sin and save the lost. Further, the zealous come-outers even held officially to the teaching that Christ is the unique divine-human Person. But they became so enamored of their own religious experiences that these "subjective" things ran roughshod over the "objective" deed of God done in, and flowing from, the Incarnation, including its communication to future generations through the "objective" medium of the historic church.

Here is the way the Mercersburg theologians expressed their conviction, using the biblical figures of life and death: We are "dead in our trespasses" and need *life.* Christ *is* Life (John 14:6). He entered our history decisively at Bethlehem. The incarnate Life dwelt among us, teaching, healing, dying, rising, ascending. As such, Christ is the *second* Adam who brings life to a world in the throes of the death inflicted by the first Adam and his heirs.

On the day of Pentecost, Christ passed on his healing, saving benefits, breathing the Spirit of Life into his earthly body "so that *we* might have life. . . ." Here in the *church* — warts and all — we are given Life. And that church with its distinctive marks — unity, sanctity, catholicity, apostolicity — has been with us ever since. As *one,* from the Christ who is not divided, we cannot rend it asunder by sectarian strife. As *holy* — by virtue of the residence of Christ — we cannot claim to *make* it holy by our good works. As *catholic,* its universality gathers to itself a variety of parts and gifts over time and space. As *apostolic,* it is given continuity with that first company by its apostolic Scripture, teaching, and ministry.

Mercersburg is a very earthy theology. God is earthed in the incarnate Christ. Christ is earthed in the tangibilities of the body of Christ. In the theological and philosophical language of their day the Mercersburg theologians stressed the "objective" and "historical":

> an objective historical form, an order of grace flowing from Christ, and altogether different from the order of nature, nothing more or less than the idea of the Holy Catholic Church. . . .[1]

These terms say to us that: (1) God takes our time and space seriously. We meet the God of the Bible in singular persons, events, and communities — not apart from them in the gardens of personal piety or universal spirituality. (2) History comes to a turning point in the incarnate Christ, hence the "christocentric" focus of Mercersburg. The Incarnation is the point of entry of the mighty God, as the second Person of the Trinity — becoming thereby the world's defining moment. (3) Christ continues unfailingly among us to complete what he started — never deserting us — "I am with you always, to the end of the age" (Matt. 28:20). Therefore the *visible* church, the body of Christ on earth, is the medium through which he is now eminently present to us. (4) The Son of the Father has risked "vulnerability," becoming accessible to us through very earthy means — water, bread, and wine. So in the simple visible objective rite of baptism, grace

---

1. John Williamson Nevin, "The New Liturgy," in *Catholic and Reformed: Selected Writings of John Williamson Nevin,* ed. Charles Yrigoyen Jr. and George H. Bricker (Pittsburgh: The Pickwick Press, 1978), p. 378.

envelops us in the arms of the body of Christ. In the tangible actions and tastable elements of Holy Communion the glorified Christ offers us the nourishment of his body and blood. And with these things, as well, Christ risks their stewardship by very ordinary people like the first apostles, and their successors in ordained pastoral ministry. (5) A *living* body is a *growing* body. "History" is where life and growth happen. So mark well the development that has taken place, and continues to do so in the church. It is a gift of the Presence of Christ and the power of the Holy Spirit.

So Christ gives *himself* to us — "vivific" Life — in the incarnate Person and atoning Work, and in their issue, the Spirit-filled body of Christ on earth. No wonder that Henry Harbaugh wrote in a much-sung Mercersburg hymn:

> Jesus, I live to thee, the loveliest and best,
> Thy life in me, my life in thee;
> In Heaven's blessed love I rest.

Objective *and* Subjective

There is another side to the Mercersburg understanding of the church, a side that gives special impetus to its ecumenical vision. We come at it here through an unexpected portal: misunderstandings of Mercersburg.

In polemical moments, the Mercersburg theologians sounded so insistent on the objective and the historical that the subjective and the personal seemed to get downplayed. But overall, and in moments of careful self-definition, the truly catholic and inclusive spirit of the Mercersburg theology shines through. Thus Schaff can even acknowledge the value of the Puritans, the very epitome of the subjectivity he assailed:

> The deep moral earnestness, the stern self-discipline, the unbending force of character must fill the unprejudiced historian with admiration. There are reasons for its war against false forms.[2]

And our personal act of justifying faith is, for him, "the article of life":

---

2. Philip Schaff, *The Principle of Protestantism,* ed. Bard Thompson and George Bricker (Philadelphia: United Church Press, 1964), p. 80.

The all-sufficient satisfaction of Christ takes hold upon the individual subjectively in justification. This is a judicial, declarative act on the part of God, by which he first pronounces the sin-crushed, contrite sinner free from guilt as it regards the past, for the sake of the only-begotten Son, and then . . . makes over to him in boundless mercy the full righteousness of the same.[3]

And Nevin echoes Schaff:

The Gospel . . . cannot save . . . without . . . experience (of) its power, on which account it is, that we need to be placed in communication with it through faith.[4]

But, so as not to be mistaken, Nevin quickly adds,

The subjective here, sundered from the objective, can give at best only a spurious evangelicalism. . . .[5]

Another place the balance of objective and subjective appears is in Mercersburg's relating of the Incarnation to the Atonement. The earlier description of the Atonement in this chapter incorporated Mercersburg's stress on the Incarnation. In contrast to popular versions of the "penal theory" associated with the sect movements, the cross was portrayed as the judgment of the righteous God falling on the Jesus who stood in our place. Forgotten here was the *divine*-human Person that did the saving Work. *God, as such,* not just a human Jesus, received the divine judgment in the Person of the Son (2 Cor. 5:19). As Luther put it, the divine mercy took into itself the divine wrath. Or in Mercersburg metaphor, the divine Life overcame the death we sinners deserved in the atoning Work of the divine-human Person. So Easter signals the triumph that took place on the cross.

Again, the sacraments, neglected by both the subjectivity-drenched revivalists of their day and the sermon-oriented preachers of their own Reformed tradition, prompted the Mercersburg theologians to so stress Holy Communion that their critics accused them of forgetting the Word *proclaimed.* Not so in the overall picture, as the Mercersburg liturgies demonstrate. *Both* Word and sacrament are means of grace. Preaching is the way

3. Schaff, *The Principle of Protestantism*, p. 99.
4. Nevin, "The New Liturgy," p. 377.
5. Nevin, "The New Liturgy," p. 377.

the Word of Life calls forth the response of faith integral to saving grace. Indeed, the widely acclaimed World Council of Churches document, *Baptism, Eucharist and Ministry,* reflects the Mercersburg spirit with its understanding of the eucharist as including the Word preached.[6] The stress on the catechism and the creeds also demonstrates the importance to Mercersburg of the communication of the Word *by* the word as well as *in* the sacrament.

Sacramental misunderstandings were also possible when it came to baptism. The stress on the objective divine initiative sounded to some like an automatic "baptismal regeneration." Not so, for Mercersburg spoke instead of "baptismal grace," a new relationship to Christ through the church that *offered* salvation, one rendered efficacious only when received by faith — that of parent and sponsor standing in for the infant, and of the baptized later come of age, or concurrently so in the case of adults.

The struggle of that day with revivalism and its subjective exuberances prompted stress on the objectivity of the pastoral office and the church's sacramental life, and did not give the attention to the partner "ministry of the laity" that was, in fact, implicit in its premises. It was there in Question 32 of its honored Heidelberg Catechism, where the continuation of the threefold ministry of Christ (prophet, priest, and king) is assigned to *laity* as well as clergy. And in the liturgies of Mercersburg, the laity play a participative role. At work here is the catholicity of Mercersburg's vision, needing further theological development. Yes, the apostolic ministry comes down to us through the pastoral office, stewarding and guarding the Life-*giving* organs of the body. But the complementary ministry of the Life-*moving* limbs — the body walking and working in the world — is a natural implication of the Mercersburg catholicity. A ministry of the laity in the "church scattered" is companion to the ministry of Word and Sacrament in the "church gathered."

Again, on the matter of the ministry, Mercersburg's "high doctrine" could be interpreted as requiring the "historic episcopate" as the bearer of apostolic succession. Indeed, Mercersburg was, and is, sometimes confused with the Oxford movement within the Anglican communion (and out of it, as with Cardinal Newman's departure to Rome). The Mercersburg theologians did value its sacramental and liturgical concerns but be-

6. See World Council of Churches Faith and Order Commission, *Baptism, Eucharist and Ministry* (Geneva: WCC, 1982), p. 10.

42

lieved that Oxford did not understand the fact of *growth* integral to the *life* of the body. Its preoccupation with the forms of the early centuries, including the historic episcopate, petrified the living and growing organism of the church. Continuing apostolic identity was crucial to the Mercersburg theologians. It was borne through apostolic Scripture, credo, and the ministry of Word and sacrament. The form of the latter was a matter of the *well*-being of the church, not its very being, to be determined by the needs of the living and growing body. Today's participants in the Mercersburg movement are in churches that do not ordain in episcopal succession, but they are, at the same time, supportive of the proposals of a threefold ministry (bishop, presbyter, and deacon) in *The Consultation on Church Union.* Here, ecumenical commitments can accept it on the basis of the *bene esse* — the well-being of a church universal.

Mercersburg theologians, with their belief in a living and growing body, were committed to recognizing their own historic limitations, as in the issues surrounding ministry just noted. Fighting battles with the unchurchly ideologies of the day meant also that they did not draw out the implications of their own christological and incarnational premises with regard to the world outside the church. Schaff, Nevin, and Harbaugh did teach that Christ, the eternal Word, brings to be, and is active in, the whole of the creation (John 1:1-4). Such a cosmic and historical Christology in the present context means sensitivity to the incognito Christ in the world wherever discerned by the revelation of Christ given to the church in Scripture. Especially so, as Matthew 25:31-46 declares, where enfleshed — incarnational — deeds of mercy and justice are done to and with the hungry, poor, abused, and disenfranchised. Hints of this are found in the Mercersburg theologians' support of the anti-slavery and temperance struggles of their day. These themes need to be more aggressively integrated into the churchly theology of Mercersburg.

The Emmaus road story gives us a clue to a larger catholicity. Christ travels in the world, incognito ("in profile") on the road alongside the disciples . . . and us. Yet, in the upper room, at the (eucharistic) meal, Christ meets the disciples . . . and us "face to face," disclosing who he is. Christ is encountered on the "road" and as Presence shared and known in the "room."

In each of the above quests for full-orbed teaching, Mercersburg's ecumenical assumption is at work: responsible doctrine and orthodox faith rise out of the church catholic; the half-truths of heresy are the predictable result of schism and sectarianism. The latter, in turn, make for reduced and distorted teaching. The catholicity of a Pauline Corinth is a good guide, bringing us back to the controlling metaphor of Mercersburg: the church as the body of Christ. The body is not whole without its many parts, each contributing to its vitality (1 Cor. 12). We welcome the gift each brings to the life and health of the body! At the same time, the pretension of a single organ to constitute the body in its entirety must be rejected. "The eye cannot say to the hand, 'I have no need of you'" (1 Cor. 12:21).

Conclusion

We desperately need the gifts the Mercersburg theologians bring to the church, and to the doctrine of the Person of Christ as it relates to the church. With it comes its catholic, Corinthian vision, an ecumenism of doctrine as well as denomination. Away with our current tribalisms, with competing groups or reductionist emphases claiming to be the whole of the church or the fullness of the gospel. Such convictions put one's feet on the Mercersburg path, and on one's lips the confession:

I believe in the holy catholic church.

CHAPTER 4

The Work of Christ and the Doing of Ministry

F or years a group of people in the Boston science community met in members' homes. Each evening a different member took the "hot seat" to talk about his or her work. Frank reported on the breakthroughs in gene splicing in his experiments at MIT. Al tested out with the group a code of ethics he developed for cancer research. Jill described a new strain of corn being studied in her laboratory and the impact it could have on hunger in Third World countries. George told of his misgivings about his company's new MX missile contract. Bill brought charts and graphs to get feedback on his effort to widen employee decision-making power in the small firm he had founded. Sandra explained the dilemmas of many science teachers these days as they struggle with the creationist-evolutionist controversy. Carl shared his attempt to alert fellow pediatricians to the medical effects of a nuclear attack and the need for a freeze on this weaponry. It is in this learning laboratory of real people, members of Eliot Church, Newton, that the following proposals have been developed and refined.[1]

1. The pastor of the congregation (Herb) and I were members of the group in our capacity as theological resources. The kind of group this is reinforces a central thesis of this essay: at the heart of the ministry of the laity is the ministry of the workplace. The latter, however, by no means exhausts the former. Ministry of the whole people of God includes those too young or too old for the work of the world, those whose "work" is neither denominated or remunerated as such, and those who live out their ministry principally in the worlds of

What is going on when Frank expresses doubt about the commercialization of gene research or Al urges protection standards for laboratory workers or Jill puts up with the hassles of her job in the interest of its far-reaching benefits?

Are they acts of moral conscience? Indeed. Is it the practicing of one's Christianity? Yes. But something more is happening. It has to do with the answer to the question, "Who carries forward the work of Christ?"

In Christian theology the "work of Christ" refers to the service Christ performed for the salvation of the world in his life, death, and resurrection. "The Son of Man also came not to be served but to serve" (Mark 10:45). His work is his *ministry*. As such, Christ is *the* minister. Therefore all those who are called to ministry are the present representatives of who he was and what he did. Christ continues his ministry in their ministry.

Christian tradition has portrayed the work of Jesus Christ as prophet, priest, and king. As prophet he foretells the truth; as priest he makes a sacrifice for our sin; and as king he triumphs over evil and death. The church has made use of this threefold office of Christ in characterizing the ministry that succeeds Christ's work. In particular, it regularly describes the functions of the clergy in these triple terms. In the Protestant tradition, "pastors are those who are at the head of a definite flock for teaching, administering the sacraments and exercising oversight."[2] In the Roman Catholic tradition, ordination to holy orders confers a threefold power: magisterial, sacerdotal, and jurisdictional.[3] While there are fundamental differences between Protestant and Roman Catholic views on ministry, it is instructive to note the agreement at this point. In both cases the ordained clergy continue the threefold work of Jesus Christ; what he did in his ministry, they do in their ministry. In the prophet office, therefore, a pastor proclaims the Word, in

---

leisure and community service/social action. Yet in all these areas it is the life and movement of the body in the world, its vitality, that constitutes the ministry entailed, as does servanthood in the workplace. This is also true for those laity for whom the institutional church itself is in an arena of significant ministry. It is carried out there as a ministry of vitality to the extent that the matters of identity uppermost in that place are shaped in the direction of the world

2. Quoted in Heinrich Heppe, *Reformed Dogmatics,* rev. and ed. Ernst Bizer (London: George Allen & Unwin Ltd., 1950), pp. 676-77. See also Augustus Strong, *Systematic Theology* (Valley Forge, Pa.: Judson Press, 1907), pp. 916-17; the charge to the minister in almost any Protestant ordination service.

3. C. Cronin, "The Sacrament of Order," in *The Teaching of the Catholic Church: A Summary of Catholic Doctrine,* ed. George D. Smith (New York: Macmillan, 1927), pp. 1025-27.

preaching, teaching, and many and various ways in both words and deeds; in the priestly office in serving at the altar, in the leading of worship, and preeminently in the celebration of the sacraments and rites of the church, along with deeds of sacrifice and suffering; in the royal office as in a leadership role, yet always in the footsteps of the One who was a "servant-leader."

The exercise of this threefold ministry has prompted Calvin to declare that "neither the light or heat of the sun nor any food nor drink, are so necessary to nourish and sustain the present life as the apostolical and pastoral office is to the preservation of the church in the world." And Luther speaks in no less exalted tones: "A Christian preacher is a minister of God who is set apart, yea is an angel of God, a savior of many people, a prince in the kingdom of Christ and among the people of God. . . ." As a "steward of the mysteries," therefore, the pastor continues the function performed by the apostles, and thus the role that is rightly called "the apostolical and pastoral office."

But there is more to be said of the ministry that continues Christ's own threefold work. A full-orbed New Testament understanding of the *munus triplex* will return us to the living room where Frank and Jill and their friends are holding forth.

The Body of Christ

We begin with a cluster of New Testament texts that deal with the image of the church as the body of Christ. The people of God together constitute that organism: "many members . . . are one body . . ." (Rom. 12:4-5). As befits a body, it "does not consist of one member but of many" (1 Cor. 12:14). Thus "there is one body and one Spirit . . ." (Eph. 4:4) that animates this community. Therefore the continuation of Jesus Christ and his ministry in our midst is his body in its *entirety* as it is empowered by his Spirit. In these key passages are materials for getting at a full understanding of the continuing ministry of Christ though his Body.

Identity and Vitality

The Ephesians passage on the body of Christ has been the subject of considerable attention in recent discussions of the ministry of the laity. The debate about "the fatal comma" has eventuated in translations of Ephesians 4:11-12 that render the text, "And his gifts were that some should be apostles, some prophets, some evangelists, some pastors and teachers to equip the saints for the work of ministry . . ." (RSV) or "to equip God's people for work in his service . . ." (NEB).[4] Thus understood, the passage provides reason for (a) extending the concept of ministry to all the members of the body and (b) viewing the particular role of pastors and teachers as that of "equipping the saints."

As valuable as these insights are, this Ephesians text needs to be enriched by themes from Romans 12 and 1 Corinthians 12, for circumstances in these other churches bring into bolder relief other aspects of collegial service. Thus Paul's counsel to the Corinthian congregation, given in the light of inordinate claims made by one or another of the parts of that community, has to do with the two-way traffic of ministry. "The eye cannot say to the hand, 'I have no need of you . . .'" (1 Cor. 12:21) applies not only to the saints who need equipping from the pastors and teachers, but to the pastors and teachers who need equipping from the saints as well. Empowering moves in two directions. It goes also from helper and healer to prophet and apostle. Earlier views of the relation of clergy to laity do indeed affirm the ministry of the laity but see the relationship as the "ordained ministry" equipping the saints for their work (the clergy as "quartermaster corps" feeding the troops, an earlier often-used figure). This is too simplistic in the light of Pauline description of *mutual* empowerment.

The Corinthian and Roman texts further refine and enrich the apostles-prophets-saints relationship of Ephesians 4 in their accent on the multiplicity of the gifts of the Spirit and thus, the plurality of non-clerical ministries within the body of Christ. An examination of this range of different services adds significantly to the clarification of the key question we are posing about the relationship of the two sub-communities traditionally referred to as clergy and laity. The services that keep company with apostle, prophet, teacher, and their equivalents — workers of miracles, healers, helpers, administrators, speakers in various tongues, interpreters of tongues, contributors, doers of works of mercy — strongly suggest a pattern of interrelationship. Taken together and interpreted in the setting

---

4. For example, see Hans-Ruedi Weber, *Salty Christians* (New York: Seabury Press, 1965). The old translation places a comma between "saints" and "for," thereby limiting ministry to apostles, evangelists, pastors, and teachers.

of the body imagery, the *commonality, particularity,* and *mutuality* of ministry emerge.

Commonality

The commonality of ministry is grounded in the body metaphor itself, that is, the ministry of Christ, which is the source and norm of all Christian ministry carried forward through the present body of Christ. All of what Christ was on earth then continues to all who compose the body of Christ on earth now. The powers and mandates of ministry are given to the one body by the animating breath of the Spirit. Thus the continuity with Christ comes through the unity of the body of Christ: as one body, all the people of God share in the common gifts and claims. It is in this sense that some of the earlier formulations on the ministry of the laity are to be understood:

(a) The people of God are the *laos,* and therefore all members, clergy included, are "the laity." (b) Baptism is the ordination into the ministry of the *laos.* Whatever particularities are acknowledged, therefore, are outgrowths of this common body that lives from the breath of the one Spirit under the work of the one Lord, to which body belongs the primal inheritance of both power and imperative.

Particularity

The particularity is as much a feature of the body image as is the commonality, for bodies are not what they are without the variety of their parts. But the question we have posed about clergy and laity and the character of the multiple gifts points us to a deeper pattern within the pluralism of ministry. Described in the Pauline imagery of these texts are some organs and limbs associated with the *vital signs* of a living self, from beating heart to moving feet. And there are some body parts associated with the *identifying marks* of a particular selfhood, from memory cells to speaking lips. One keeps the body alive and alert, and the other remembers and declares whose body it is.

The signs of life in the earliest Christian community — helping, healing, miracle working, tongues, acts of mercy, serving, contributing — all are ministries of *vitality*. Those reminders within the body of the source of that life — apostle, prophet, pastor, teacher — are the ministries of *identity*. The gifts of vitality give the body life and locomotion. They empower it to walk and work in the world. They move it in pilgrimage on the way to God's future. As stewards of its *hopes*, they preserve the church from nostalgia. Those members of the body, oriented in their calling to the secular arena (outside the institutional church) whom we have called the "laity," constitute these ministries of vitality. As the *church scattered*, they take the body into the world and are the body in its vital movements of outreach; they are the Spirit's organs of mission.

The gifts of identity give the body self-identification. They empower it to know and to be who it is. As the stewards of its memories, they preserve it from amnesia. They point the Christian company to its "whence" so that it may better know its "whither." These members of the body, directed in their calling to the churchly arena and whom we have identified as "the clergy," constitute the ministries of identity. In serving the *church gathered*, they are called to a vocation of empowerment of the community at the place of in-reach; they are the Spirit's organs of *nurture*.

Mutuality

The mutuality of ministries is fundamental to their communality and inseparable from their particularity. As parts of a body animated by the breath of the same Spirit, they cannot perform their functions without being in living interrelationship. The head cannot say to the feet, "I have no need of you" (1 Cor. 12:21). The ministries of identity require the ministries of vitality to carry out the very purposes of identity.

Can Herb preach on Sunday in the most meaningful way to a congregation that includes Carl and Al and Jill if he does not know what happens in their lives on Monday afternoon or, perhaps, has not been helped by them in a Tuesday evening group to ask the right questions of the text he explores in his study on Wednesday morning? And the ministries of vitality require the ministries of identity in order to be the church on their terrain. Can Frank make his most effective witness in his MIT laboratory without the perspective brought by the lore of Scripture and tradition in which Herb is trained and called to share with him in preaching, teaching, and worship?

Mutuality of ministry entails not only the enrichment of each by the other but also the active participation of each in the very being and work of the other. As in the ancient trinitarian doctrine of "perichoresis" in which the Persons in the divine being enjoy their own individuality but at the same time have such a unity that they "coinhere," so the ministries of identity and vitality have a genuine particularity but at the same time live in mutual participation.

George, as longtime advisor of the Eliot Youth Group, has had a very strong influence on a generation of young people. In that outreach role he has performed a ministry of nurture, representing and sharing the identity of Christian faith in the church gathered. Herb, the pastor, on the other hand, is known throughout the city for his active part in community organization of the poor and aged and his leadership in the peace movement. In that outreach role, he performs a ministry of vitality, representing the mission of the church scattered.

There are several ways in which this mutuality and interpenetration come to expression. The expression may rise out of the weakness or undeveloped nature of a body part, as yet incapable of performing its function. In such moments another body part takes up the responsibility of the dysfunctional or undeveloped limb. As such, it plays either a vicarious role doing what must be done in the absence of the appropriate organ or a modeling role in which something is done that will help the undeveloped part find its own way toward its proper function. (The body metaphor breaks down here and a pedagogical one takes its place.) Thus, Al may decide to organize a prayer and Bible study group in the congregation. Herb's reticence about pietism inhibits him from giving leadership. And Herb may find himself assisting Ken in circulating petitions to city physicians appealing for a nuclear weapons freeze in the hope that Al may catch the vision.

Mutual interpenetration may take place out of strength as well as weakness. Thus a person may have a plenitude of gifts that exceed the boundary of the area of his or her primary ministry. There is a proper permanent place, not just a pioneering and pedagogical role, for a ministry of vitality like that of George sharing his gift and strength with youth. In the same way, a minister of identity, like Herb, is called to share the strength of his gifts of social passion in movements of humanization.

While mutuality means both enrichment and interpretation, it cannot be forgotten that these are movements from points of primary particular ministry. The "pastor and teacher" exist to equip the saints for their ministry, not to preempt it. And those called to the church scattered cannot domesticate their gift and claim it in the household of the church gathered. If the particularity of these ministries is neglected, the body is seriously crippled. That particularity is, as we have seen in our reflection on mutuality, not the monopoly by the ministers of identity and vitality of these functions, but their faithful *stewardship of* them. This stewardship entails seeing that the tasks get done by whoever can best do them, not by the stewards' compulsion to perform all of them by themselves. Particular ministry therefore is custodianship of those special ways that keep the body of Christ alive in its vitality and awake in its identity.

The Contexts for Interpreting the Texts of Ministry

The foregoing discussion of the identity and vitality aspects of ministry assumes that there are people within the Christian community primarily responsible for these functions, those traditionally called clergy and laity whom we have designated as ministers of identity and vitality. But the facts of the matter are that (a) those we call clergy and laity are not identified as such in the New Testament (*klēros* does not appear, and *laos* refers to the people of God), (b) there is much more interest in the New Testament in an exploration of the variety of those charged with the identity function and the qualities they need than there is in the definition of clerical offices as such, and (c) there is much more attention to the particular contributions to the body of those with the gifts of vitality than to the definition of an entity, "the laity." Does this not suggest, then, that faithfulness to the Scriptures requires that we abandon the very distinction represented by the words "clergy" and "laity"? Are we not continuing to cripple the laity by perpetuating the distinction between ministries of identity and vitality?

These questions must be seriously confronted by all who take the Scriptures as normative and who are committed to the affirmation of the ministry of the whole people of God. The answer to them drives us beyond the particular issue of ministry to fundamental matters of authority and revelation. What finally determines our theological assertions?

The authority for theological statements here assumed is threefold. The Scriptures of the Old and New Testaments as they witness to Christ and the gospel constitute the *source*. The church and its traditions comprise the *resource*, and contemporary human experience constitutes the *setting* for our views on ministry. Therefore, it is the New Testament perspective on ministry, as it has been in dialogue with the church over two thousand years and is now in conversation with us today, that shapes the position to be taken. This means that the emergence of a pastoral office expressed in different ways and described in different language and its function in the life of the church universal provide the horizon against which we interpret Scripture. The doctrine of ministry, therefore, *develops* from this given as "ever new light breaks forth from God's holy Word." Christian doctrine is enriched as faith learns from and speaks to each new context in which it finds itself. The setting of the world in which we think through our faith and do our mission is the environment in which the resource of tradition and the source book of Christian faith join to answer Bonhoeffer's question, "Who is Jesus Christ for us *today?*"

Our discussion of the ministry issue is the outworking of these authority-revelation assumptions. We take our setting seriously when we respond to the coming-of-age movements of those formerly treated as dependent, invisible, marginalized nobodies — in our ecclesial context, "the laity." We take our resource seriously when we relate the new perspectives to the valid and invalid claims of the tradition — the developed office of identity and the undeveloped office of vitality. We take our source seriously when we test the setting, resource, and perspectives against the biblical norm and source. It is this method that prompts us to cast the question in terms of the relation of the pastoral office to a reformulation that challenges its hegemony while retaining its valid functions.

This contextual approach to theological issues — addressing the Scripture in the light of ecclesial and historical context — means that in another time with a different set of dynamics the identity-vitality distinction might not be the most fruitful category for the exploration of ministry. But for now, both the hard-won wisdom about the stewardship of identity and the yet-to-be-won affirmation of the stewardship of the church's vitalities must find their rightful place in a quest for the ministry of the whole people of God.

The Threefold Office

We have taken the first step toward enlarging the continuation of Christ's ministry by seeing that it is the whole body of Christ and not just a small part of it that is heir to his work. And we have sought to show how the traditional distinctions of clergy and laity are, in fact, coordinate activities of this organism that assure its identity and vitality. A deepening of our understanding of who carries forward Christ's ministry and how that may be done moves us now from our scriptural inquiry about the body of Christ to an exploration of a formula from the Christian tradition: the threefold office of Christ.

We have noted how the doctrine of the threefold office has directly or indirectly reinforced the idea that those ordained are the true bearers of Christ's ministry. There is another small voice in Christian tradition, however, that points in a different direction. This second scenario of the threefold office of Christ has its roots in the early centuries. Thus Chrysostom comments on the baptism of the Christian believer: "So also art thou thyself made king and priest and prophet in the laver."[5] The unction associated with baptism in the ancient church was understood as anointing into the threefold office, a practice and formulation noted in the Decree on the Apostolate of the Laity of Vatican II and used today in Roman Catholic rites of Christian initiation.[6] The Reformation gave special accent to this wider concept of the triple office, as stressed in questions 51 and 52 of the Heidelberg Catechism.[7]

While there is this significant expansion of the principle of who and what continues Christ's mediatorial office, its radical implications have yet to be drawn out. Most traditional interpretations stress consideration of personal piety but give no attention to matters of structure and power. These general urgings to "confess his name" (prophet), "present myself a living sacrifice of thankfulness to him" (priest), and "fight against sin and Devil"[8]

---

5. Cited by Hans-Ruedi Weber in "The Spontaneous Missionary Church," *Laity*, November 1957, p. 8. Reprints for nos. 2-6 (Geneva: Department of the Laity, World Council of Churches, 1962), p. 78. The gathering of important documents like this one in *Laity* and other former publications of the World Council of Churches continues today through *Laity Exchange*, edited by Mark Gibbs of the Audenshaw project. For example, see an update on the thinking of pioneer Hans-Ruedi Weber, "The Battle Is Not Yet Won," *Laity Exchange* 6 (April 1979).

6. "Decree on the Apostolate of the Laity," *The Documents of Vatican II*, ed. Walter M. Abbott, S.J. (New York: Association Press, 1966), p. 491.

7. *The Heidelberg Catechism* (Philadelphia: Board of Christian Education of the Reformed Church in the United States, 1902), p. 145.

8. *The Heidelberg Catechism*, p. 145.

(king) are expressions of the life of individual piety that have not yet reached the corporate level of ministry in the body of Christ.

Prophetic, priestly, and royal work in Israel were ministry within a covenant community. The threefold work of Christ rose out of the dynamics of the trinitarian life together. Pastoral ministry is exercised within the ecclesial community. The full significance of the threefold office of the ministry of vitality comes clear only when we inquire about its communal function and powers.[9] In doing this, we shall draw a line of precedents that runs from the original models in Judaism of prophet, priest, and king through the transfiguration of these offices in the threefold work of Christ to their present limited articulation in the pastoral ministry.

The Prophetic Office

The prophet brings a word from the Lord. Christ, the prophet, announces the coming of the kingdom. The pastor is called to the pulpit to proclaim the Good News. Prophecy is the power and commission to testify. The form of prophecy is the speaking of the right word at the right time. The prophetic office of the ministry of the laity, like its antecedents, is the prerogative and command to bear witness to what has been seen and heard. The prophet of vitality tells the Story. But this tale is told fundamentally in the place where this minister of the Word has been called and in a manner befitting that location. The place is "outside the gate of the temple," in the worlds of work, play, family life, and in the structures of political, social, and economic vitality. And the manner in which the Word is set forth is commensurate with these life worlds and in relationship to the issues that excite and agitate them.

Under the prophetic imperative, the minister of vitality is called to "name the name." But the naming that is fitting in this secular setting is not the uncritical transfer to the secular setting of the code language of the

---

9. Another matter of undrawn conclusions also awaits examination. If ministry entails a call — a personal inner call and an ecclesial outer call — must not the rite of Christian initiation, infant or adult, be followed by a rite of vocational maturity in which the claims of the threefold office made in baptism are accepted in all their personal particularity? So it is with the ordination of the ministers of identity. Can it be otherwise with the ministers of vitality? We leave this derivative question unanswered and concentrate on the nature of the prophetic, priestly, and royal offices conferred upon the entire *laos* in baptism.

ecclesial community. The task of translation belongs to the ministry out-side the gate. As Christ comes to this arena, hidden in the concerns that swarm through the world, so the ministers of vitality are beckoned to keep company with him there and to speak for him and about him in terms of these living issues and in the midst of involvement in them.

The work of evangelism is one of the expressions of the prophetic of-fice speaking the word. But evangelism that takes seriously the secular set-ting and the incognito Christ (Matt. 25:51-46) names the name and tells the story in the midst of the struggle to make and keep life human. Thus when Bill is asked by business colleagues why he is trying to develop his firm in the way that he is, he not only cites the models of co-management he learned in Harvard Business School, but he also testifies how his faith and his church have helped him to question the worship of the almighty dollar and autocratic views of life and work. As in the apostolic model of engaged evangelism, the deed of healing and hope "indigenizes" the word of truth. Since the prophet is called to name the name in worldly context, that ac-tion cannot be either wordless deed or deedless word, but a word in the midst of deed.

The work of apologetics is another form of the prophetic office of the ministers of vitality. Their ministry is among a people who talk in another tongue. Apologetics is the setting forth of the Word in response to the questions put by the people of a given time and place. And so Sandra ex-plains to her colleagues how she differs from fundamentalists on the one hand and atheists on the other in her belief that the first chapter of the Christian story has to do with the "whys and wherefores" of creation — that the good world is brought to existence by and is accountable to God and is not a creation of fate and chance — and not the "how, when, and where," which are subjects appropriate to scientific inquiry.

The prophetic office, as embodied in its antecedents, is one of seeing visions as well as speaking words. The visionary mandate is part of the call to prophecy. What that has meant for Amos and Isaiah, for prophetic clergy, and most of all for the chief prophet, Jesus Christ, is the setting forth of the claims of the vision of shalom. The "things that shall be" call into question the things that are. The collision between God's ultimate fu-ture and the world's self-serving agendas for tomorrow results in pain for the visionary in the church scattered. When Fred tells his boss that his commitments to peace will not allow him to work on a missile system that accelerates the arms race and then Fred takes the consequences of that decision, the prophetic voice is being heard on Boston's high-technology Route 128. There is no escape from the world's hostility for those God calls to exercise prophetic ministry.

In the living out of the ministry of the Word and vision, the structures of support and preparation are important: a community that stands by in the moment when the prophetic stance must be taken; equipment with the hard-won theological wisdom that enables a minister of vitality to know the possibilities and limits of historical hope; girding with a spiritual discipline that can save the prophet from self-righteous fury and draw on the grace of Another that finally sustains all ministry. Thus Bill and Sandra and George are supported and their vision is clarified by the life together they have in their Tuesday-night group with those who share common history and circumstances. The cost and the joy of prophetic discipleship are made possible and real through these means of grace.

The Priestly Office

The Letter to the Hebrews describes Jesus as high priest who understands the human condition in its weakness and vulnerability, from within the human condition, and who makes sacrifice and supplication to God for us. The pastoral ministry has been viewed as successor to this priesthood in its sacramental celebration, its leadership in prayer and praise, its sharing in the sorrows and bearing the burdens of the people of God. Long ago the clerical monopoly of this office was challenged by the Reformers. The priestly order is in fact the whole baptized people of God who, for good order, delegate the exercise of its power to its representatives. Sacerdotal delimitation and the polemics of the sixteenth century tended to cause the priestly office of the whole *laos* to be thought of principally in terms of the relocation of the right of access to God from the few to the many. The note of particular responsibility was muted and with it the definition of the priestly role of the church scattered.

Priestly ministers of identity care for the organs of identity in the church gathered: baptism and eucharist through which the birth and nurture of Christian believers take place, the rites that mark the decisive events in the journey of faith, the rhythms of worship. The ministers of vitality carry on a companion work in the institutions in and for which they take responsibility. The Reformers early saw that this meant the care of souls within the household, as in the "family altar." But the church scatters far beyond residential walls. Ministers of vitality are called to prayer and praise in all the yonder places. Surely this has to do with the life of personal devotion that offers work and play to God. But ministry is much more than individual piety. It entails leadership in community. We are only beginning to understand what this might mean and what forms such "priesting" should take. For example, might there be equivalents in the church scattered to the sacraments of birth and nurture celebrated in the church gathered? Are there peak (or valley) internal experiences in secular institutions that might be liturgically acknowledged and enabled by the ministers of vitality? If a code of ethics developed by Al and his friends wins approval at the next professional society meeting, there will be rejoicing among all in his laboratory. Will Al take his colleagues out to a celebration luncheon that day and maybe offer a prayer of thanksgiving to catch up the feelings of that grateful group?

As with the custodians of identity, so with the stewards of vitality, the priestly office continues the witness of solidarity and vulnerability. Christ, our high priest, bends low to share our maelstrom and miseries. He calls his ministers to join him in his passion. The priestly ministers of vitality bear the burdens of the forlorn and forgotten in those places of living and dying in which Christ has put them. How that ministry is carried out depends on particular gifts given to the priest set there: counselors, listeners, pray-ers, supporters, helpers, healers, and so on. When Sally comes to Jill with her anxiety about the son who is threatening suicide, and when even the boss consults Jill about how the results of their company's research can be used overseas, then the work of priesting is not absent from the workplace.

How important the task is of identifying the gifts of ministry that the Spirit has distributed throughout the body! Whatever the gift may be that determines the way priesthood is exercised, the office is common to all ministers of vitality. We are co-bearing the burdens assumed by the One present there before us, no stranger to sorrow and acquainted with grief.

The Royal Office

Jesus Christ makes things happen. He defeated the forces of sin, evil, and death on Easter morning and now empowers his purpose in the world, assuring its ultimate victory. When kings were kings, they also made things happen. Thus the victory and power of Christ are described in the classical tradition in regal idiom. And as prophet and priest were anointed, so in Israel the king assumed rulership by the same sign, providing further warrants for the threefold office of Christ the Anointed One.

While the potency of kings has passed and the masculine image does not do justice to the inclusive rule of Christ, regency does strike the note of *leadership* — indeed, a different kind of leadership, for here the symbol is broken and remade.

Christ reigns from the cross. The victory over the powers and principalities was won through suffering love and continues through vulnerability. This leadership is the power of powerlessness, the potency of servanthood.

The pastoral stewardship of the royal office takes place in the church gathered. When faithful to the crucifixion-resurrection mode of leadership, the pastor is "the servant of the servants of God." Christ came not to be ministered unto but to minister. As Christ called into question the ways of the ancient despot by manifesting leadership through solidarity and suffering, so too the minister of identity lives out the leader role from a position of alongsidedness and serves as a resource and enabler rather than source or Oriental sovereign. Servant leadership is no less leadership. Initiative, ingenuity, and boldness are necessary for the effective equipping of saints for their own work of ministry. Christ's ministers of vitality are also called to the royal office of initiative, ingenuity, and boldness. In a way this office is the most demanding ministerial role. It is an unambiguous statement of the imperatives of leadership. This royal mandate makes it impossible to view the life of faith in conventional or solitary terms. Leadership requires community; the king needs a kingdom. The institution(s) in which the minister of vitality lives and moves is to that minister what the organized ecclesial community is to the minister of identity. The secular institution exists under the sovereignty of Christ, who has called the minister of vitality to give leadership in obedience to that rule of suffering love. And the way in which leadership is exercised is commensurate with the nature of Christ's mode of ruling, as resource and enabler, as servant-leader. When Carl determines in his gracious but firm way that all the doctors in pediatrics should get to see the statistics on burn victims in a 20-megaton bomb holocaust, or when Frank organizes a weekly luncheon meeting with colleagues to think about the moral issues related to genetic manipulation, then there is a royal role of servant leadership being exercised in "the church in this (work) place."

Anxiety about the claims of the ministry of the laity, among laity themselves, is not infrequently related to the burdens of this royal office. While unfamiliar with the theological categories, they intuitively grasp its meaning, sensing the analogy of clerical responsibility in the ecclesiastical setting. They recognize that ministry is far more than the ill-defined "being a good Christian," for it demands leadership in the secular context. When this leadership is further clarified in terms of the prophetic and priestly tasks, then this vocation becomes a profound challenge. It is difficult to think of those who choose to walk this way as anything less than heirs to Christ's own ministry.

Conclusion

Why all this talk about the ministry of the laity? There are a gift given and a claim made on our Frank and Jill, Paul and Sandra, which place them in direct succession to the ministry of Jesus Christ. Some familiar lines of poetry take on fresh meaning against the backdrop of these questions from the ministry of the whole people of God.

Christ has no hands on earth but yours, no feet but yours. . . .

To know that herein lies a charge for the responsibilities of the vital signs and the identifying features of this body is an awesome thought indeed. What if the word were out that all the helpers and healers and risk-takers on the Route 128s of this world were gifted and claimed for the prophetic, priestly, and royal ministry that was and is Christ's own work? And what if this act of theological imagination were matched by ways of support, training, accountability, and legitimation by and for these ministries of vitality? We would soon enough be remarking upon the new outpouring of the Spirit in our midst.

PART III

JESUS CHRIST AND
PARISHIONER QUESTIONS

CHAPTER 5

Jesus Christ and the Angels

"Angels we have heard on high . . ." "Gloria in excelsis Deo!" "Christian, dost thou see them on the holy ground, how the powers of darkness compass thee around?"

In song, Scripture, and stained glass, the inhabitants of an angelic "higher cosmos" and the night powers of "nothingness" are much among us. Our inquiry here will be from within this world of the pastor and teacher — the "strange new world of the Bible" never far from the local congregation.

Is that probe made harder or easier when the magazines parishioners read and the television specials they watch feature stories of angel encounters and devil worship?[1] Yes and no. On the one hand, a subject too long ignored in mainline pulpits and classrooms is now breakfast talk. On the other hand, angels who fix flat tires and run errands in the snow do not sound much like Isaiah's six-winged seraphim circling the throne of God.[2] At the very least, media angelology and demonology can make this a moment for theological distinctions.

Today's popular interest in angels is not only the preoccupation of New

---

1. So the major stories on angels in the December 27, 1993, issues of both *Time* and *Newsweek,* the May 1994 two-hour network special on the same, and so on.

2. On current angel experience, see Sophy Burnham, *A Book of Angels: Reflections on Angels Past and Present and True Stories of How They Touch Our Lives* (New York: Ballantine Books, 1990).

Age pieties. The demythologizers, busy since the Enlightenment, are also much with us. Fiction and fantasy! And then there are the postmodern remythologizers finding psycho-social meanings hidden from Enlightenment eyes. Loudest of all is the apocalyptic thunder. Graphic depictions of Things-to-Come give the New Age angels and the Satanist scenarios a good run for their money.

To clear the ground for this ecclesial inquiry, a proviso from Karl Barth is in order.

> Our reference is . . . to the Christian use of the term "angel." What has been meant and thought and written and maintained in both ancient and more modern times concerning the being and existence and activity of the possible hypostases and mediators of other gods, we commit into the hands of the inventors and adherents of the relevant systems and messages and writings in which these figures occur. We are obviously unable to prevent them from using the word "angel" for what they think they may know and accept and believe in this respect. We insist, however, that whatever lies to the right hand or to the left of the reality whose concept is decisively given by its relationship to the living active and revealed God of Holy Scripture, does not correspond to the Christian idea of angel and does not deserve to be called an angel according to the Christian use . . . including . . . angels of so many mythical, spiritualistic, occult, theosophical and anthroposophical systems . . . those of popular fantastic imagination of so many individual dreamers or whole circles of such. Nor are the beings under which this name has met with so much ridicule and skepticism and denial. . . . As Christians and theologians we must refrain from speaking of such beings as angels, and . . . we must certainly not be so foolish as to try to learn from an acquaintance with such beings what is to be understood as angels in the Christian sense of the term.[3]

Barth's advice is lodged within a 160-page guidebook to "the higher cosmos" of Scripture in the third volume of his *Church Dogmatics*.[4] No churchly travel over this terrain can ignore Barth and his maps. We shall be in conversation with him, following his pointing finger much of the way.

3. Karl Barth, *Church Dogmatics*, III/3, ed. G. W. Bromiley and T. F. Torrance (Edinburgh: T. & T. Clark, 1960), p. 514.
4. Barth, *Church Dogmatics*, III/3, pp. 369-531.

But not all of the way. While Barth is a good guide, others know some trails he has either missed or been reluctant to tread.

The Other Dimension of Creation

"Your will be done, on earth as it is in heaven." What is this "heaven"? The answer takes us into a doctrine of creation. The world God brought to be includes the elusive dimension of "heaven." Created, but transcending our mortal coil, it is a "counterpart of the earth . . . the sum of all that which . . . is unfathomable, distant, alien and mysterious in creation."[5] Scripture has no interest in its typography (contra the long history of its mapmakers), but the canonical pattern of teaching about "the kingdom of heaven" holds it to be

> the Whence, the starting point, the gate from which [God] sallies with all the demonstrations and revelations and works of His action on earth. . . . Heaven is a place: the place of God in view of which we have to say that God is not only transcendent in relation to the world but also immanent and represented within it; the place of God from which His dealings with us, the history of the covenant, can take place in the most concrete sense, and His majesty, loftiness and remoteness can acquire the most concrete form. . . .[6]

While little is said in Scripture about origins, a long tradition in Christian theology interprets Genesis 1:1 — "In the beginning God created the heavens and the earth . . ." — as the making of celestial as well as the terrestrial heavens and thus the creation of angels and their abode.[7] The heavenly kingdom, as the created place under the rule of God and the "Whence" of the divine purposes among us, is in perfect conformity with the divine will. No surprise, then, that the biblical angels who dwell there are unswervingly obedient to the ways of God. So ordered to divine ends, they can be "messengers of God" as their name declares, instruments among us of the purposes of heaven.

5. Barth, *Church Dogmatics*, III/3, p. 424.
6. Barth, *Church Dogmatics*, III/3, pp. 433, 437.
7. On the interpretation of the Genesis verse and its linkage with the ancient creeds, especially the Nicene: "We believe in one God, Father Almighty, maker of heaven and earth, of all that is seen and unseen," see Mortimer J. Adler, *The Angels and Us* (New York: Macmillan, 1982), pp. 37-40.

Talk of this other dimension of creation is a shock to secular contemporaries, including many Sunday worshipers on whose lips is routinely found the Lord's Prayer entreaty. A heavenly kingdom? The habitat of angels? Counter-secular, yes, but the biblical narrative is incomplete without its many allusions to this invisible[8] order of created transcendence and its agents.

"Your will be done on earth as it is (done) in heaven." Christ prays: let heaven's allegiances find their way to earth! The upper cosmos is there to show us how this world should work. What's there has to be communicated to what's here. Accordingly, angels in Scripture appear regularly at critical junctures of God's history with us, manifestly so at its centerpoint — the annunciation, birth, temptations, actions, suffering, death, resurrection, and ascension of Jesus Christ.

As the biblical picture of the upper cosmos and its relation to us begins to develop, our inclination is to hasten it along. Sharpen those lines! Give us more color! What do angels look like? How many are there? How can I get in touch with one? Here Scripture is much more elusive, restrained, modest, and paradoxical than our aesthetic, philosophical, and cultural impulses. The Bible affords no straightforward, coherent angel ontology. We learn regularly of the doing of angels, but not the details of their being:

We know nothing of their essential being and its particular nature. We know nothing of their mutual relationship and distinction. We know nothing of the way in which they are a totality yet distinct. But we do know that even in the mystery of their being, they exist in and with the kingdom of God coming and revealed to us. . . . They are in the service of God.[9]

---

8. Barth questions St. Thomas's philosophical reading of the "heavenlies," and Thomist interpreter Mortimer Adler in his widely read book *The Angels and Us,* declares him, in turn, to be too restricted to Scripture and apologetically weak (pp. 26-29). While Barth has a better biblical compass and can steer us between the Scylla of New Age angelologies and the Charybdis of Enlightenment orthodoxies, there are significant convergences between the views of both. Also, here and there, Adler appears to be more faithful to the biblical accounts, as in the symmetry of creation's nature, human nature, and supernature.

9. Both Christian and traditional theology have contributed much to these preoccupations. For a review of this see Theodore Ward, *Men and Angels* (New York: Viking, 1969), passim.

With even greater reserve, Barth's view of critical transcendence disallows a systematic demonology. The "opponents of the heavenly ambassador of God" are consigned to the regions of "nothingness" in a concluding brief discourse appended to the long investigation of angelic realities.[10] While no doctrinal locus on demons is possible, we must wonder if Reformed preoccupation with the divine sovereignty and too much talk in the Heideggerian idiom of Nothingness combine in Barth's account to obscure another aspect of created — and fallen — transcendence. While the angels do belong to the fore in doctrinal explorations of Scripture's landscape, the demons must also be given their due. Creation's "lower cosmos" can describe not our plane (contra Barth) but a depth dimension of powers and principalities (contra Tillich) that have set their face against the divine purposes. After Easter, they deserve neither high profile nor equal time (contra modern apocalyptics). While not in the main body of this inquiry, we will make more than passing reference to them.

The Angel Office

What do biblical angels do? In a second-floor chapel of the sixteenth-century *Antonierhaus* in Berne, Switzerland, now housing a Lutheran congregation, a Fritz Pauli fresco shows an imposing angel on the ground pointing to the newborn Jesus. Here is the angel of God directing us to Another. Barth singles out this painting as more worthy than most angel art. The pointing finger, of course, is reminiscent of similar comments on Grunewald's John the Baptist.[11] Angels do not call attention to themselves but exist to witness to the Word. As noted, Scripture is not so much in their nature as their mission.[12] We have no doctrine of their "person," but do learn of their "work." Angels are apertures of the divine light. They give glimpses of the way and will of God, as that will and way come to singular focus in Jesus Christ.

10. Barth, *Church Dogmatics,* III/3, p. 451.

11. Barth, *Church Dogmatics,* III/3, pp. 492-93.

12. For an illuminating trail of the teaching from the Fathers on the mission of angels — the law, world religions, nativity, ascension, church sacraments, death, and so on, see Jean Daniélou, *The Angels and Their Mission: According to the Fathers of the Church* (Westminster, Md.: Christian Classics, 1976).

On the face of it, angels as messengers exist to execute an epistemological mission. Barth, with his focus on revelation, predictably gives angelology that turn. But the two testaments do not limit their role to acts of disclosure.[13] They act as well as speak. As angels that point to Christ — as angels of Christ — the 311 references to them in the New Testament (and, by anticipation, Old Testament counterparts) can be read as a reflection of the *munus triplex* of Jesus Christ: a prophetic, priestly, and royal office that accompanies and instruments Christ's own threefold work. While not taken up in conventional angelology, we pursue here the implications of a christological angelology with its threefold ministry.

1. Prophetic

The first office of Jesus Christ is "to be our chief Prophet and teacher, who fully reveals to us the secret counsel and will of God concerning our redemption. . . ."[14] This is the atoning work of disclosure, both then and now.[15] The angels of Christ are themselves bearers of that revelatory work, forth-telling the Word and deeds of God.

The prophetic work of angels in Scripture and tradition turns the Christian eye away from "I, me, and mine." Here is an alternative understanding of God's ambassadors for pastors and teachers confronted by today's popular god-of-the-gaps spiritualities, now taking shape as angels-in-the-breach. Biblical angels are not at our beck and call. They fix our attention on God. And that attention is regularly at cross-purposes with our agenda and expectations. The prophetic ministry of Gabriel and the angelic hosts leaves no doubt about the surprise and unexpected otherness of angel epiphanies. They inspire awe and even fear and, accordingly, they counsel "be not afraid." Then comes yet more of the unexpected, this time good news.

13. Barth, indeed, somewhat grudgingly acknowledges some truth in Peterson's doxological stress. Barth, *Church Dogmatics*, III/3, p. 483.

14. *The Heidelberg Catechism* (Philadelphia: Board of Christian Education of the Reformed Church in the United States, 1902), Question 31.

15. On the prophetic office as part of the doctrine of the atonement, see Gabriel Fackre, "Atonement," *Encyclopedia of the Reformed Faith*, ed. Donald McKim (Louisville: Westminster John Knox, 1992), and *The Christian Story*, vol. 2, *Scripture in the Church for the World* (Grand Rapids: Eerdmans, 1987), pp. 135-54.

Greetings, favored one! The Lord is with you. . . . Do not be afraid, Mary, for you have found favor with God. And now, you will conceive in your womb and bear a son, and you will name him Jesus. (Luke 1:28, 30, 31)

Do not be afraid, for see — I am bringing you news of great joy for all of the people. . . ." (Luke 2:10-11)

Angels bring good news. Not only at the beginning of the central story, but at every turn and at the end.

Do not be afraid. I know that you are looking for Jesus who was crucified. He is not here, for he has been raised. (Matt. 28:5-6)

Men of Galilee, why do you stand looking up toward heaven? This Jesus who has been taken from you into heaven will come in the same way as you saw him go into heaven. (Acts 1:11)

In season and out, the congregation is reminded in its hymnody of the angels who bring the good word at these turning points. In well-known refrains:

Hark the heralds angels sing,
Glory to the newborn King.
Peace on earth and mercy mild,
God and sinners reconciled.

And in less familiar ones:

An angel . . . spake unto the three, "Your Lord does go to Galilee."
(Jean Tisserand, d. 1494)

In passing, we note that hymns and liturgy keep the angelic presences before us, for, as our congregations sing and say them, they instinctively employ the "divinatory imagination" that Barth sees as Scripture's own way of portraying the heavenlies among us:

Why should not imagination grasp real history, or the poetry which is its medium be a representative of real history, of the kind of history that escapes ordinary analogies . . . ?[16]

---

16. Barth, *Church Dogmatics,* III/3, p. 375.

Created transcendence makes its way into our world through saga, symbol, and story, a "real history," but one requiring its own mode of discernment.

Biblical angels bring bad news as well as good news. Again, sharply distinguishing from today's popular angelologies, we have to do with a tough love as well as a tender love. Stretches of the book of Revelation challenge both our pious and secular predilections.

> The third angel poured his bowl into the rivers and springs of water, and they became blood. And I heard the angel of the waters say, "You are just, O Holy One, who are and were, for you have judged these things. . . ." (Rev. 16:4-5, as typical of chapters 14–18)

Prophets tell it like it is. Likewise, the prophetic office of angels is a megaphone of the justice as well as the mercy of God.

And the prophetic office of Jesus Christ is not only exercised in Galilean ministry, but also is a "continuing Work." The prophetic ministry of angels is still among us. Wherever the Word of truth, justice, and mercy is spoken, can the angels be far away?

> Where God is — the God who acts and reveals Himself in the world created by Him — heaven and the angels are also present. . . . At bottom a piety or theology in which there is no mystery, which lacks the mirror or self-representing deity, and in which there are therefore no angels, will surely prove to be a godless theology.[17]

2. Priestly

> And suddenly there was with the angel a multitude of the heavenly host, praising God and saying, "Glory to God in the highest heaven, and on earth peace among those whom he favors." (Luke 2:13-14)

With angelic news comes angelic praise. Once again, biblical angels are pointers to Another, this time "practicing what they preach." And again, good hymnody and liturgy may keep our theological work on track when our preaching and teaching wander and falter. What congregation rightly ordered has not had some hint of this office in its opening act of worship when it has joined the angels in adoration, singing:

17. Barth, *Church Dogmatics*, III/3, p. 477.

Holy, holy, holy, Lord God Almighty!
. . . Cherubim and seraphim falling down before thee. . . .

The priestly office of Jesus Christ in Reformation confession and catechism is to make sacrifice: the eternal Son of God suffering and dying for the sins of the world. The Reformation saw this office carried forward in the Body of Christ on earth in the priesthood of all believers who "make a living sacrifice of thankfulness to Him. . . ."[18] The angels of Scripture as messengers of God model this "sacrifice of praise and thanksgiving."

> In the year King Uzziah died, I saw the Lord sitting on a throne, high and lofty; and the hem of his robe filled the temple. Seraphs were in attendance above him. . . . As one called to another and said, "Holy, holy, holy, is the Lord of hosts; the whole earth is full of his glory." (Isaiah 6:1-2, 3)

Isaiah's angels teach us the heart of worship: not our issues and needs to the fore, but the glory of God.

Leander Keck, in his Beecher lectures, *The Church Confident*, charges mainline churches with the loss of the biblical praise of God, it being "displaced by anthropocentric utilitarianism."[19] Interests that run from the therapeutic to the political have so intruded themselves into our Sunday services that the "theocentrism" of Isaiah's temple has disappeared:

> If praise is the heart of worship, then making worship useful destroys it, because it introduces an ulterior motive for praise. And ulterior motives mean manipulation, taking charge of the relationship, thereby turning the relationship between the Creator and creature upside down. In this inversion, the living God, whose biblical qualities like jealousy and wrath have been tamed, has been deprived of freedom, having been reduced to the Great Enabler, now has little to do but warrant our causes and help us fulfill our aspirations. . . . The opening of the Westminster Confession is now reversed, for the chief end of God is to glorify us and to be useful to us indefinitely.[20]

---

18. *Heidelberg Catechism*, Question 32.

19. Leander E. Keck, *The Church Confident: Christianity Can Repent but Not Whimper* (Nashville: Abingdon Press, 1993), p. 34.

20. Keck, *The Church Confident*, pp. 36-37.

The charge of reversal — glorifying ourselves rather than God — is not limited to mainline churches, for evangelical David Wells has indicted modern evangelicalism for the same anthropocentrism.[21]

Can the angels teach us, once again, what it means to praise God? Not those of pop culture. The reports of their presence have consistently to do with their usefulness to our needs and wishes. On the other hand, biblical angels have a priestly office, a psalmic turning of the eyes of faith in the direction of the divine glory. In liturgical worship, the praise of God reaches a stirring climax in eucharistic prayer and seraphic hymn:

> Thee mighty God . . . we magnify and praise. With apostles and martyrs . . . with the innumerable company of angels round about thy throne, the heaven of heavens and the powers therein, we worship and adore thy glorious Name, joining in the song of Cherubim and Seraphim — "Holy, Holy, Holy, Lord God of Sabaoth, heaven and earth are full of thy glory. . . . Hosanna in the highest!"[22]

The priesting work of angels helps us to join them in that ascent.

3. Royal

Christ the king, according to the Heidelberg Catechism, "governs us by his word and Spirit, and defends and preserves us in the redemption obtained for us."[23] The royal office of angels is executed in kind. Angels save Lot and his family from destruction (Gen. 19:1-19), protect Daniel in the lions' den (Dan. 6:22), care for Jesus after his temptations (Matt. 4:11), and strengthen him in the garden (Luke 22:43). They are, throughout the Bible, "ministering spirits" (Heb. 1:14). Angels do deeds as well as praise God and bring news.

Does the royal office sound a little like Sophy Burnham's "reflections on angels . . . and true stories of how they touch our lives"?[24] Some crucial distinctions are in order:

---

21. David Wells, *No Place for Truth; or, Whatever Happened to Evangelical Theology?* (Grand Rapids: Eerdmans, 1993).

22. The eucharistic prayer and seraphic hymn, "Order for Holy Communion," *The Hymnal, Evangelical and Reformed Church* (St. Louis: Eden Publishing House, 1947), p. 25.

23. *Heidelberg Catechism*, Question 31.

24. The subtitle of her *A Book of Angels*.

1. Biblical angels are about God's business. In each case beneficent powers are released to accomplish something integral to the divine purposes. All actions comport with and contribute to that end. Read christologically, these deeds are under Christ's regency and testify to his truth. The critical test that all claims to angel visitation must pass is: Do they serve the realm of God and testify to Jesus Christ?

2. As part of a threefold office, the angelic act is never separable from angelic Word and worship. The deed done carries with it the expectation of hearing the Word and making the act of thanksgiving. Is a life changed, a truth gained, God praised? Is the act of deliverance accompanied by a new will "to deny oneself" and to "take up the cross"?

3. Popular testimonies to angel aid speak regularly of one's "guardian angel," or rescue by a single supernal being. Of the hundreds of biblical allusions to angels, only two references to individual guardianship appear, Job 33:23 and Acts 12:15. Neither requires a theory of full-time oversight. And a canonical hermeneutic would not build an angelology — or any "ology" — on such slender evidence.

To challenge the narcissism of New Age angelology is not to deny the present deed-doing ministry of beneficent powers. As the angels still speak the Word and praise the Lord, they continue with us also as ministering spirits. But biblical sobriety calls us to "test the spirits to see whether they are from God" (1 John 4:1), as in the above scrutiny. Yet Scripture, as judicious as it is, in another sense, is more exuberant about angel presences than are most modern claimants. Here the always-sober Calvin has a surprise for us. Guardian angels? Why settle for one? There are hosts about us:

> We ought to hold as a fact that the care of each one of us is not the task of one angel only, but all with one consent watch over our salvation. . . . For if the fact that all of the heavenly host are keeping watch for his safety will not satisfy a man, I do not see what benefit he could derive from knowing that one angel has been given to him as his special guardian.[25]

And of a piece with this challenge to individualistic preoccupations is the Reformer's wariness of personal hoverings diverting attention from the real Source:

25. John Calvin, *Institutes of the Christian Religion*, ed. John T. McNeill (Philadelphia: Westminster Press, 1960), vol. 1, p. 167.

Thus it happens that what belongs to God and Christ alone is transferred to them. . . . Even John in Revelation confesses that this happened to him, but at the same time he adds . . . "You must not do that! . . . Worship God."[26]

Angel Experiences and Realities

Popular angelologies revel in angel experiences. In contrast, Martin Luther prayed that he would not meet one. St. Paul talked about them in his letters. Whole stretches of Scripture have nothing to say about them. Hymnody helps again to put things in perspective: "I ask no dream, no prophet ecstasies . . . no angel visitant, no opening skies. . . ."

Why this reserve? Surely it has to do with the believer's experience of God. For Christians, over time, the divine encounter has to do with pneumatology, not angelology. The richness of meeting Jesus Christ by the power of the Holy Spirit empties the soul of all craving for angel visitations. Is a culture devoid of classical piety fertile soil for the claims of other encounters?

The account of Abraham's meeting with the three strangers in Genesis 19:1-20 suggests another reason for experiential modesty. The visitations had to do with three travelers welcomed to the table, no winged creatures of supernatural appearance. Only after their departure did Abraham realize he had entertained "angels unawares." Angel epiphanies in Scripture regularly take place in earthly and ordinary circumstances. They require the gift of discernment. Their presence is empirical but not experiential, embodied in our space and time, but not self-evidently so:

> The angels keep their ancient places —
> Turn but a stone and start a wing!
> 'Tis ye, 'tis ye, your estranged faces
> That miss the many-splendoured thing.[27]

Here the studies of Walter Wink make an important contribution to the theological discernment of the powers among us. In his trilogy, *Naming the Powers, Unmasking the Powers,* and *Engaging the Powers,* care-

---

26. Calvin, *Institutes,* vol. 1, p. 170.

27. Francis Thompson, "The Kingdom of God," in *The Oxford Book of Mystical Verse,* ed. D. H. S. Nicholson and A. H. E. Lee (Oxford: Clarendon Press, 1917), verse 245.

ful exegetical work and insightful psycho-social analysis combine to give us one contemporary understanding of Scripture's references to *exousia, archai, dynameis, thronos, kyriotēs, angelos.*[28] Finding these terms fluid and largely interchangeable, he argues that they refer not to

> separate heavenly or ethereal entities but . . . the inner aspect of material or tangible manifestations of Power. I suggest that the "principalities and powers" are the inner or spiritual essence, or gestalt, of an institution or state or system. . . . "[T]he Powers" should no longer be reserved for the special category of spiritual forces, but should rather be used generically for all manifestations of power, seen under the dual aspect of their physical or institutional concretion, on the one hand, and their inner essence or spirituality on the other.[29]

Wink makes a persuasive case that New Testament allusions to "powers and principalities," "thrones," and "authorities" can be understood to be spiritual dynamisms associated with experienced phenomena, the institutions and forces of our day-to-day world.

Wink's insights have enabled clergy better to understand peculiar forces alive in the church as institution, the "angels" of the congregation in which we live and work. They are data for a "theology of institutions," shedding light for laity on the meaning of their workplace as an "authority" that is both a locus for their secular ministry and a "power" called biblical angelology. Human life, in this case in its institutional expression, is the medium through which the angels come among us "unawares." Indeed, they do so for ill as well as good, a topic to which we will subsequently turn.

Wink's interpretation of the human and institutional expression of angelic powers, however, must be related to the larger threefold office. As such, his proposal to interpret biblical angelology only in terms of psychosocial and institutional dynamics must be challenged as reductionist. Biblical powers are for telling and praising as well as institutional "doing." And the mysterious More of the Scripture's "ethereal entities" cannot be reduced to modern plausibilities.[30]

---

28. Walter Wink, *Naming the Powers* (Philadelphia: Fortress Press, 1984), *Unmasking the Powers* (Philadelphia: Fortress Press, 1986), and *Engaging the Powers* (Minneapolis: Fortress Press, 1992).

29. Wink, *Naming the Powers,* pp. 104-5.

30. Robert Webber in *The Church in the World* (Grand Rapids: Zondervan, 1986) strives to hold together the structural and the ontological dimensions of powers and principalities.

The tracing of the threefold "work" of angels in Scripture also poses the postmodern question: Are we drawing a picture of the biblical cosmos and sketching in some neglected characters? Is this a storybook world into which we invite the reader, one with its own counter-cultural expectations and demands juxtaposed to society's values? Yes. But "no" to the sometimes-assumed corollary that no claims can be made for the correspondence of this narrative to the real state of affairs. The upper cosmos is not a fictive realm. Biblical ontology, while modest, is not missing. Angels are true messengers of a true God. A world "strange" to cultural categories can no more be reduced to the stories of postmodernity than to the institutions of modernity. Accounts of the angelic legions do conform to the "real order" of things.

Dealing with the Demons

Both Satanist cults and "post-trib pre-mils" have much to say about the immediate regency of dark powers. Ironically, the extremes meet in their mesmerism with evil. Again, the ideologies of the hour — very different here than the sunnier New Ageisms — make for a teaching moment, this time on the "fallen angels."

The biblical story — at its beginning, middle, and culmination — does indeed speak about tempters and seducers. The world did fall away from the divine purpose. (Eden, understood theologically as the divine intention for creation, carried down with it elements of a good created transcendence.) In Christian tradition, more is said about Satan than any leading angelic counterpart. And in the earlier twentieth-century recovery of a biblical theology of principalities and powers, with its background struggle against modern "isms," the emphasis was often on "rebellious powers."[31] The demonic is more remarked upon than the angelic, as in Tillichian analysis[32] and Niebuhrian realism about "immoral society."[33] The popularity of C. S. Lewis's *Screwtape Letters* is yet

---

31. See Albert H. Van den Heuvel, *These Rebellious Powers* (New York: Friendship Press, 1965). Pioneering work was done by George Caird, *Principalities and Powers* (Scottdale, Pa.: Herald Press, 1962).

32. Paul Tillich, *The Religious Situation* (New York: Henry H. Holt and Co., 1932).

33. Reinhold Niebuhr, *Moral Man and Immoral Society* (New York: Scribner's Sons, 1932).

another testimony to the power of the Christian imagination in our troubled time.[34]

Sobriety, sensitivity to the dark side, realism — yes. However, they have to do with the penultimate, not ultimate, reality. Luther, who was no stranger to such struggles, left us a reminder of that finality:

> The prince of darkness grim, we tremble not for him;
> His rage we can endure, For lo his doom is sure;
> One little word shall fell him.

Although we confront "a world with devils filled," the enemy has met its Match: "He disarmed the rulers and authorities and made a public example of them, triumphing over them" (Col. 2:15). Because Christ "made captivity . . . captive" (Eph. 4:8), we do not tremble at the saber-rattling of the powers.

In his memorable Letter to Great Britain, with bombs falling on London, Barth echoed this powerful "because . . . therefore":

> The world in which we live is the place where Jesus Christ rose from the dead . . . since this is true [it] is not some sinister wilderness where fate or chance hold sway or where all sorts of "principalities and powers" run riot unrestrained and range unchecked. . . . We Christians . . . have no right whatsoever to fear or respect them or resign ourselves to the fact that they are spreading throughout the world as though they knew neither bounds nor lord. We should be slighting the resurrection of Jesus Christ and denying his reign on the right hand of the Father, if we forget that the world in which we live is already consecrated, and if we did not, for Christ's sake, come to grips spiritedly with these evil spirits, and smite them.[35]

To the young who flirt with the satanic and the old who are fearful of the demonic, the message is "Be not afraid. . . ." The Christ to whom the angels point rule even these ominous powers. They should worry about us with our "one little Word," not the other way around. For all its peculiarities and popular distortions, the rite of exorcism practiced in some Chris-

---

34. C. S. Lewis, *The Screwtape Letters* (New York: Macmillan, 1944).

35. Karl Barth, *A Letter to Great Britain from Switzerland* (London: Sheldon Press, 1941), pp. 10-11.

tian traditions is rooted in this conviction of the regency of Jesus Christ. And that same trust in the royal office of Christ (and the angels) fortifies us in the struggle against political, social, and economic powers as real in our time as in other eras.

But now comes the Enlightenment caveat: "Along with all the high theology, Luther hurled an inkpot at the Devil. Are you inviting us back into the pre-critical world?" Wink's studies take this question seriously but invite the critic toward the post-Enlightenment times, ones that are able to appreciate at least the experiential underside of the biblical realm of thrones and authorities. Scripture speaks of discussable realities that make their presence known in our historical and personal tumults.

The damaging work of rebellious powers looks a lot like the reverse of the royal office of the angels: done deeds of bondage not deliverance. Do the demons have their own threefold office? In Scripture, there seem to be false prophets of the upper cosmos who bring bad news and untruth, and fallen priests who blaspheme. Are the heirs today of the "father of lies" (John 8:44) the prophets of institutional untruth and the false priestcraft in the cult of corporations who demand sacrifice rather than offering it?

To name the spirituality of institutions in the language of Scripture has an apologetic force, especially for those at home in metaphor, symbol, and story. But as with angels, so with demons; we cannot reduce the biblical characters to our conventions. There is a More here in things demonic. What that More is takes us to questions beyond "mission" to "nature." But again we meet with biblical reserve about angels fallen as well as unfallen, giving us no clear ontology of the demonic. Indeed why would there be such if Satan has already fallen (Luke 10:18) and Jesus has already led captivity captive?

There seems to be a correlation between those with elaborate descriptions of the demons and the devil and the belief that the latter are now in charge; again the cultists and apocalyptics join forces.[36] While the story tells us that we struggle with evil until the end, that end has already begun, the enemy already having been dealt a mortal wound.

---

36. Clinton Arnold's careful study *Powers of Darkness: Principalities and Powers in Paul's Letters* (Downers Grove, Ill.: InterVarsity Press, 1992) makes a strong evangelical case for the personal ontology of the "dark powers," but forcefully asserts the "defeat of the powers at the cross" (pp. 100-109) and challenges apocalyptic preoccupations with the devil's present rule. In a similar vein see also J. I. Packer, "The Devil's Dossier," *Christianity Today*, June 21, 1993, p. 24.

The Old Dragon under ground,
In straiter limits bound,
Not half so far cast his usurped sway,
And, wroth to see his Kingdom fall,
Swings the scaly horror of his folded tail.[37]

Metaphor here serves better than metaphysics. And with it mission: exorcizing the remnants of demonic presence wherever they appear in the arrogance of institutional power or the subtle temptations and seductions of the soul.

Conclusion

We began with our sanctuaries and congregations and ended there. Much soul-searching goes on these days about what transpires in our pews and pulpits. Have the seductions of culture emptied the former and eroded the message of the latter? It is no accident that Barmen's call to listen to "the one Word of God . . . Jesus Christ as he is attested to us in Holy Scripture . . ." is now increasingly heard as a challenge to the church's acculturation. With it, we should remember the words of the author Barmen quoted earlier that "a piety or theology in which there is no mystery . . . no angels . . . is a godless theology." The work of Christ in Scripture is inseparable from the work of the angels.

For all that, biblical angels are on the edge, not the center, of Christian faith, in the stained-glass windows but not on the altar. That they are very much in our songs, texts, and sanctuaries should give us, as too-often-forgetful teachers and preachers, some pause. Their prophetic, priestly, and royal work under and for Jesus Christ has made a difference in the life and witness of other generations. And not to remember the demonic counterparts to the angelic hosts is the best assist we can give the angels of nothingness. In re-centering in Jesus Christ we may better see the demons lurking and hear the angels singing.

---

37. John Milton, "On the Morning of Christ's Nativity."

CHAPTER 6

Jesus Christ, and Those Who Haven't Heard

In the nineteenth century the gospel had been carried from Boston to the mid-Pacific Sandwich Islands. Thousands of Hawaiians were converted. After awhile a troubling question arose among the new Christians: "What will happen to our ancestors of blessed memory? They never heard the Good News." Could the Congregational missionaries give them an answer?

In New England during the late 1800s, the subject of the unreached was much to the fore. Missionaries brought the Hawaiians' question back with them to the theologians, the churches, the clergy, the laity. Different answers were debated in church papers, on mission boards, in seminaries. The discussion became so heated that an artist for the famous New York magazine, *Puck,* drew a cartoon showing one group of professors pushing another group out of a boat, each brandishing their theories of salvation. Out of the controversy grew a point of view among many of the missionaries much like the one taken up here.[1]

This "postmortem" conviction, however, did not get its start just one hundred years ago. It appeared early in Christian history and has been ad-

---

1. For a summary of the issues and events as they came to a head in North America in the late nineteenth century, see Thomas P. Field, "The 'Andover Theory' of Future Probation," *The Andover Review* 7, no. 41 (May 1887): 461-75, and *The Andover Case* (Boston: Stanley and Usher, 1887).

vocated here and there ever since, especially when issues of evangelism or "pluralism" came front and center. Some great souls have declared for it. And, of course, those who believe that death is no barrier to Christ pursuing the unreached hold that it can be found at the heart of the Bible.

Can this view, discussed so intensely in the missionary struggles of another age, have something to say to us today? I believe it can. While it has yet to achieve widespread recognition, like many other Christian teachings, "soaking time" is needed for a clear picture to develop. It took four hundred years of "christological controversies" in the early centuries for Christians to come to a mind on what Scripture says about who Jesus Christ is — "truly God, truly human, truly one."[2] We are in the middle of a churchwide conversation right now on yet another disputed question, this very one on the destiny of the unevangelized. And there is no "knock-down" argument for any one position. We have to search the Scriptures and be in conversation with one another. This book is a step in that direction.

Our own issue is prompted by the experience of *today's* parishioners as well as by yesterday's missionaries. Through travel, communication, and our increasingly diverse society, we have come more and more into close contact with people of different religions and people of no religion at all. This is a world of billions of people, many of whom never hear the gospel. How then can Christ say: "I am the way, and the truth and the life. No one comes to the Father except through me" (John 14:6)? The question is urgent. Will the church come to a common mind on this after awhile, as it did on the Person of Christ?

Divine Perseverance

A sign of an unsettled question is how varied the ways are of talking about it. The names were shifting (and complicated!) in the debates of the first four centuries about who Jesus really is vis-à-vis God. A string of movements that stressed Jesus' humanity but played down his divinity arrived on the scene with their pet terms and ideas: "Ebionism," "Adoptionism," "Arianism," etc. And then there were the opponents who stressed the divinity of Christ but neglected the Scripture's teaching that he also was a real

---

2. The definition of who Christ is vis-à-vis God, held by most Christians and worked out at the Council of Chalcedon in A.D. 451.

human being: "Docetism," "Apollinarianism," "Monophysitism," etc. We have the same varieties of names and factions on the subject at hand, the destiny of the unreached. Especially so, with the labels for the view to be discussed here. It is variously called "future probation," "second probation," "eschatological evangelism," "postmortem evangelism," "P.M.E.," etc.

We need a name that better expresses the main conviction of this point of view. Here it will be called *divine perseverance*. Of course, we have in the tradition the "doctrine of perseverance."[3] That old idea has to do with the "perseverance of the *saints*," true believers given the power never to backslide. This one has to do with the *perseverance of God*. God is resolute, never giving up on getting the Word out. In this world, God will give us the power to spread the gospel far and wide. But to those we can't reach, the Word will also be declared, even if it takes an eternity. The poet Francis Thompson had it right: Christ . . . is the "hound of heaven," pursuing us to the end. We shall make a case here for Divine Perseverance.

Learnings from Our Forebears

Any case for such a Christian teaching rests on Scripture. Why not immediately go to the relevant texts in the Bible? We *are* going to defend Divine Perseverance by a careful look at the biblical evidence. But first we have to be clear about *how* the Bible is rightly read. Scripture tells us that Scripture can be quoted in the wrong way (Matt. 4:5-6). So we shall take a longer path to our destination by dealing with a few important preliminaries on the "how" before we consider the "what" of the matter. And we'll get some help on this from the great debates about the Person of Christ earlier mentioned.

One thing they taught us about the interpretation of the Bible was the importance of "the analogy of faith." That is, Scripture has to interpret Scripture. Since the Bible has an overall unity in its teaching, we'll get help on difficult passages by comparing them with analogous ones that are clearer. Therefore, we have to read any one part of the Bible in the light of the whole Bible, the "canon" of all the accepted books. This is a "canonical approach" based on the belief that the God who inspired the Scripture is of one mind. The true meaning of a passage cannot be out of sync with the

---

3. For an explanation of perseverance in the "order of salvation" see John Murray, *Redemption — Accomplished and Applied* (Grand Rapids: Eerdmans, 1980), pp. 151-60.

rest of the Bible's teaching. When we come to investigate some crucial passages about Divine Perseverance, we shall do it canonically, with the help of overall biblical teaching.

Another very similar learning from the early centuries was the realization that not only *texts* but also *teachings* hang together. (Actually, it's hard to separate texts from teachings.) What is true in one doctrine sheds light on what is the case about others. In some circles of theology then (and now), "analogy of faith" meant just that, tracing out the harmony of all Christian teachings.

An example of that harmony is the relationship of the Person of Christ to the Trinity. The two doctrines developed parallel to one another. Church thinkers of that day reasoned: the Son is a Person "of the same substance" as the Person of the Father — so said the Nicene Creed in 325 A.D. Again, they concluded from Scripture that the Holy Spirit is not just an impersonal power but also a personal Subject. That would make God three separate Subjects. But God cannot be three separate Gods — that's polytheism! The God of the Bible is *one* God. The Persons are so intimate, so mutual ("co-inherent" as the church fathers put it, in one loving Life Together — 1 John 5:6-8), that the Three are really One, the *triune* God of classical Christian faith. Thus what is taught about the Person of Christ (that Christ is God — along with the Father and the Holy Spirit) has to fit with what is taught about God (God is One). True doctrines will be harmonious, integrated with one another, and shedding light on one another.

Following this lead of seeing how one doctrine sheds light on another, we are going to compare the question of the unreached to another knotty Christian issue, the *problem of evil*. It has many similarities to our own question. The same fundamental teachings of Scripture that have to fit together in it have to mesh in our question. And the history of the debate about "theodicy," as the problem of evil is called, has produced parties very similar to those found in the debate about the destiny of the unreached.

Divine Perseverance and the Problem of Evil

Theodicy poses this question: How do you justify the ways of God in a world so full of evil? This comes up for Christians day in and day out when we see the suffering of people who don't seem to deserve it. In the face of these agonies, how can a believer hold together three basic, non-negotiable, biblical teachings: (1) God is *almighty,* (2) God is loving and *all-good,* and (3) Evil is *real.*

The popular "solutions" to this mystery — which are, in the end, no so-lution — have a common tendency. Each *eliminates* one of the basics. You've heard all the answers:

1. Yes, God is all-good and evil is utterly real, but God is not almighty. Evil things happen that even God can't deal with. God is powerful, but not *all-*powerful. You've got to live with these limitations as best you can, and accept the unfair suffering of the innocent. Rabbi Harold Kushner has given this view high profile in our day in his book *When Bad Things Happen to Good People.*

The reality of evil and the goodness of God are taken seriously here. But what happened to God almighty?

2. Yes, God is almighty, presiding over everything, justly punishing evil and rewarding good. Where there is suffering, there is a reason for it. While it doesn't seem just, it's part of the plan. Accept it and learn to live with it. Job's counselors sounded this note.

The power of God is stressed here, and so is the reality of evil. But what happened to the love and goodness of God?

3. Yes, God is almighty and all-good. In this kind of a world with this kind of a God, what looks like evil can't really be that. You have to change your attitude, see things in their true light. Christian Science is a variation on this theme of misperception.

The love and goodness of God are stressed here, and the power of God is assumed. But what happened to the reality of evil?

There are many parallels between the solutions offered to the problem of evil and those proposed on the question of the unevangelized. On the latter issue:

1. One view puts a big emphasis on the goodness and love of God and counts on the power of God to back them up. The world is made up so that everybody in some way will find out what is right and then do the right thing. It will turn out that way because a loving God would not condemn anybody. This is the doctrine of "universalism." It holds that everyone will finally be saved.

But, if everyone is saved, what happened to the reality of evil?

2. Another view stresses the divine power and also takes account of the reality of evil. Because God is all-powerful, things will be settled on God's terms. That can mean either that the Almighty chooses some sinners ahead

of time and passes over the rest, or that God restricts the offer of Good News to some, denying it to others. These are variations on a "restrictivist" view.

But if some are arbitrarily excluded, what happened to the goodness of God?

3. Another view stresses the goodness of God and the reality of evil by giving everyone a chance for a decision for Christ in this world. If they are prevented from knowing Christ directly they will be given a choice indirectly, through another kind of knowledge of good and evil. This is an "inclusivist" view.

But if worldly limits are set to when and how Christ can work, what happened to the power of God?

Of course, neither the question of theodicy nor that of the unevangelized can be settled by these generalities. But they do tell us something. An opinion may fix on an important truth, but ignore or reject other truths. In fact, in this case, positions 1, 2, and 3 may be *right* in what each affirms, but *wrong* in the one point each denies. These right but "reductionist" perspectives push us to look for a bigger picture that includes all three of the non-negotiables.

Divine Perseverance is key to getting this bigger picture on both the problem of evil and the problem of the unreached. We'll look at the parallels, and then go from this general discussion to the scriptural evidence.

Theodicy and Divine Perseverance

None of the three basics can be eliminated. But one of them has been misunderstood: the *power of God.*

Our fallen human nature often tempts us to let our surrounding society's ideas wander into our reading of the Bible. For a long time, "power" in the world outside of the faith has had a take-charge ring to it. In the old days, kings and emperors ran things with an iron hand. They were the way the world understood power. In our time, power (on TV and in the movies, for example) is understood in a similar fashion, symbolized for example by . . . the "terminator."

The secular idea of power, as this kind of instant-and-everywhere domination of things, too often gets read into what the gospel means by *God's* power, both in the old days and in our time. Yes, power does mean the ability to win through, to achieve the goal. No, God's power does not do it the way human power works. Instead, "God's *weakness* is stronger than human strength" (1 Cor. 1:25). The power of God is the power of the *cross*. As Christians, we get our understanding of power — and everything else we believe about ultimate reality, for that matter — not from "human wisdom" (1 Cor. 1:25) but from the Word of God — the Word made flesh in Jesus Christ as testified to by the biblical Word.

When we come at the problem of evil from this angle, things look very different. The "power of God" has nothing to do with Arnold Schwarzenegger. Yes, God's whole being is set against evil. Yes, nobody is going to get away with anything. But no, God does not treat us as things to be pushed around. We are given an *invitation* to say "Yes," or "No" to God's will. "Choose this day whom you will serve . . ." (Josh. 24:15). The whole history of salvation we read about in Scripture is the story of God's quest to win us, the Divine Perseverance that relentlessly pursues us, calling for our response. And it's a tale of our nay-saying, with all the destructive consequences that follow. Not only human beings, but the "powers and principalities" are bent on going their own way.

At the very center of this Story, God makes the decisive move to turn the world around: the conception, birth, life, preaching and teaching, miracles, sufferings, death, resurrection, and ascension of Jesus Christ. His Incarnation and Atonement determine and disclose how it all, finally, will turn out. There's a "great Day comin'"! In that kingdom, every wrong will be righted, every flaw mended, and God will "be all in all" (1 Cor. 14:28). No wonder we read Romans 8 at Christian burial. We declare then for a final victory in the *future* tense: nothing "*will* be able to separate us from the love of God in Christ Jesus our Lord . . . neither death, nor life, nor angels, nor rulers, nor things present, nor things to come, nor height, nor depth, nor anything else in all creation . . ." (Rom. 8:39, 38).

What comes clear here is that the power of God is, mysteriously, the way of the cross, the "weakness of God." The ultimate power is not *machismo* but the *divine vulnerability*. That means God does not run roughshod over us, but allows the world to range about in its rebellion — even to the point of crucifying the Son of God. Suffering and evil do have their day in the great drama that is unfolding in our midst.

God's love is *patient* and *persistent*. It outlasts us. It is a "weakness" that is *stronger* than our rebellion. God's weakness is a *powerful* powerlessness, a *victorious* vulnerability. For the final victory of this powerful patience, however, we must await the *End* of the story. Only then will the kingdom come — the resurrection of the dead, the return of Christ, final judgment, and everlasting life. In the End, God will settle accounts, vindicate the sufferer, and validate the divine purposes.

For believers, Easter morning is the demonstration of the coming Reign of God. Confidence in the risen Christ and the kingdom to come *empowers* us to stand fast against the powers of evil, and struggle with, and live through, the suffering that is part and parcel of a world still short of the End. A strong "eschatology" makes for a deep piety and a powerful ethics.

Christians live by hope in the "eschatological" power of God, an almightiness that establishes itself on God's patient and persistent terms in the Last Things, rather than on our own impatient timetable. To that God of power and love — in the face of the world's worst evil — be all the honor and glory!

The Unevangelized and Divine Perseverance

Eschatological theodicy — the divine perseverance in bringing together the goodness and power of God in the face of evil — has its counterpart in *eschatological evangelism* — the divine perseverance in bringing together the goodness and power of God in the face of the unreached.

Christian faith entails a passion for conversion. The Good News changes lives. We have found "a pearl of great price" and want to share it. The Word comes: "Go into all the world and proclaim the good news to the whole creation" (Mark 16:15). And because the world cannot "hear without someone to proclaim him . . ." (Rom. 10:14), the messengers go out with the gospel.

But our question here is: What of those we *do not* reach? Those who by circumstance are denied the saving knowledge of Jesus Christ?

To believe in Divine Perseverance is to be confident that the reality of evil, the goodness of God, and the power of God are biblical non-negotiables. In Jobian theodicy, "evil" has reference to the problem of *suffering*. In "evangelistic theodicy," it is the problem of *the unreached*. How can we justify the existence of the unevangelized? With a loving and all-powerful God, how can sinners who need salvation receive it if they don't hear the Good News? Any answer to this question has to do justice to all three of the biblical basics — the *reality of evil*, the *goodness of God*, the *power of God.*

The answer has to do with the same Story that speaks to the problem of evil, the narrative of God's persistent and powerful love. The three basics are the same. They have to be held together.

1. Evil Is Real

In this case, "evil" goes back to original *sin*. Sin is universal — "There is no one who is righteous, not even one" (Rom. 3:10). Sin is too deep for our best moral and spiritual efforts. "All have sinned and fall short of the glory of God" (Rom. 3:23). We stand exposed before the majesty of God for what we are. Only something and Someone not our own can change the picture. "God, be merciful to me, a sinner!" (Luke 18:13).

2. God Is All-Loving and Good

"There is a balm in Gilead that makes the wounded whole." In Jesus Christ, the good God has entered our sin-sick world. In the life, death, and resurrection of Christ, the powers of sin, evil, and death have met their match. On the cross, Jesus Christ took the punishment for our sins.

> For while we were still weak, at the right time, Christ died for the ungodly. (Rom. 5:6)

In biblical teaching, especially emphasized in the Reformation tradition, the forgiveness of sin, accomplished on the cross alone, is imparted to us by the grace of Christ alone and received by us through faith in Christ alone.

> Therefore, since we are justified by faith, we have peace with God through our Lord Jesus Christ. (Rom. 5:1)

Faith receives the grace that justifies. God gives us access to Calvary's saving work through the personal response of faith in Jesus Christ. As all-loving, the One who went to the wall for us — to the cross — will leave no stone unturned to get this message out.

3. God Is Almighty

The saving love of God in Jesus Christ presupposes the *power* of God. But there is a special form of it associated with our third non-negotiable. As almighty, the One who created the world and defeated sin, evil, and death in the Person and Work of Christ can "do all things." No limits can be set to the triune God, except Self-chosen limits. The divine love and power call the church into being to spread the Good News. God's tender love places the treasure of the gospel "in earthen vessels" (2 Cor. 4:7), risking the proclamation of the Word in this world on evangelizers like *us* — the "weak things of this world" (1 Cor. 1:27). And God's *powerful* powerlessness sustains the church in its mission, sending it to the very ends of the earth.

The reality of sin and our creatureliness enter to limit the range of the church's mission in time and space. We have not gotten the Word out to the last and the least. Yet the goodness of God will not relent in the face of these realities. And the power of God breaks through their limitations. The *gates of death*, as well as the "gates of hell," cannot prevail against the Divine Perseverance. The powerful love of God assures us that the saving Word will be proclaimed to those who have not heard it, even beyond the gates of death.

As a powerful *powerlessness,* no one is going to be forced to accept the offer. God's power is so great that it can restrain the very imposition of itself on those it seeks out. Yes, the love of God "desires everyone to be saved and come to the truth" (1 Tim. 2:4). While the power of God will patiently *persist* in that desire, it will *not insist* upon its compliance. We are free to say "No" into eternity itself. To demand that God save everyone — "universalism" — is to violate both the freedom of God and human freedom.

Divine Perseverance so understood holds together the three basics involved in the question of the unreached. It's an example of the "analogy of faith" at work in Christian teaching, the harmonizing of basic Christian beliefs. But can we actually find this view of Divine Perseverance in the pages of the Bible?

Scripture

1 Peter

Those who have believed deeply in God's unlimited power and love to reach the unreached have returned again and again to 1 Peter 3:19-20 and 4:6. We shall begin our look at the biblical evidence here with these much-discussed texts, expanding them to include the chapters in which they appear and the setting of the letter as a whole. As one commentator says about 3:19-20: "These verses have been called the most difficult in the N.T."[4] Our search for their meaning will include what is often missing in the explanation of these verses: "the analogy of faith" as a canonical reading of texts in Scripture.

All commentators agree that the question uppermost in the mind of the author of 1 Peter is the *suffering* of the early church.[5] Its members asked: How come we, as the people of God, have all this suffering? In the same letter, therefore, there is a striking combination of the two problems we have been discussing: the problem of evil and the problem of the unreached. And the way 1 Peter addresses both is by proclaiming God's persevering love and power beyond the doors of death.

The response of 1 Peter to the first question — Christian theodicy — is: look at Jesus. He suffered and triumphed. Take courage. If he suffered and overcame, you can too. As God raised him from the dead, so God will vindicate you:

> By his great mercy he has given us a new birth into a living hope through the resurrection of Jesus Christ from the dead, and into an inheritance that is imperishable, undefiled, and unfading, kept in heaven for you who are being protected by the power of God through faith for a salvation ready to be revealed in the last time. (1 Peter 1:3-4)

---

4. Benjamin W. Robinson, "First Peter," *The Abingdon Bible Commentary,* ed. Frederick Carl Eiselen, Edwin Lewis, and David Downey (New York: Abingdon Cokesbury Press, 1929), p. 1342.

5. From the most conservative: Henry H. Halley, *Pocket Bible Handbook: An Abbreviated Bible Commentary* (Chicago: Henry H. Halley, 1941), pp. 434-37, to the most critical: Edward Schillebeeckx, *Christ: The Experience of Jesus as Lord,* trans. John Bowden (New York: Seabury Press), pp. 223-37.

Eschatological vindication is the answer to the agony of innocent suffering, suffering for "doing good" (1 Peter 3:17). This is the same point we made earlier in our discussion of the problem of evil. The Word is: "Christian, persevere, because God perseveres, overcoming suffering and death by the power of the resurrection in the End."

In the midst of 1 Peter's witness of Things to Come, based on the reality of the crucified and risen Lord, appear the verses under study. They also speak of the death and resurrection of Christ, of "the living and the dead," of Christ's dealings with the dead. Could these verses be addressed to the same question posed to the Hawaiian missionaries?

In the third chapter, Peter urges believers to stick to their convictions in spite of persecutions. After all, "Christ also suffered" (3:18), going all the way for us. As an example of this divine perseverance, Peter then cites Christ's determination to breach the very walls of death to make a "proclamation to the spirits in prison" (3:19). Christ's resolute power and love will persist to and through the final barrier of those imprisoned in death. Even this last enemy is not strong enough to prevent the declaration of the Word.

Who were these prisoners? They were the dead who "in former times did not obey, when God waited patiently in the days of Noah . . ." (3:20). They were not among the chosen few, "eight persons saved through water" (3:20) who prefigure "baptism, which . . . now saves you . . ." (3:21). Read canonically (Gen. 5:28–10:32), the reference is to *all* those outside of God's special saving history in Israel and Christ — human beings who, since Noah, right up to the present moment and into the future, are accountable to the patient God. They are accountable in another way, through what our forebears called that covenant established in "the days of Noah," the *Noachic covenant.*

We have taken up in this volume the covenant with Noah, marked by the rainbow sign. After the creation of the world and its fall "the wickedness of humankind was great in the earth . . ." (Gen. 6:5); God put up with the worst the world could do, even waiting "patiently in the days of Noah." Then judgment descended. Nevertheless, the long-suffering *patience of God* persisted. It manifested itself in a special grace toward Noah and his family, "saved through water" (1 Peter 3:20), anticipating for 1 Peter the baptizing church. But more, a rainbow "sign of the covenant" (Gen. 9:12) was given between God "and *every* living creature of all flesh" (Gen. 9:15). God promised therein to stick by the world even in its waywardness. Of a piece with that promise was knowledge of the rules for life together on earth (Gen. 8:16–9:7) that are necessary to keep the world going, given by God to Noah and all his descendants.

The covenant of Noah is, therefore, a gift and a demand. God is gracious, sustaining the world even in the face of its continuing rebellion. As part of that promise, God gives the world an awareness of what it takes to make life livable. In theological language, this universal gift and expectation is, as noted, "general revelation" made possible by a "common grace": enough light to live by, even though it is regularly ignored, for "the inclination of the human heart is evil from youth" (Gen. 8:21).

On the basis of divine patience and its subsequent Noachic covenant, "Gentiles . . . living in licentiousness, passions, drunkenness, revels, carousing and lawless idolatry" (1 Peter 4:3) will have to "give an accounting to him who stands ready to judge the living and the dead" (1 Peter 4:5), for not living up to the light and the moral law of general revelation. Yet the graciousness of God is such that *even these*, failing to live up to the rainbow light they are given (sinners "judged in the flesh as everyone is judged" — 1 Peter 4:6), will not be denied the Good News proclaimed to all sinners — "for this is the reason the gospel was proclaimed even to the dead" (1 Peter 4:6). Sinners who die outside the knowledge of the gospel anywhere in the world, then or now, will not be denied hearing the Word of judgment with its offer of forgiveness achieved by the saving Work of Christ.

The verses in 1 Peter 4 here correlate exactly with those in 1 Peter 3. As in chapter 4, the dead hear the gospel, so in chapter 3, those in the past who have the light of general revelation and even then "did not obey" will not be refused Christ's ultimate Word of judgment and forgiveness. "He went and made a proclamation to the spirits in prison, who in former times did not obey, when God waited patiently in the days of Noah . . ." (1 Peter 3:19-20).

The gospel that announces God's offer to forgive the sinner goes against every human instinct. As Paul says, it contradicts our reason, being "foolishness to Gentiles" (1 Cor. 1:23 KJV). And it goes against our sense of righteousness, being "a stumbling block to Jews" (1 Cor. 1:23 KJV). Christ's offer of mercy to sinners in the *here and now* is as offensive to human wisdom as is Christ's proclamation of the gospel to sinners in the *hereafter*. But in both cases, "God's foolishness" (1 Cor. 1:25) outwits us, and the justice of God outruns our standards of justice, as the divine perseverance leaps over every boundary, death included. If in this life alone humans have hope, then we are miserable indeed (1 Cor. 15:19). But such is not the lot of those born out of time or place. To them also comes the Good News of Jesus Christ. "To him belong the glory and the power forever and ever. Amen!" (1 Peter 4:11).

John and Paul with Peter

The Gospel of John, as well as the first letter of Peter, had its concerns about the unreached. John assures us that there are "other sheep that do not belong to this fold" (John 10:16). And this gospel knows of a Christ who promises that "I must bring them also, and they will listen to my voice. So there will be one flock, one shepherd" (John 10:16). That voice will surely sound through those who travel the length and breadth of the world to preach the gospel. And what of those unreached in this world by the most determined efforts of our evangelism? Does the voice of Christ go silent before them? Are the unreached dead denied the Word? In John a firm "No" is said to all our delimited maps and timetables:

> Very truly, I tell you, the hour is coming, and is now here, when the dead will hear the voice of the Son of God, and those who hear will live. (John 5:25)

Paul adds his testimony to that of Peter and John, speaking of the freedom of Christ to cross the lines we like to draw. So he takes to the heights those he has brought from the depths:

> Therefore it is said, "When he ascended on high he made captivity itself a captive; he gave gifts to his people." When it says, "He ascended," what does it mean but that he had also descended into the lower parts of the earth? (Ephesians 4:8-9)

Jesus Christ is Lord of both the depths and the heights and is free to bring those he calls from one to the other. He will descend to the depths of death to achieve his purposes. The same presence, freedom, and regency of Christ in the place of death spoken of here are echoed in parallel passages elsewhere in the New Testament (Matt. 12:40; Rom. 10:7; Phil. 2:10; Rev. 1:18; 5:13; 21:25).

The Biblical Story

Specific passages and verses can make a case for the reach of Christ's Word beyond the boundaries of death. But we are brought to those texts, and gain light from them, because they are part of the larger sweep of the biblical Story. That narrative tells of God's resolute will to reconcile a rebel world. It is about

> God our Savior, who desires everyone to be saved and to come to the knowledge of truth. (1 Tim. 2:4)

God's desire to save — with our freedom to resist — *is* the "storyline" of Scripture, clear at every turn of the tale — from creation to fall, to the covenants with Noah and Israel, to the Person and Work of Jesus Christ, to the pouring out of the Holy Spirit on the church, in the redeemed, and on the world, and finally to the consummation of all things in the resurrection of the dead, the return of Christ, the final judgment, and everlasting life in the reign of God.[6]

The sweep of this Story shows us that God's pursuit of the divine purpose is indefatigable. The "long-suffering" One will not give up on us. In each chapter of the Great Story — chapters that have subsequently become the traditional doctrines of the church: anthropology, Christology, soteriology, ecclesiology, eschatology — a *divine* perseverance is at work. Of a piece with this grand drama of salvation is the will of God to have all "come to a knowledge of the truth." The last and least, in time and eternity, will not be overlooked or denied access to the saving Word of Jesus Christ, a Word to which they, like we, may say a "Yes" or a "No."

The Early Centuries

The biblical pattern of God's patient pursuit was taken up by believers in the early centuries. Biblical texts that pointed to "an intermediate state" and the "descent of Christ" into the realm of the dead increasingly received attention. The latter subsequently found its way into a sentence in the Apostles Creed: "He descended to the dead. . . ." In his comprehensive

6. For a primer on the chapters in this story, see Dorothy and Gabriel Fackre, *Christian Basics* (Grand Rapids: Eerdmans, 1991).

study of this issue, John Sanders takes up the early church teaching, beginning with a reference to a generalization by J. A. MacCulloch:

> "From at least the second century there was no more well-known and popular belief, including the Descent to Hades, the overcoming of Death and Hades, the Preaching to the Dead, and the Release of Souls, and its popularity steadily increased" (*The Harrowing of Hell,* p. 45). That the doctrine was taken for granted by A.D. 150 is evident from the fact that the heretics Marcion and the Valentinians, who were criticized on most of their beliefs by the early Church Fathers, were not challenged at all on this point. Both the early Fathers and the heretics agreed that Christ descended into hell. . . . It can be concluded from this that the doctrine of Christ's descent into hell and the release of souls therefrom was well established by the end of the first century. The only question through this time involved *who* was released.[7]

Modern Times

"Modern times" means our own day-and-age of expanded horizons, the realization of how big and diverse the world is, the Age of Enlightenment that began two hundred years ago, when science and industry, travel and communication, knowledge and criticism of things past and expectations about the future, began their spurt forward. The ocean ventures of the nineteenth-century missionaries, and their theological quandaries earlier mentioned, were part of that new world. With it came the church's effort to respond to the questions posed by "modernity."

The view of Divine Perseverance held by the missionaries in question was one such response. It thought along the same lines as the early church fathers, faced now with the same religious pluralism but increased a thousand-fold by contact with new cultures and faiths across the sea and around the world. But the New England travelers were not alone. European theologians, confronted more by the Enlightenment's demand to cross new mental boundaries, rather than the missionaries' physical ones, were asking about the divine love and justice. How could God be fair to the

---

7. Cited in John Sanders, *No Other Name: An Investigation into the Destiny of the Unevangelized* (Grand Rapids: Eerdmans, 1992), pp. 183-84.

countless millions before and since Christ who never heard the saving Word? Could the hard teaching of Scripture still be believed: "There is salvation in no one else, for there is no other name under heaven given among mortals by which we must be saved" (Acts 4:12)?

Those Christian traditions that stressed the necessity of personal belief were the hardest put to answer this question. This included the evangelicals with their missionary passion, as was the case with the New England Congregationalists. The question also troubled many in the mainline churches, especially those influenced by Martin Luther. If "justification by faith" is at the heart of the matter, as Luther said, then God must make possible to all the response of justifying faith. And if "faith comes from what is heard" (Rom. 10:17), then everyone must have the chance to hear the Word. It was not long before Isaac Dorner, Julius Mueller, and others began to turn their attention to the texts we have discussed.[8] And their exegesis, drawing on that of some of the nineteenth century's leading interpreters of 1 Peter (biblical scholars Plumptre, Olahansen, Meyer, Godet, Alford, Smith)[9] came to similar conclusions: the Divine Perseverance sets before each of us "the ways of life and death," if not in this world, then in the next.

While traditional Roman Catholicism was challenged and criticized by Luther's clarion call to "justification by faith alone,"[10] personal response has always been part of Catholic teaching as well. On this question it began to show up in the nineteenth century (under some of the same pluralistic influences) in a teaching that came later to be called "final option." It could not be the same as the Protestant teaching about Divine Perseverance after death (named in those days "future probation") because of the Roman

---

8. For current Lutheran thinking, see George Lindbeck, "*Fides ex auditu* and the Salvation of Non-Christians: Contemporary Catholic and Protestant Positions," in *The Gospel and the Ambiguity of the Church*, ed. Vilmos Vajta (Minneapolis: Fortress Press, 1974), and George Lindbeck, *The Nature of Doctrine: Religion and Theology in a Postliberal Age* (Philadelphia: Westminster Press, 1984), pp. 46-72. For a discussion of Lindbeck's views, see Sanders, *No Other Name*, pp. 200-205.

9. Cited in Field, "The 'Andover Theory' of Future Probation," pp. 469-72.

10. Now Catholics and Lutherans are talking together about this. Indeed, they produced a joint statement saying there is more agreement on this point than the angry exchanges of the sixteenth century allowed for. See T. Austin Murphy and Joseph A. Burgess, eds., *Justification by Faith*, Lutherans and Catholics in Dialogue VII (Minneapolis: Augsburg, 1985), and the famous 1999 Augsburg accord of Lutherans and Roman Catholics, "The Joint Declaration on the Doctrine of Justification."

Catholic doctrine of purgatory. That doctrine allows for the postmortem change of destiny only for those with smaller sins — "venial sin," not eternal life and death ones — "mortal sin." That is, physical death is the end of all opportunity for choices that affect the alternative between heaven and hell. However, prominent nineteenth-century Catholic theologians like Cardinal Newman began to speak of the *moment* of death itself as a time of encounter with Christ by all people, believers and those who never knew him, a "final fundamental option." Added by most of these interpreters was the idea that what a person did before that with his or her life counted toward how that decision for Christ would be made (a notion hard for Protestants to hold because of their belief that sin is so deep-going that only a graced faith in Christ can save). As religious pluralism becomes more pervasive, the teaching of a moment at death of final decision grows in Roman Catholic circles, competing with the notion of "anonymous Christianity" (those who do not know Christ can be saved by following their best lights and are, therefore, Christians without knowing it).[11]

The Reformed tradition with its accent on the divine sovereignty had less to say about all this. It has stressed *God's* choices, not ours. In its strictest forms, God's eternal decree of double predestination decides things. In variations of this emphasis on the divine majesty and initiative, Reformed teaching can, ironically, be used to support universalism: The divine will settles everything, for what God desires, God does (1 Tim. 2:4). In more subtle formulations, as in Karl Barth, the matter has been settled *in principle* for all, by the universal saving act on Calvary, but remains to be applied *in fact* as God so chooses. That divine decision could go either way, although we have a right to hope for universal salvation.[12]

An interesting example of Reformed efforts to face into nineteenth-century questions of divine love for those that are unevangelized, along with stress on the divine majesty, appears in the Princeton theologians, Charles Hodge and Benjamin Warfield. For them it was the question of what happens to the multitudes who die in infancy. The answer given was that the benefits of Christ are applied automatically by the sovereign will

---

11. For example, in the works of Ladislaus Boros, especially his *The Mystery of Death*, trans. Gregory Bainbridge (New York: Herder & Herder, 1965). See also Edmund Fortmann's discussion of this in *Everlasting Life after Death* (New York: Alba House, 1976), pp. 78-82, 154-55.

12. Karl Barth, *Church Dogmatics*, IV/3, first part, trans. Geoffrey Bromiley and T. F. Torrance (Edinburgh: T. & T. Clark, 1961), pp. 477-78.

of God to all those who never reach the age of discretion.[13] Of course, this is not exactly the same as our question. But it does reflect the nineteenth-century Christian encounter with the "fair-play" issues about those who do not hear the Word.

The twentieth century — the "brothers and sisters" of the present who join the earlier "fathers and mothers" of the past — has had many proponents of Divine Perseverance among both evangelicals and "ecumenicals." The former's concern is deeply connected to their strong belief in evangelism, as it was with their nineteenth-century missionary forebears. Ecumenicals come at the issue more from the direction of religious pluralism, as with their Enlightenment-preoccupied predecessors. Among evangelicals currently espousing this view is Donald Bloesch.[14] Brian Hebblethwaite and Russell Aldwinckle are ecumenical theologians who defend it.[15]

The Covenant with Noah: Amplifications

In both Scripture and Tradition, the earlier-mentioned covenant with Noah has an important bearing on the question before us. We return to it.

In Judaism, the rainbow promise has reference to the light given to those outside God's special saving covenant with the Jewish people. That is, God will judge human beings — Christians included — by the response

13. Charles Hodge, *Systematic Theology,* vol. 1 (New York: Charles Scribner & Co., 1872), pp. 26-27.

14. Donald Bloesch, *Essentials of Evangelical Theology,* vol. 2 (San Francisco: Harper and Row, 1978), pp. 226-28, and Donald Bloesch, "Descent into Hell," *Evangelical Dictionary of Theology,* ed. Walter Elwell (Grand Rapids: Baker, 1984), pp. 313-14.

15. See Carl Braaten, *The Flaming Center: A Theology of Christian Mission* (Philadelphia: Fortress Press, 1977), p. 117; Brian Hebblethwaite, *The Christian Hope* (Grand Rapids: Eerdmans, 1984), pp. 218-19; and Russell F. Aldwinckle, *Jesus — A Savior or the Savior? Religious Pluralism in Christian Perspective* (Macon, Ga.: Mercer University Press, 1982), pp. 179-215. Among the evangelicals: Stephen T. Davis, "Universalism, Hell, and the Fate of the Ignorant," *Modern Theology* 6 (January 1990): 173-86, and Wayne Grudem, "Christ Preaching Through Noah: I Peter 3:19-20 in the Light of Dominant Themes in Jewish Literature," *Trinity Journal* 7 (1986). Evangelical Clark Pinnock combines in a unique way themes from eschatological evangelism and "inclusivism" in his book *A Wideness in God's Mercy: The Finality of Jesus Christ in a World of Religions* (Grand Rapids: Zondervan, 1992); see esp. pp. 168-80.

they make to the universal hints of what is true and good and holy given from Noah's time on. God pledged the same by the rainbow sign and will follow through.[16]

In Christian teaching, the same belief is held, but is understood and applied differently. Given our fallen world, "special revelation" of the will and ways of God is required. It comes decisively in the fulfillment of the Old Testament promise in the saving Person and Work of Jesus Christ. But also, God "has not left himself without a witness . . ." (Acts 14:17) to those outside the range of these special deeds and words. Here, in "general revelation," is the way for the world to "search for God and perhaps grope for him . . ." (Acts 17:27). Our first biblical clue of this "common grace" given in and to all creation came up in our cross-reference to Genesis 6 while investigating 1 Peter 3–4. God gives to "all flesh" an awareness of basic moral and spiritual standards and expectations — don't shed the blood of humankind for it is made in the divine image . . . (Gen. 9:6-7); know and love your Creator and Sustainer . . . (Gen. 11:1-9). How much we honor these graces of preservation is shown in the very moments of their being given, as in Noah's own conduct (Gen. 9:20-27), and in succumbing to the temptation to build our towers of Babel (Gen. 11:1-9). Yet even this ingratitude does not turn aside God's promise and good gifts of providential light and love.

God's fidelity to the covenant with Noah in the face of our wandering ways is yet another manifestation of Divine Perseverance. Thus the doctrine we are exploring has a *temporal* as well as an eternal expression. In *this* world, as well as the next, God does not give up on us. But we must be clear about what that divine faithfulness entails, and see how the common grace of God given to all flesh relates to the particular grace of God in the one Word made flesh in Jesus Christ.

The covenant with Noah is not the end of the tale. Its purpose is to keep the biblical story going forward. Its promise is to sustain creation with enough power and light for the great drama to be played out — the election of Israel, the coming of our Lord and Savior, and finally the consummation of all things. The Noachic covenant is necessary to restrain the world from the self-destruction to which we sinners might drive it by our

---

16. See Eugene Borowitz, "A Jewish Response: The Lure and Limits of Universalizing Our Faith," in *Christian Faith in a Religiously Plural World*, ed. Donald G. Dawe and John B. Carman (Maryknoll, N.Y.: Orbis Books, 1978), pp. 59-60.

arrogance and animosities. We desperately need this common grace to make and keep life human.

Read from the angle of the New Testament, Jesus Christ himself is party to the covenant with Noah. The triune God is the author and sustainer of this work that saves the world from its own self-inflicted wounds. Thus the Son, as well as the Father and the Spirit, is the giver of the gift of common light, the "light, which enlightens everyone . . ." (John 1:9).

The famous story of the sheep and the goats puts things in this perspective. Simple, basic acts of compassion, ones that relieve the miseries of human life — feeding the hungry, giving water to the thirsty, clothing the naked, caring for the sick, welcoming the stranger, visiting the prisoner — are given an unexpected interpretation by Christ:

> Truly I tell you, just as you did it to one of the least of these who are members of my family, you did it to me. (Matt. 25:40)

Those who did not know they were dealing with Christ — "Lord, when was it that we saw you hungry and gave you food . . . ?" (Matt. 25:37) — had to be told. Christ is present "incognito" in these acts of care and concern. The Good Samaritan love of the New Testament here expresses the standards of the Old Testament's covenant with Noah, deeds of mercy and justice that make human life livable.

When the covenant with Noah is so honored, human life is *saved* from hate and hurt, from suffering, sickness, misery, pain, and violence. Cruden's venerable concordance of the Bible recognizes this *other* dimension as it adds to the standard meaning of salvation as "deliverance from sin and its consequences," a second definition, "preservation from trouble or danger," and lists all the Scripture references to both kinds of salvation. In the Bible, persons, cities, and nations are saved from the sicknesses, sorrows, and sufferings of this life; persons are also saved from sin and guilt. The former is "horizontal" salvation — before and in the midst of temporal things. The latter is "vertical" salvation — how you and I stand before the eternal God. And both are salvation by grace alone, not by our good works. Both are by Christ alone. In human affairs, we are saved by the grace of Christ from the miseries of this world. In divine affairs, we are saved by the grace of Christ from our sin and guilt before God.

We can't confuse these two dimensions of Christ's saving work. Our "horizontal" attitudes and acts of love are *always* short of what they might be, always frail and flawed by our sin, and therefore they cannot justify us "vertically" — before God. The rules for living that we know from the universal covenant with Noah, and the promise of a common grace that goes with them, are enough to make life livable. But they are *not* enough for the salvation of souls before God. Instead they expose us for who we are; the "law" does not save us from sin but judges us. We need a Savior. Hence the sequel to the covenant with Noah, the crowning covenant in Jesus Christ. So too the *particular* grace of the gospel that evokes the justifying faith in Calvary's cross.

> For God so loved the world that he gave his only Son, so that everyone who believes in him may not perish but have eternal life. (John 3:16)

Christ came to rescue us from the death that is "the wages of sin." That stunning offer is made to "everyone who believes," the good Word of God's deed of redemption in Jesus Christ. Faith comes from *hearing* this Word, "and what is heard comes from the preaching of Christ" (Rom. 10:17). Personal salvation — our righteousness before the holy God — is inseparable from hearing, believing, and confessing Jesus Christ.

> If you confess with your lips that Jesus Christ is Lord and believe in your heart that God raised him from the dead, you will be saved. For one believes with the heart and is justified, and one confesses with the mouth and so is saved. (Rom. 10:9-10)

The evidence from Scripture that so hearing, believing, and confessing the reconciling work of God in Jesus Christ is integral to personal salvation is overwhelming. John 3:16 — ". . . whoever *believes in him* . . ." is echoed throughout the New Testament.[17]

---

17. Matt. 8:10-13; 9:1-8, 19-22, 23-38; 10:32-33, 37-40; 11:27-30; 12:36-37; 17:19-20; Mark 2:5-12; 5:34; 8:34-38; 9:23-25; 10:52; 11:22-26; Luke 5:20-25; 7:9-10, 50; 8:48-50; 10:25-28; 15:7; John 1:12-13, 16-18; 3:3-8, 16-18, 28, 36; 4:10-14, 22, 42; 5:24; 6:29, 33-40, 47-51, 53-58, 68-69; 10:10; 11:25-26; 12:25-26, 50; 14:1-7, 23-24; 15:1-11; 17:1-5, 25-26; 20:30-31; Acts 2:36-39, 47; 3:17-19; 4:11-12; 8:21-22; 10:43; 11:13-18; 13:38-39, 48; 15:6-11; 16:30-34; 20:21, 32; 26:16-18; Rom. 1:16-17; 3:21-22, 25-31; 4:3-17; 5:1-2, 8-11; 6:23; 8:28-30; 10:9-13; 11:1-6, 11, 13-14, 21-22; 1 Cor. 1:9, 18-19, 21-24; 3:15; 5:5; 6:9-11; 15:1; 2 Cor. 2:14-16; 4:4, 14; 5:18-21; 6:2; 7:9-10; 8:7-9; 10:7; 13:4-5; Gal. 1:4; 2:15-16, 19-21; 3:6-14, 22-29; 4:4-7; 5:4-6; 6:8-9, 15; Eph. 1:4-7; 2:3-5, 8-9, 13, 16, 18-19; 3:10-12, 17-19;

As noted earlier, a canonical interpretation of biblical truth searches for the pattern of teaching found throughout Scripture. Here is a manifest one that supports the inseparability of personal salvation from personal belief, and thus the necessity of hearing the gospel proclaimed. The Divine Perseverance will not deny the saving Word to any, and will contest all the makers of boundaries, including the final boundary, "the last enemy, death."

Evangelism: Affirmations

If a patient and pursuing Christ can call in eternity those who have not heard the gospel in time, why the need *now* to proclaim the gospel to all the world? Doesn't eschatological evangelization cut the nerve of mission? The answer is a resounding "No!"

Why does any Christian want to share the gospel? Especially so, those of evangelical faith? For one, or all, of these three reasons:

1. As we have found treasure, a "pearl of great price," we just can't keep quiet about it. Come over here! See what we have found! It's for you too! Once the Word of salvation has come to us, something inside of us (the Holy Spirit) opens our mouths. We want to share the Good News. We have "a story to tell to the nations." A basic motivation for evangelism is this joy in the Lord. We've heard the Good News, and we want to pass it on. No belief in the divine perseverance after death is going to still this Story.

2. Yet it is we *sinners* saved by grace who do the passing on. We are still in this mortal frame with all its troubles and temptations. Joy in the Lord is not a constant twenty-four-hour state. Along with those times of spontaneous sharing of the faith, there are other times when we have to be *reminded* of our responsibility to proclaim the gospel. So evangelism is a duty as well as a joy. We do it because we are told to do it. Our hope for those we cannot reach in this life does not affect one whit our need to obey Matthew 28:19 here and now: "Go . . . make disciples of all nations. . . ."

4:30-32; 5:8; Phil. 2:12-13, 15-16; 3:8-11; Col. 1:12-14, 20-23, 26-28; 2:2, 6, 12-13; 3:1-4, 12-13; 1 Thess. 1:9-10; 2:2-12, 16; 4:12, 14, 16; 5:5, 23-24; 2 Thess. 1:3-10; 2:10, 12; 3:1-2; 1 Tim. 1:16, 19; 2:3-6; 4:1, 16; 5:8; 6:12; 2 Tim. 1:5-10, 18; 2:11-13, 15; Titus 1:1-3; 3:5-8; Heb. 4:2-3; 5:9-10, 12; 6:5-6; 7:24-25; 9:14-16; 10:32-36, 39; 13:20-21; James 1:17-18, 21; 2:5, 20-26; 5:20; 1 Pet. 1:5-9, 19-23; 2:23; 4:17-19; 5:10; 2 Pet. 1:3-4, 10-11; 1 John 1:1-7; 2:1-3; 3:1-4, 23-24; 4:9-10, 13-15; 5:4-5, 11-13; 2 John 1:9; Jude 1:20-23; Rev. 14:12.

3. Christians are thinking people. They can put two and two together. They experience joy in the Lord and all the other marvelous fruits of the Spirit: "love . . . peace, patience, kindness, generosity, faithfulness, gentleness . . . self-control" (Gal. 5:22-23). They know the countless spiritual benefits that come from life in the church and personal communion with Christ. How much richer life in *this world* is when one has the confidences and consolations of the gospel!

Here is yet another motivation for evangelism. While the unreached will not be denied the Word of eternal salvation in the world to come, its blessings are the fruit of an evangelism that shares it with them in the here and now.

Divine Mystery

This last point raises a question. The teaching of Divine Perseverance goes a long way toward demonstrating the love and justice of God toward the unreached. The divine goodness will not abandon them. The divine justice will keep faith with them. They will not be denied the offer of eternal salvation. But point three above acknowledges that those unreached by evangelism in this world *will not* have the temporal benefits of the Good News. This does not square with our standards of compassion and fair play. While the blessings of eternity are not foreclosed, those of time are.

Like the question of theodicy with which we began, so here in these matters of the unreached, there is still a loose end. As in theodicy, so in eschatological evangelization; the shadow of mystery as well as the light of understanding attend our best efforts. We are left with similar puzzles from every other attempt at a solution — "universalism," "restrictivism," "inclusivism," etc. (Far more darkness in those cases, we believe, than the traces of shadow here!) This tells us something about the love and justice of God: "For my thoughts are not your thoughts, nor are your ways my ways, says the Lord" (Isa. 55:8). We cannot catch God in the nets of human logic. This is true of all basic Christian doctrines, from creation to the covenant with Israel, to the Person and Work of Christ, to the nature and mission of the church, to salvation, to the consummation of all things. Everywhere we run into "paradoxes," mysteries that can be *explored* but not *explained.*

Indeed, one is mixed right in with the issues of evangelism, what some call the "paradox of grace."[18] On the one hand, we have been saying throughout that a *decision* of faith is necessary for salvation, while on the other we are saying that we are *not* saved by works . . . not *even* our work/ decision of faith. We can make that act of faith only by the grace of God. Here is a *paradox* that we can't sort out with our feeble human reason. It is true because Scripture says so ("I have outdone them all — not I, indeed, but the grace of God working in me" — 1 Cor. 15:10). And that truth is confirmed by the Spirit within us as we take on the burden of our free decision for Christ, yet after the fact, recognize that it was "the grace of God working in me."

We have sought to probe as deeply as we can into the mystery of the unreached. The Scripture and some wisdom gained from our forebears in the church put us on the trail of the Divine Perseverance. But at the end we must add this footnote of modesty: Divine Mystery is the companion of Divine Perseverance. And to God be the glory.

18. See D. M. Baillie, *God Was in Christ: An Essay on Incarnation and Atonement* (New York: Scribner, 1948), pp. 106-32.

CHAPTER 7

Christ and the People of Israel

Has the Church replaced Israel in the drama of redemption? Have the chosen people been superseded with the coming of Christ? Are anti-Semitism and its most horrifying result, the Holocaust, caused by replacement and "supersessionist" views in Christian theology? If the covenant with Israel continues after Christ, does that include the promise of ancestral lands? Where does the "uprising of the Palestinian people" fit into the purposes of God for the Jewish people?

Wrenching theological questions underlie the political issues in the Middle East and interfaith matters very close to home. Pastors and congregations face them daily with Jewish (and Arab) neighbors. Theologians have agonized over them in a rash of volumes since World War II that could fill a library. And official church bodies have produced a shelf of their own of studies and statements. What follows is a proposal based on an interpretation of Paul's struggle with these issues in Romans 9–11 as that is read canonically:

1. "The gifts and call of God are irrevocable . . . all Israel will be saved" (Rom. 11:29, 26). These are two of fourteen references in Romans 9–11 to the positive role and destiny of Israel in the purpose of God. (Other themes vis-à-vis Israel: the urging of Gentiles to value their engrafting [11:17-20]; the hardening/disobedience of Israel [11:7]; affirmation of a remnant in Israel who received Christ, among them Paul [11:1-5]; etc.) A

105

major theme in these chapters, consonant with canonical accents, the irrevocability of the covenant, including the promise of salvation for "all Israel," is a fundamental New Testament teaching.

2. From the same chapters: "If you confess with your lips that Jesus is Lord and believe in your heart that God raised him from the dead, you will be saved. . . . How are they to believe in him of whom they have never heard? . . . How beautiful are the feet of those who preach the good news!" (Rom. 10:9, 14b, 15b). This "scandal of particularity," repeated hundreds of times throughout the New Testament, is *also* integral to Christian teaching (so argued in *The Christian Story,* volume 2, *Authority: Scripture in the Church for the World* [Grand Rapids: Eerdmans, 1987], pp. 254-340). The affirmation of christological singularity, the new covenant/New Testament in Jesus Christ, is a Christian non-negotiable.

3. The partnership of new and old covenants is not an innovation. The covenant with Abraham does not eliminate the covenant with Noah. The covenant with Moses does not revoke the covenant with Abraham. Each new chapter in the great Story incorporates the earlier ones. This is a canonical refrain. The difficult question is *how* the covenants in Abraham/Moses/David continue in the time of the new covenant in Christ. A minimalist view is content to assert the partnership and not explore it further. But this ignores Paul's profound struggle with the question, and too quickly settles for what appears to be a flat contradiction.

4. How does Israel's covenant continue after the unique deed of God in Christ? Christians believe that in Christ's life, death, and resurrection the powers of sin, evil, and death were finally defeated. Paul's effort to hold together both the continuing old and the new covenant, read canonically, can be understood this way:

a. Israel plays a unique role in the salvation story. "To them belong the sonship, the glory, the covenants, the giving of the law, the worship, and the promises. . . . And of their race is the Christ" (Rom. 9:4). Indeed, Abraham is "the father of faith," and those who are his true children in Israel before Christ are "saved" — albeit by the retroactive "application of the benefits of Christ," as the traditional teaching has it. Yet Paul extends this special claim *forward* as well as backward. Thus the future tense: "All Israel *will* be saved." The "all," however, must be read in the light of Paul's statement that "not all who are descended from Israel belong to Israel" (Rom. 9:6b). Only those of true Abrahamic faith are heirs. By implication, those in the future (after Christ) who stand in this faithful line constitute "all Israel." Where there is Abrahamic faith, then and *now,* there is saving faith.

b. Yet how can Paul say this if *knowledge of* Christ is the need and goal of all humanity? And this entails a *confession of* Christ in the "heart" and with the "lips." Some resources from the early Church Fathers, and from Karl Barth, give help here. The Fathers, interpreting the descent of Christ to the place of the dead on Good Friday (see 1 Peter 3 and 4, the Apostles' Creed, etc., discussed in *The Christian Story,* vol. 1, pp. 288-92), believed that the faithful in Israel before Christ were confronted by him in his descent into death, evoking confession of Christ as the fulfillment of their proleptic faith. Barth, in a complementary line of thought, held that *all* humanity died and rose again in Christ. Christian mission tells the world what it does not yet know about its already reconciled life in the New Age. Pressing the Fathers' insight beyond Good Friday, and limiting Earth's neo-universalism to the Israel of Romans 11, points to an *eschatological* encounter of Christ with all of Abrahamic faith. Those redeemed in that faith come to know the reconciler, Jesus Christ. In this way both the christological centralities and the irrevocable covenant with Israel are affirmed.

c. Another consideration is closely related to Paul's own personal journey. "I myself am an Israelite, a descendant of Abraham . . ." (Rom. 11:1b). Before the Damascus Road, Paul was no Abrahamic believer, but a devotee of the law, one who "did not pursue it through faith, but as if it were based on works" (Rom. 9:32a). Yet there was hope even for this "chiefest of sinners," saved by grace through faith in Christ. He puzzled over why only a "remnant" in Israel so responded, but went on to urge the proclamation of faith to Jews as well as Gentiles. With him, and those few who believed, faith is not only *noetic,* as in b., but *also fiducial,* a saving faith contingent on the knowledge of Christ. Might Paul's "all Israel" also include those zealous for the law who must also first meet Christ — in time or eternity — as Paul did on the Damascus Road, to learn of that kind of gracious faith which saves? Did Paul have a special place in his heart for others, like himself, whose ardor for God proved to be the first step on the path from works to faith?

Anti-supersessionism as described above does not forbid sharing the gospel with Jewish people. Exclusion, in fact, is a subtle form of discrimination, denying to Jews what Christians believe to be their own most precious gift. *How* this non-exclusionary mission mandate is carried out, while honoring the continuing covenant of God with Israel, is not clear.

What is clear is that targeting Jews for evangelism, on the grounds that they will not be saved without Christian ministrations, appears to conflict with Paul's judgments in Romans 11.

5. Paul struggles mightily with how the continuing covenant with Israel worked, *collectively*, as well as personally. He does so with an eye on symbiosis: what happens to Israel affects the church in a salutary way.

One sign of the symbiotic relation today is Israel's custodianship of basic codes of human life together. The heirs of Amos and Isaiah are regularly found in the front ranks of causes of justice and peace. As Reinhold Niebuhr observed, one soon learns that it is Jews in the community who can be counted on as allies in the struggles for humanization. Indeed, the witness of Israel reminds the church of its own historical commitments, and often saves it from Marcionite temptations to write off the Old Testament and over-spiritualize the gospel. As a special community of conscience to both church and world, it reminds Christians, "It is not you that support the root, but the root that supports you" (Rom. 11:18).

6. Does a continuing covenant entail the promise of land? For many Jews what Christians have to say on this subject is of more interest than the strictly theological questions addressed above. Christian Zionism to the contrary notwithstanding, there are no direct biblical warrants for the reacquisition of the soil of ancient Israel. Nor can there be any straight-line theological endorsement of the modern state of Israel. The uncritical identification of the will of God with human institutions violates the divine sovereignty. In the Romans passage no linkage is made between the continuing covenant and a future nation-state.

However, an excessive disjunction between land and covenant is not in order, either. This is for the following reasons:

a. The God of Abraham and Sarah, the same God incarnate in Jesus Christ, is One who lives and acts in human history, and thus is active in our political moil and toil.

b. The hardships of the people of Israel over time are directly related to its stewardship of God's Torah. As conscience of the human community, this people evokes the hostility of a fallen creation. As such, space is needed to assure its continued witness, geography "with defensible borders" — especially in the face of the twentieth-century record of hate toward the bearers of the prophetic tradition.

c. Geographic stewardship is inseparable from the covenant mandate: a land flowing with the milk and honey of the law and the prophets. The most painful testing place for such a model of Shalom in the late twentieth century is on the fertile crescent where marching armies from North and South have ever and again challenged this vision, and from whose womb three great religions, all proclaiming Shalom, were born. Here is an opportunity for the state of Israel to be what it is, the world's community of conscience, demonstrating what life together can mean. No realization of this vision is possible without the partnership of the Palestinian people. What more dramatic witness could there be to a political life together in our time than such a "light to the nations"?

Conclusion

The conversation on the place of Israel in Christian faith — both the ecumenical exchange and the internal evangelical dialogue — is far from over. Critical to its advance is an understanding of the range of alternatives. So too are a close reading, and canonical interpretation, of the relevant biblical texts. This chapter is a contribution to both of these tasks.

PART IV

CHRISTOLOGY IN DIALOGUE

CHAPTER 8

Christology in Evangelical Perspective: Donald Bloesch

I n the early 1950s Donald Bloesch and I entered the ordained ministry of
the Evangelical and Reformed Church, now part of the United Church
of Christ.[1] In this half-century we have been in many of the same church
struggles for christological integrity. Both of us played active roles in organizing neo-confessing movements in the United Church of Christ, each
helping to draft their initial documents, looking on these movements as
the last best hope of an acculturated Protestantism.[2] In 1978 we each

1. We were both under care of the Northern Illinois Synod of the Evangelical and Reformed Church, seeing each other briefly at a Commission on Ministry meeting but going
our separate ways.

2. Bloesch drafted "The Dubuque Declaration" of the Biblical Witness Fellowship, and I
wrote portions of the first "Witness Statement" of the Craigville Colloquies (1984) and the
Statement of Purpose of the Confessing Christ movement (1993). Bloesch notes that "theologians of various persuasions are beginning to speak of a new confessional situation, a *status confessionis,* as the church finds itself engulfed in a crisis concerning the integrity of its
message and the validity of its language. . . . People of faith may be called again . . . to engage
in a new *Kirchenkampf* (church struggle)" (Donald G. Bloesch, *Jesus Christ: Lord & Savior,*
Christian Foundations 4 [Downers Grove, Ill.: InterVarsity Press, 1997], pp. 243-44). I have
made a similar case for the importance of centrist/confessing movements in "The Church of
the Center," *Interpretation* 51, no. 2 (1997): 130-32. Currently both of us have written critiques
of *The New Century Hymnal,* seeing it as a characteristic example of obeisance to ideologies
of the day. Donald G. Bloesch, *Essentials of Evangelical Theology,* vol. 1: *God, Authority and*

launched long-term projects in systematics, concerned as we have been for the recovery of Christian foundations.

The *kind* of theological renewal we sought reflects both the similarities and the differences to be detailed in this chapter. The convergences and divergences are a showcase of how two kindred commitments — Donald Bloesch the "ecumenical evangelical" and his friend the "evangelical ecumenical" — strove to keep company with their "Savior, Redeemer, and Lord."[3]

"Christology" as a systematics locus has a long association with the doctrine of the incarnation.[4] In this sense, Christology as the person of Christ — humanity, deity, and unity — is distinguished from the atonement, the work of Christ as "objective soteriology." However, there is also a long tradition of Christology interpreted as both person and (objective) work.[5] In the latter case, it is succeeded by the locus of salvation-soteriology in its subjective tense or present tense, taking up the "application of the benefits of Christ."[6] None of the above quite fits Bloesch's doctrine of Christ. As developed in the recent volume of his systematics series, *Jesus Christ: Savior and Lord*, and earlier analyses in *The Christian Life and Salvation, Jesus Is Victor!*, and *Essentials of Evangelical Theology*, Christology is both person and work *and* both objective and subjective soteriology. The inclusion of "application" in Christology puts Bloesch in continuity with other major works in the broadly evangelical tradition, such as those

---

Salvation (New York: Harper & Row, 1978) — hereafter referred to as *Essentials* 1, and Gabriel Fackre, *The Christian Story: A Narrative Interpretation of Christian Doctrine* (Grand Rapids: Eerdmans, 1978). Later came Bloesch, *Essentials of Evangelical Theology*, vol. 2: *Life, Ministry and Hope* (New York: Harper & Row, 1979) — hereafter referred to as *Essentials* 2, and Fackre, *The Christian Story* (Grand Rapids: Eerdmans, rev. ed., 1984; 3rd ed., 1996); and *The Christian Story*, vol. 2, *Authority: Scripture in the Church for the World* (Grand Rapids: Eerdmans, 1987).

3. The ecumenical evangelical/evangelical ecumenical distinctions are made in Fackre, *Ecumenical Faith in Evangelical Perspective* (Grand Rapids: Eerdmans, 1993), pp. vii-x. The conjunction "Savior, Redeemer, and Lord" is from Question 60 of the Evangelical Catechism, learned by Bloesch in his early years in the Evangelical Synod of North America.

4. A usage Bloesch himself employs in his early work *The Christian Life and Salvation* (Grand Rapids: Eerdmans, 1967), p. 53.

5. See George S. Hendry, "Christology," in *A Dictionary of Christian Theology*, ed. Alan Richardson (Philadelphia: Westminster Press, 1969), pp. 51-64.

6. As in John Murray, *Redemption Accomplished and Applied* (Grand Rapids: Eerdmans, 1955, 1978).

of Charles Hodge and Augustus Strong. For example, in Hodge's *Systematic Theology,* "Soteriology" is the major locus that includes "The Person of Christ," "The Mediatorial work of Christ" (past and present), and the application of the benefits of Christ described by the familiar *ordo salutis.* Hodge's soteriology also includes a long initial section on the "plan of salvation" and concluding sections on "the law" and "the means of grace," matters also dealt with in Bloesch's Christology but not in similar detail in this locus.[7]

The inclusion of the believer's appropriation process within Christology is also related to the influence of two of Bloesch's mentors, P. T. Forsyth (to whom he dedicates *Jesus Christ*) and Karl Barth, who returns ever and again as Bloesch's interlocutor. Forsyth insists on the *moral* dimension of doctrine with the subjective work *in us* inseparable from the objective work of Christ on the cross. While the soteric weight of the subjective is quite different in Barth, volume four of his *Church Dogmatics* integrates the applicatory work of the Holy Spirit in faith, love, and hope with his revised version of the natures, states, and offices of Christ.

A case could be made that an even wider circle needs to be drawn to encompass Bloesch's Christology. In *Jesus Christ* "anthropology" is integral to the development of the doctrine of Christ, and election, ethics, and eschatology are discussed. This larger web of doctrine also appears in *Christian Life, Jesus Is Victor!,* and *Essentials.* In addition to these subjects a long investigation of Mariology is undertaken in *Jesus Christ.* While allusion will here be made to these matters, the limits of space and focus preclude detailed exploration. The discussion of Bloesch's Christology will, therefore, take up his view of the divine-human person and its entailments, and the work of that person, both objective and subjective. General reference to pertinent writings will be made throughout with supportive quotation at places where Bloesch is breaking new ground or entering hotly disputed terrain.

---

7. Charles Hodge, *Systematic Theology,* 3 vols. (New York: Charles Scribner's Sons, 1872), 1:313-732; 3:3-709. See also Augustus Strong, *Systematic Theology: A Compendium* (New York: Revell, 1907), pp. 665-888, with person, work, and application, but only short discussions of election and law and "the ordinances of the church" discussed under the separate rubric of "Ecclesiology."

Formative Factors

Traditions

Bloesch's periodic self-descriptions and general orientation point to three theological traditions that inform his Christology: (1) evangelical, (2) Reformed, and (3) catholic. Their interaction contributes to the distinctive way in which the doctrine of Christ is interpreted, one, indeed, that varies from current treatments of Christology in each of these three traditions.[8]

Bloesch is one of North America's best-known evangelical theologians, *evangelical* understood as the interiorization and radicalization of the formal and material principles of the Reformation (the authority of Scripture and justification by faith).[9] For Bloesch, Scripture is read with an "infal-

---

8. Representative systematics include the following:

EVANGELICAL SYSTEMATICS: Millard Erickson, *Christian Theology* (Grand Rapids: Baker, 1983-85), part 7, "The Person of Christ"; part 8, "The Work of Christ"; part 10, "Salvation" (the *ordo*, including predestination); James Leo Garrett Jr., *Systematic Theology: Biblical, Historical, and Evangelical*, 2 vols. (Grand Rapids: Eerdmans, 1990-95), part 5, "The Person of Jesus Christ"; part 6, "The Work of Jesus Christ"; part 8, "Becoming a Christian and the Christian Life" (the *ordo*, including predestination); Gordon R. Lewis and Bruce A. Demarest, *Integrative Theology*, 3 vols. (Grand Rapids: Zondervan, 1987-94), vol. 2, part 2, "Christ's Atoning Provisions" (including person and work); vol. 3, part 1, "Personal Transformation."

REFORMED SYSTEMATICS: Louis Berkhof, *Systematic Theology*, 4th rev. and enl. ed. (Grand Rapids: Eerdmans, 1939, 1941), part 3, "The Doctrine of the Person and Work of Christ" (including natures, states, and offices); part 4, "The Doctrine of the Application of the Work of Redemption" (the *ordo*, with predestination treated in part 1, "The Doctrine of God"); John H. Leith, *Basic Christian Doctrine* (Louisville: Westminster John Knox, 1993), part 8, "Jesus Christ"; part 9, "The Work of Christ"; parts 12-14, on faith, justification, and sanctification; Daniel L. Migliore, *Faith Seeking Understanding: An Introduction to Christian Theology* (Louisville: Westminster John Knox, 1991), part 8, "The Person and Work of Jesus Christ"; part 9, "The Holy Spirit and the Christian Life" (justification, sanctification, vocation).

ROMAN CATHOLIC SYSTEMATICS: Francis Schussler Fiorenza and John P. Galvin, *Systematic Theology*, 2 vols. (Minneapolis: Fortress, 1991), part 5, "Jesus Christ" (person and objective work); part 6, "Church"; part 7, "Sin and Grace"; Richard McBrien, *Catholicism* (Minneapolis: Winston, 1981), part 3, "Jesus Christ" (including person, work, and sacramental presence); part 5, "Christian Existence — Ethical and Spiritual Dimensions" (including conversion, faith, discipleship).

9. Assuming the definition of *evangelical* in the entry, Gabriel Fackre, "Evangelical, Evangelicalism," in *The Westminster Dictionary of Christian Theology*, ed. Alan Richardson and John Bowden, rev. ed. (Philadelphia: Westminster Press, 1983), pp. 191-92.

libilist" hermeneutic,[10] and justification is seen as experiential appropriation of Christ's penal substitution evidenced in personal holiness and evangelistic intent. In Christology these evangelical stigmata are evident in Bloesch's insistence on the scriptural basis of all assertions with extensive biblical documentation, and as noted, in the inseparability of subjective soteriology from the doctrine of Christ.[11]

Bloesch is also a self-described Reformed theologian. This identity is borne out in the regular appearance of the characteristic Reformed emphases of *sovereignty* and *sanctification*.[12] His choice of Barth as conversation partner is a natural corollary. Formation in the Evangelical Synod wing of the Evangelical and Reformed Church contributes to the Reformed influence. However, the dual Reformed and Lutheran heritage of this "Prussian union" church helps Bloesch appreciate the Lutheran contributions to theology and sheds light on his interest in Reinhold Niebuhr, whose roots also lie in the Reformed-Lutheran conjunctions of that same church.[13]

Asserted in Bloesch's early works[14] and gaining high visibility in *Jesus Christ* is the Great Tradition, the doctrinal heritage and sensibilities of pre-Reformation Christianity and current Roman Catholic and Eastern Orthodox thought. Thus the section on Mary in *Jesus Christ* engages the Marian dogmas and the role of saints in Christian faith. Critical appropriation of the Great Tradition reflects also an "evangelical catholicity" with affini-

---

10. An evangelical "infallibilism" in the sense of unfailingly trustworthy in matters of faith and morals, rather than "inerrant" in science and history as well. See my distinctions and discussion of Bloesch's hermeneutic in Fackre, *The Christian Story*, vol. 2, pp. 71-72.

11. Bloesch is an "evangelical" also in its sixteenth-century Reformation meaning, as in his Evangelical Synod of North America origins and nurture in the Evangelical Catechism of that church.

12. Distinctive aspects of Reformed theology discussed in Gabriel Fackre, "What the Lutherans and the Reformed Can Learn from One Another," *The Christian Century* 114, no. 18 (1997): 558-61, 563-65.

13. Bloesch's father was a friend of Reinhold Niebuhr, and Bloesch wrote his doctoral dissertation at the University of Chicago Divinity School on Niebuhr. While much influenced by the Reformed Barth, Bloesch's evangelical differences with him appear regularly. For example, in anthropology vis-à-vis Christology, Barth takes up "pride, sloth and falsehood" in turn after each christological theme (priest, king, and prophet), whereas Bloesch deals with the Fall *before* the specifics of Christology. Here also is an example of Bloesch's appreciation for the Lutheran law-gospel distinction, albeit dealt with by Bloesch christologically.

14. For example, Bloesch, *Christian Life and Salvation*, pp. 13-18.

ties to the Mercersburg theology of John Williamson Nevin and Philip Schaff. Catholic identity in this sense has to do with the desire to honor all the theological charisms in the body of Christ, marking Bloesch as an *ecumenical* evangelical.

Polemics

The convergence of these three streams has caused a mighty Bloeschian wave to roll over the parched shores of contemporary theology. Over the years Bloesch has made an increasingly sharp contrast between his evangelical, Reformed, and catholic perspective and the "neo-Protestantism" and "neo-Catholicism" in mainline churches and their ideological counterparts in the academy. The attack on the acculturated theologies of the day has been accompanied by institutional efforts in theological reform, with special reference to his own denomination, the United Church of Christ. In addition to drafting the Dubuque Declaration of the Biblical Witness Fellowship (a conservative evangelical group in the UCC), he continues as an important resource to that constituency.[15] Recently he has written sharp indictments of *The New Century Hymnal* published by an agency of the UCC.[16] The polemic plays out in Bloesch's Christology. The development of any given aspect of the doctrine is prefaced by and permeated with analyses of present heterodoxies. In *Jesus Christ,* he views these deviations collectively as "a new theological paradigm," a capitulation to "Romanticism with its emphasis on individualism, pluralism and relativism."[17] The response to cultural captivity requires a Barmen-like *No!*

Christology and Its Contexts

Christology constitutes the heart of theology, since it focuses on God's work of salvation in the historical figure, Jesus of Nazareth, and the bearing it has on humankind. . . . To know the plan of God we must see the

15. See "Reflections on the Theological Drift of the UCC: An Interview with Donald Bloesch," *The Witness,* Winter 1996, pp. 13, 16.

16. See his review of the *New Century Hymnal* in *Christianity Today* 40, no. 8 (1996): 49-50, and comments on inclusive language in Bloesch, *Jesus Christ,* pp. 75-79.

17. Bloesch, *Jesus Christ,* pp. 229-30.

plan realized in the cross of Christ and fulfilled in his resurrection and second advent.[18]

Christology so understood is, as noted, conceived soteriologically, "God's work of salvation" as "realized" on Calvary and "fulfilled" at Easter and the eschaton. Yet only the person ("God . . . in the historical figure, Jesus of Nazareth") can do the work. The soteriological exposition of Christology begins, accordingly, with the *context* (the problematic of *sin*) to which God's saving action is addressed, with anthropology playing an introductory role in a christological volume.

The prominence of harmatology appears in historical as well as theological context: the need to deal with Christology in a culture that must be asked, "Whatever became of sin?"[19] Context in this latter sense is reflected in *Christian Life, Essentials,* and *Jesus Christ,* where the doctrine is expressed in the setting of modern debates about the meaning of Christ. The discussion of each facet (humanity and deity, pre-existence, virgin birth, atonement, finality, *ordo salutis,* etc.) entails a polemic mounted against current alternative views.

Chapter 1 *of Jesus Christ* illustrates this contextuality. The stage is set for the general christological inquiry by a rapid survey of deficient views, such as those of the Jesus Seminar and "Christology from below," as well as liberationist, feminist, pluralist, process, and postmodern perspectives. Theologians and New Testament scholars questioned to one degree or another include John Dominic Crossan, Marcus Borg, Wolfhart Pannenberg, John Macquarrie, Hans Küng, Stanley Grenz, John Hick, Jürgen Moltmann, Jon Sobrino, and Peter Hodgson.

On the other hand, twentieth-century theologians and traditions that have sought to maintain an "orthodox Christology" include "traditional Catholicism, Eastern Orthodoxy and conservative evangelicalism," and at least on Chalcedonian matters, "neo-orthodox theologians like Karl Barth and Dietrich Bonhoeffer." While their new interpretations go against the modernist stream, Emil Brunner and Reinhold Niebuhr are seen as less orthodox. Evangelical compatriots cited in the struggle for christological orthodoxy include Leon Morris, Howard Marshall, David Wells, Millard Erickson, and David Parker.

---

18. Bloesch, *Jesus Christ,* p. 15.

19. The title of the well-known book by Karl Menninger, *Whatever Became of Sin?* (New York: Hawthorne, 1973).

This overall critique of the new theological paradigm in chapter one resurfaces in the analysis of each particular aspect of Christology in *Jesus Christ*. The discussion of "the finality of Christ" is representative. Current heterodoxies are traced historically to Schleiermacher, the History of Religions school (E. Troeltsch, H. Gunkel, and J. Weiss) and William James. Bloesch then criticizes contemporary pluralist, historicist, and immanentist views of Paul Knitter, John Hick, Gordon Kaufman, Langdon Gilkey, Marjorie Hewitt Suchocki, Edgar McKnight, David Griffin, John Cobb, Marcus Borg, Matthew Fox, and Rosemary Ruether.

Developing the doctrine of Christ in the context of a "battle for Christology"[20] entails institutional as well as theological warfare. Bloesch sees his work as undergirding a needed new confessional movement: "It is my hope that the Spirit of God will use my theology to prepare the way for a confessing church for our time."[21] However, in both the theological and institutional struggles Bloesch distances himself from fundamentalists: political and apolitical, hyper-Calvinists, and other defenders of the tradition whose own distortions and repristinations fail to honor properly the evangelical essentials, the *semper reformanda* of the Reformed tradition or the catholicity of the Great Tradition.

The Person of Christ

While soteriology is the framework for the doctrine of Christ, it is necessary to establish *who* is able do the work of reconciliation before investigating *what* that work is. Thus, with Charles Hodge and Augustus Strong, Bloesch takes up the person before the work. Chalcedon sets the stage:

> Even when acknowledging that Greek philosophical categories were used to produce the Chalcedonian formula, I unashamedly stand by Chalcedon as an enduring expression of the faith once delivered to the saints. With the church fathers I affirm that Jesus was consubstantial with the Father, according to his divinity, and consubstantial with us mortals (except for sin) according to his hu-

20. A characterization that comes to mind as parallel to the title of a book by Bloesch, *The Battle for the Trinity: The Debate over Inclusive God-Language* (Ann Arbor, Mich.: Servant, 1985).

21. Bloesch, *Jesus Christ*, p. 13.

manity. . . . Chalcedon does not explain away the paradox of the incarnate Christ in human flesh but lets it stand as a depiction of mystery at the outer limits of human reason.[22]

Following Chalcedon, all three motifs (the divinity, humanity, and unity of the person) are investigated in *Jesus Christ,* as in Bloesch's other christological analyses, with the struggle against human-scale reductionisms always to the fore.

In the general discussion of the person of Christ these refrains appear:

1. Jesus Christ is truly God, the unique incarnation of Deity as the second person of the Trinity, "an irreversible union between the Word as God and Jesus as man."[23]

2. Jesus Christ is truly human, sharing all our human characteristics (body, mind, and spirit), sin excepted. The New Testament "insists on his true humanity . . . born of woman, born under the law (Gal. 4:4)."[24]

3. Jesus Christ is truly one, the hypostatic union (not moral union) of the eternal Word with Jesus of Nazareth, the second person's assumption of an individual human nature constituting the unity, a "union . . . unique and incomparable."[25]

4. Jesus had no independent personal existence *(anhypostasia)* but had real human personality in God *(enhypostasia).*[26]

5. While "God is the acting subject" in Jesus, his human temptations and obedience were a genuine struggle, not an illusory one.[27]

6. Jesus Christ "became sin" in his identification with fallen humanity, but did not succumb to sin. The sinlessness of Jesus, a sign of his person, is related to the presence of the divine nature but is not predetermined by it.[28]

7. While the human nature of Christ did not literally precede the incarnation, it was integral to the divine plan of salvation; in that sense it is eternally inseparable from the person, constituting thereby "the pre-existence of Jesus Christ."[29]

---

22. Bloesch, *Jesus Christ,* pp. 69-70.
23. Bloesch, *Jesus Christ,* p. 56.
24. Bloesch, *Jesus Christ,* p. 55.
25. Bloesch, *Essentials,* 1:129.
26. Bloesch, *Jesus Christ,* p. 56.
27. Bloesch, *Jesus Christ,* pp. 57, 73.
28. Bloesch, *Jesus Christ,* p. 54.
29. A theme anticipated in earlier works (Bloesch, *Essentials,* 1:130) but developed in detail in conversation with Barth in Bloesch, *Jesus Christ,* chapter 5.

8. The person of Christ (as well as the work) expresses itself in the full career of Jesus from pre-existence through virginal conception, life, teaching, miracles, suffering, death, resurrection, ascension, and session at the right hand of the Father to personal return.[30]

9. The virginal conception is a biblical teaching (an "essential truth of the catholic tradition") grounded in the historical core of "folkloric" biblical narratives, a necessary sign of the divine initiative which "safeguards" the central paradox of the Incarnation, but not an essential of faith indispensable for salvation.[31]

10. The Chalcedonian definition invites *exploration* ("faith seeking understanding") but does not attempt *explanation,* since the incarnation is a "paradox" impervious to human reason, accessed only by faith as it encounters Scripture through the work of the Holy Spirit.[32]

11. The "finality of Christ" is integral to the doctrine of the person with consequences in the work. Only in this man does God enter the world to redeem it from sin, suffering, death, and the devil, the "scandal of particularity." Here is a radical exclusivity, albeit associated with an inclusivity that entails the relationship of everyone to Jesus Christ, whether that be unto salvation or damnation.[33]

12. To affirm the deity of Christ, the Council of Ephesus declared Mary to be the "Mother of God." The wider church's assertion of further privileges of Mary presses evangelicals to explore what "may well be the new frontier in ecumenicity."[34] While there is no solid biblical basis for the belief that Mary is free of original sin, or is queen of heaven or coredemptrix, she is

> an exemplar of faith . . . special covenant partner with Christ in making . . . salvation known and in communicating its fruits to both church and world . . . a means of grace . . . but never a necessary means of grace . . . an intercessor as are all the saints . . . and we may perhaps in our prayers ask for their intercession, but we do not go to them first in order to get to Christ or to God.[35]

---

30. Bloesch, *Essentials,* 1:120-80, 2:174-210.
31. Bloesch, *Jesus Christ,* pp. 83, 93, 104.
32. Bloesch, *Essentials,* 1:122, 127; Bloesch, *Jesus Christ,* p. 57.
33. A full chapter (10) is devoted to this in Bloesch, *Jesus Christ.*
34. Bloesch, *Jesus Christ,* p. 107.
35. Bloesch, *Jesus Christ,* pp. 118-19.

13. A sound doctrine of the incarnation entails language commitments. Biblical authority supported by church tradition requires the retention of *Son* for the second person, signifying as it does a filial relation to the Father. The pronoun *he* for Christ signals a real flesh-and-blood incarnation, applicable to the unity of the divine-human person as well as the real humanity of Jesus. Because the privileged masculine images of Scripture and tradition can be misunderstood as human projection, their meaning can be clarified by usage in personal piety of maternal images from Scripture, as for example the Wisdom figures that have been applied to Christ.[36]

The Work of Christ

Bloesch develops his own "biblical-evangelical" understanding of Christ's saving work in sympathetic-cum-critical conversation with "classical and Latin theories" and such theologians as Calvin, Barth, Forsyth, Anselm, Aquinas, Aulen, and in sharper exchange with current advocates of process, Bultmannian, liberal, and neoliberal theologies of the left, and hyper-Calvinists on the right. He weaves together the following strands:

1. While there is "some truth" in varied theories of atonement that view Christ as saving from corruptibility or demonic powers, revealing God's love or reuniting the soul with God,[37] we must go to "the heart" of the matter:

Evangelical theology affirms the vicarious, substitutionary atonement of Jesus Christ. It does not claim that this theory does justice to all aspects of Christ's atoning work, but it does see substitution as the heart of the atonement. The crucial point is that Jesus suffers in our stead, and he also conquers in our stead.[38]

Variously characterized as "satisfaction," "expiation," or "propitiation," substitutionary atonement has to do with the suffering and death of Christ as the fulfillment of the reconciling purpose of God "before history," accomplished on the cross by Christ receiving the divine wrath and

36. For a discussion of the same see Bloesch, *Is the Bible Sexist?* (Westchester, N.Y.: Crossway, 1982), pp. 61-83; Bloesch, *Battle for the Trinity*, pp. 1-67 and passim; Bloesch, *Jesus Christ*, pp. 75-79.

37. Bloesch, *Jesus Christ*, pp. 144-58.

38. Bloesch, *Jesus Christ*, p. 158.

judgment (the punishment as well as the penalty) we deserve, the result being removal "not simply of the sense of guilt but the very stain of guilt."[39]

2. The satisfaction of God and the forgiveness of sin achieved by the sacrifice of the God-Man is a "happy exchange" (Luther) of Christ's righteousness for our sin, a gift of both the divine holiness and mercy.[40]

3. The demands of divine holiness and the consequences of its violation are satisfied by God himself in the person of his Son, an atonement wrought in sovereign freedom by the divine initiative through the agency of the divine-human Mediator. This is God's own act, the "suffering of God" in the person of the Son, not the appeasement of God by Jesus.

4. In this turning point in God's history with the world, the varied biblical metaphors express one or another aspect of the fulfilled will of God: "reconciliation" — God is reconciled to the world, and the world to God; "expiation" — the human race's "stain of guilt" is removed; "propitiation" — the divine anger is turned aside and God's righteous judgment is satisfied.

5. The life of Christ as well as his suffering and death are included in the objectivity of the atoning work, albeit in an "anticipatory" sense, for we are saved not "by the sacrifices in his life but the sacrifice on Calvary that purchased our redemption."[41]

6. The resurrection is essential to the atonement in that the victory over sin (1-5 above) is revealed, and the defeat of other foes (the devil, death, and hell) is achieved.[42]

7. The work of atonement continues after Calvary and Easter, because Jesus Christ, at the right hand of the Father, intercedes for sinners and empowers believers.[43]

8. Christ's work also continues in the present kingdom of grace, "a hidden rule working as yeast and seed in church and world, a progressive lordship whereby the victory of Christ is carried forward into history through the outpouring of the Holy Spirit."[44]

---

39. Bloesch, *Jesus Christ*, pp. 157, 162.
40. Bloesch, *Jesus Christ*, pp. 159-62.
41. Bloesch, *Jesus Christ*, p. 161.
42. Bloesch, *Jesus Christ*, p. 161.
43. Bloesch, *Jesus Christ*, pp. 158, 160.
44. Bloesch, *Jesus Christ*, p. 226.

9. Christ's atonement is universal but universalism is a heresy. Hell is real.

God's election and predestination are realized in a different way for those who spurn the gospel; yet we can still hope and pray even for these condemned mortals, since we know they are in the hands of a God whose justice is evenhanded but whose mercy is boundless. I affirm no ultimate dualism (as in Augustinianism and Calvinism) but a duality within an ultimate unity, and this means that the pains of hell will be made to serve the glory of heaven.[45]

10. Again, atonement is universal in that all the race is included and no one will be unrelated to the love of God in Christ, but atonement is limited in that it is applied only in those who believe because of an efficacious grace that brings that faith to be:

> All people, irrespective of their moral and spiritual condition are claimed for the kingdom, but only some respond in faith and obedience. . . . All are heirs of the kingdom, but not all become members of the church of Christ. . . . The gates of the prison in which we find ourselves are now open but only those who rise up and walk through these gates are truly free.[46]

That the act of faith itself is integral to Christ's saving work leads to the third major aspect of Bloesch's Christology, its application.

The Application of the Benefits of Christ

The subjective is inseparable from the objective, for "His reconciliation needs to be fulfilled in the experience of redemption made possible by the Holy Spirit. . . . It is only in this subjective experience . . . that the Atonement becomes real."[47]

What has taken place *de jure* requires the *de facto* application of the benefits of Christ. Bloesch's evangelical encounter with Karl Barth, and entailed disagreements, helped to underscore for him the inseparability of objective and subjective soteriology.

45. Bloesch, *Jesus Christ,* p. 170.
46. Bloesch, *Jesus Christ,* p. 169.
47. Bloesch, *Jesus Christ,* pp. 162-63.

In an early work Bloesch quotes Barth's assertion: "To *be* apprehended is enough. It requires no correlative on my side, and can have none."[48] Bloesch says that such a view

> lends itself to misinterpretation. Indeed in the framework of Barthian theology it reinforces an objectivist as over against a paradoxical way of thinking. It is true that we are elected by virtue of the mercy of God and not because of deeds done by us in righteousness (Tit 3:5). Yet if this election is to benefit us we must believe in it.[49]

Thus Barth's delimitation of the status of faith to the noetic, excluding its ontic weight, must be challenged (although Bloesch acknowledges that Barth makes a place for the subjective in some sense, especially in his later writings). Contra Barth, the act of faith as a gift of grace has eternal import, as testified to by both Scripture and tradition.[50] Evangelicals who are drawn to Barth credit Bloesch with identifying "the Barthian error" at this point.[51]

Rationalism attempts to solve the problem of grace-faith (the divine initiative and our response) by erring in a hyper-Calvinist determinism or a Pelagian indeterminism, obscuring thereby the biblical paradox that cannot be penetrated by human reason. While faith is integral to salvation, it is not a "precondition": "We are not justified on the ground of our faith or works but on the grounds of God's free, unmerited mercy."[52] Inseparable from personal saving faith is "the Christian life," faith's obediential service. In a pithy aphorism typical of his writings[53] Bloesch declares, "We are justified by faith alone, but faith does not remain alone."[54] The work of the Holy Spirit in us generates a faith busy in love.

The insistence on sanctification is one of the gifts that the evangelical heritage brings to the Christian church and theology:

48. Barth in *The Epistle to the Philippians,* cited in Bloesch, *Christian Life,* p. 63.

49. Bloesch, *Christian Life,* p. 64.

50. Bloesch, *Christian Life,* pp. 64-83. See also Bloesch, *Jesus Is Victor! Karl Barth's Doctrine of Salvation* (Nashville: Abingdon Press, 1976), pp. 118-22.

51. See Waldron Scott in *Karl Barth's Theology of Mission* (Downers Grove, Ill.: InterVarsity Press, 1978), pp. 40-43.

52. Bloesch, *Jesus Christ,* p. 179.

53. For a collection of the same, as well as longer commentaries, see Bloesch, *Theological Notebook,* 2 vols. (Colorado Springs: Helmers & Howard, 1989-91).

54. Bloesch, *Jesus Christ,* p. 185.

The German Pietists saw that salvation is not only something done for man but also something done in man. . . . Eighteenth-century Evangelicalism in England and America shared a similar concern for the Christian life, with emphasis now being placed on the crisis experience of conversion.[55]

On occasion the emphasis on subjective soteriology in all its facets is summarized in the language of the *ordo salutis:*

> Regeneration is the inward cleansing that is done by the Holy Spirit as he applies the fruits of Christ's redemption to the sinner. Justification is the act by which God imputes the perfect righteousness of Christ to the one who believes. Sanctification is the act by which God separates his people from the pollution of the world and remolds them in the image of Christ. Vocation or calling is the grace that equips the Christian for service in the world. Adoption is the privilege of being made a son or daughter in the family of God. Election and predestination refer to God's prior act of love that shapes human decision and commitment. Glorification is the final transformation of the sinner by the glory of God so that he or she becomes transparent to this glory.[56]

Bloesch notes that various Christian traditions have gravitated toward one or another of these dimensions of salvation. While there may be a *kairos* for bringing a given aspect to the fore (Luther on justification), all are needed to understand the application of the benefits of Christ's saving work.

Commentary on Bloesch's Christology

In the thirty years from *The Christian Life and Salvation* (1967) *to Jesus Christ* (1997), a remarkable consistency is apparent in the christological content of Bloesch's work, and with it the evidences of evangelical, Reformed, and catholic characteristics. Indeed, many of the same formulations reappear in the five Bloesch volumes directly related to our topic.[57]

---

55. Bloesch, *Christian Life*, pp. 30-31.
56. Bloesch, *Jesus Christ*, pp. 176-77.
57. *Christian Life and Salvation;* Bloesch, *Jesus Is Victor;* Bloesch, *Essentials*, 1 and 2; and Bloesch, *Jesus Christ.*

I share with Donald Bloesch the Reformed, catholic, and evangelical markers, but the ordering is different — as will be apparent in this commentary. The same overlap, with variations, can be seen in our critic-in-residence relationships to the United Church of Christ, differences that reflect "ecumenical evangelical" and "evangelical ecumenical" commitments. To the three major divisions of Bloesch's Christology we now turn.

Atonement

Atonement is the heart of the matter. But there are different ways to construe it, as is suggested by this encyclopedia entry:

> As the work of reconciliation wrought by God in Christ, atonement has been central in the Reformed tradition. Interpretations of the saving deed have ranged from an encompassing at-one-ment of God and the world accomplished by a manifold ministry of Christ (the threefold office) to a delimited focus on a penal substitution carried out on Calvary to render the sinner acceptable to God. . . . Calvin's threefold office returns time and again to provide a vehicle for integrating the various accents of the Reformed tradition and for developing a more ecumenical framework for understanding the atonement.[58]

While Bloesch speaks from time to time of a many-faceted atonement, he is much closer to the "delimited focus" than to the "encompassing" view. Here the evangelical aspect of Bloesch's formation leaves its mark on Christology.

Given the Pelagian captivity of American culture and the temptation of the mainline churches to accede to it, and recognizing its weakening effects even in self-identified evangelical circles,[59] the emphasis placed by Bloesch on the priestly office is exactly right. So too is its underscoring by the incorporation of anthropology into his christological presentations, and Bloesch's frank, albeit nuanced, talk of total depravity. His dedication of *Je-*

---

58. Gabriel Fackre, "The Atonement," in *Encyclopedia of the Reformed Faith,* ed. Donald K. McKim (Louisville: Westminster John Knox, 1992), pp. 13, 16.

59. As documented by David F. Wells in *No Place for Truth; or, Whatever Happened to Evangelical Theology?* (Grand Rapids: Eerdmans, 1993).

sus Christ to P. T. Forsyth, with the latter's ardent witness to the "cruciality of the cross," is especially fitting.

In addition to bringing the cross to the center, Bloesch enriches the evangelical essential of penal substitution by relating it to the "classic motif," interpreting Calvary as through and through the work of God the Son, and sounding the note of Christus Victor. In contrast to the separation of the divine and human natures in piety and theology that view the cross as the appeasement of the wrathful God by the gentle Jesus, Bloesch sees the cross as a divine self-sacrifice made through the human nature of Jesus Christ on the cross. Here is a profound grasp of the suffering of God in the divine-human person of the Son. Again the salutary influence of both Barth and Forsyth is at work in acknowledging the divine passibility and rejecting the philosophically controlled concept of divine impassiblity.

Another enlargement and correction of the traditional penal substitutionary theory is at work in Bloesch's desire to honor the contribution of both mystics and moralists in holding up the Galilean ministry of Christ and its call for subjective response. Here is an expression of the catholicity to which Bloesch is committed, the reach for a full-orbed understanding of Christ's work by including the varied theological charisms within the church, while at the same time challenging the reductionisms to which they are prey.

While substitution and the forgiveness of sin are central to the doctrine of atonement, there is a rich and crucial circumference to this center. It is developed in the Reformed tradition by the threefold office of Christ, as exemplified in major expositions by Calvin and Barth, two of Bloesch's chief mentors. While Bloesch makes random reference to the *munus triplex*, he does not use it as a framework for his Christology.[60] This is a puzzle to me, for it has functioned historically to express the full-orbed understanding of the atonement to which Bloesch points on occasion, and is a major accent in and contribution of Reformed theology.[61]

The "encompassing view" of atonement expressed in the *munus triplex* bears witness to Christ the Victim through the priestly office, Christ the Victor through the royal office, and Christ the Revealer through the prophetic office. Each is often related to a phase of Christ's ministry (although not exclusively so, as each office permeates the others): prophetic

---

60. See the paragraph reference to it in Bloesch, *Jesus Christ*, p. 158.
61. As, for example, in the theologies of Hodge, Berkhof, and Barth.

— life, teachings, miracles; priestly — suffering and death; royal — resurrection and ascension. The work of Christ viewed as *only* one or another (either life or death or resurrection, or prophetic or priestly or royal) is exemplified in the historic reductionisms of the moral, penal, and triumphal models of the atonement, all challenged by the holism, interrelationships, and priorities of the *munus triplex*. When the incarnation is viewed as the presupposition of the atonement, both the contribution and the reductionist temptation of the Eastern tradition are recognized, for only the divine-human person can do the saving work of prophet, priest, and king.[62]

This friendly critic wonders if the evangelical aspect of Bloesch's theology, with its tendency to give exclusive attention to penal substitution, obscures the fuller understanding of the atonement pointed to in the threefold office, a framework R. S. Franks asserts to be one of the lasting contributions of Reformation theology.[63]

The threefold ministry of Christ also has a history, past and present, in the wider church. The catholicity of its usage, albeit undeveloped, can be seen in such varied theologians as Eusebius of Caesarea and Thomas Aquinas. It also appears in a decree of the Second Vatican Council, where the ministry of the laity is conceived as the outworking in the secular world of Christ's prophetic, priestly, and royal offices, a concept anticipated by questions thirty-one and thirty-two of the Heidelberg Catechism.[64] Here Bloesch's catholic as well as his Reformed identity invite more consideration of the threefold office in articulating the work of Christ.

The linkage of Christology to the ministry of the laity in both Roman Catholic and Reformed traditions poses a related question: Has the influence of an evangelical pietism reduced the impact of the social-ethical concerns of the other two formative Bloesch traditions? Both Reformed

---

62. An understanding of the atonement argued in Fackre, *Christian Story,* vol. 1, pp. 134-51.

63. So stated by Robert S. Franks in *The Work of Christ: A Historical Study of Christian Doctrine* (London: Thomas Nelson, 1962), p. 348. While the Heidelberg Catechism, one of the three doctrinal symbols of Bloesch's Evangelical Synod and Reformed roots, features the threefold office in its christological section (Question 31), the Evangelical Catechism of Bloesch's early training has no reference to it.

64. See "The Decree to the Apostolate of the Laity," in *Documents of Vatican II,* ed. Walter Abbott, S.J. (New York: Association Press, 1966), pp. 491-95. See also Questions 31 and 32 of the *Heidelberg Catechism* (Philadelphia: United Church Press, 1962), pp. 36-39.

and Roman Catholic theologies and histories are "world-formative,"[65] each holding that the church qua church must make a *systemic* witness. Bloesch also is concerned about the accountability to God of political, economic, and social systems. However, he maintains the key to social transformation is wrought by the Spirit of God in the awakening to faith in Jesus Christ. A society can advance toward greater justice only when it contains within it a church that reminds it of a higher claim and a higher morality, a church that functions as an agent in bringing people a new life orientation and the spiritual gifts that enable them to realize this orientation in their thoughts, words, and actions.[66]

Or again, the "cultural mandate" of the church is executed through the church's

> teaching and serving ministry. The church must never become a political lobby. . . . It is up to individual Christians as citizens of the state to apply the teachings of the church to the political arena. The church as church points directions but must take care not to propose political solutions, though there may be rare occasions when this is necessary.[67]

Personal transformation is surely a key to social transformation, but not the only key according to Reformed and catholic perspectives. The church as church has a responsibility to challenge the "principalities and powers" directly in the public square, as well as indirectly through the conversion and nurture of individuals and their personal witness. Indeed, the political fundamentalists on the right and the "justice and peace" evangelicals on the left have raised legitimate questions about the apolitical tendencies of traditional evangelicalism, tendencies reflected in Bloesch's comments, albeit with his recognition that a systemic witness may also have to be made on "rare occasions."

We do need the *intra-institutional* witness of transformed persons to which Bloesch points. But partnership with the counter-institutional heritage of the Reformed and catholic traditions is also required. Necessary as

---

65. Nicholas Wolterstorff, *Until Justice and Peace Embrace* (Grand Rapids: Eerdmans, 1983), pp. 2-22.

66. Donald G. Bloesch, *Freedom for Obedience: Evangelical Ethics in Contemporary Times* (San Francisco: Harper & Row, 1987), p. 234.

67. Bloesch, *Jesus Christ*, pp. 242-43.

well is the *para-institutional* approach of the left-wing Reformation reflected in current "resident alien" ecclesiologies. All must be done concomitantly, and one or another must come to the fore as the "mind of the church" under the Word can best discern. Here, as elsewhere, catholicity strives to avoid the reduction of Christian mission to one organ of the body, for "there are varieties of gifts but the same Spirit; and there are varieties of service but the same Lord" (1 Cor. 12:4-5).

Incarnation

Bloesch is a stalwart defender of the historic teaching on the person of Christ held by evangelical, Reformed, and catholic traditions. He sets it forth with biblical warrants, attention to learnings from the early christological controversies and respect for the Chalcedonian formula, which is still the standard belief of ecumenical Christianity. He is also right in his defense of the doctrine of Christ as a "paradox" that has been distorted by rationalist efforts on both left and right to explain what can only be explored. Further, he effectively challenges the many and varied current distortions of the person that continue either the early Ebionite or Docetist reductionisms.[68]

Along with the affirmations, however, questions must be raised, initially, of a diagnostic sort: "The Christ of Chalcedonian orthodoxy is in palpable eclipse in most circles except those of the old Roman Catholicism, confessional evangelicalism and Eastern Orthodoxy."[69] This sweeping judgment does not take into account (a) the emerging centrist/confessional movements in mainline churches, (b) the "silent center" in clergy and congregations to which the former is seeking to give voice,[70] (c) the current vital bilateral and multilateral ecumenical ventures whose charter documents all assert classical Christian teaching, including the doctrine of the person of Christ[71] and (d) the reclamation in mainline seminary sys-

---

68. While Bloesch associates Docetism today with views that reduce Jesus to a universal idea, this appears rather to be yet another version of Ebionism in which Jesus is an exemplar of a human value.

69. Bloesch, *Jesus Christ,* p. 234.

70. See *Interpretation,* April 1997, an issue devoted to the centrist phenomenon.

71. Most recently, the Lutheran-Reformed Formula of Agreement and its antecedents, the Leuenberg Concord, the Lutheran-Episcopal Concordat, the Roman Catholic–Lutheran

tematics departments of the Great Tradition.[72] The discernment of this wider circle of orthodoxy is not unrelated to participation in it. One of the sad consequences of evangelical-ecumenical polarization is the neglect of, and antagonism toward, outstanding evangelical theologians like Donald Bloesch by the ecumenical movement and the mainline churches and seminaries. This invites, in turn, lack of appreciation by evangelical theologians, including the best of them like Bloesch, for the theological ferment and re-centering current in those places.

In a similar vein Bloesch is sometimes dismissive of the mainstream allies he has in the retrieval of Chalcedonian orthodoxy. Two cases in point are George Lindbeck and Wolfhart Pannenberg. Contrary to Bloesch's reading and rejection, Lindbeck does make ontological truth claims for his cultural-linguistic view of doctrine, as Bruce Marshall has shown in a study of *The Nature of Doctrine,* with an agreement expressed by Lindbeck.[73] For all the rationalist tendencies of Pannenberg's theology, with which both Bloesch and I disagree, Pannenberg is a strong advocate of classical Christianity and holds to both the deity and humanity of the one person, albeit interpreted within his unique eschatological framework.[74]

Mariology

On another point, by giving it the attention not often found among Protestant theologians, Bloesch makes an important evangelical contribution to a broadly conceived Mariology cum Christology. He rightly sees the virginal conception as a crucial sign of, though not proof of, the incarna-

---

Agreement on Justification, and the nine-denomination Consultation on Church Union with its doctrinal COCU Consensus. The World Council of Churches also has in its brief doctrinal statement the confession of Jesus Christ as "God and Savior," and its Faith and Order Commission's two documents *Baptism, Eucharist and Ministry* and *Confessing the Apostolic Faith* (based on the Nicene Creed) presuppose and/or articulate Chalcedonian orthodoxy.

72. See Gabriel Fackre, "Reorientation and Retrieval in Seminary Theology," *Christian Century* 108, no. 20 (1991): 653-56.

73. Bruce Marshall, "Aquinas as a Post-liberal Theologian," *The Thomist* 53, no. 3 (1989): 353-402, and its sequel, George Lindbeck, "Response to Bruce Marshall," 403-6.

74. See especially Wolfhart Pannenberg, *Systematic Theology,* trans. Geoffrey W. Bromiley (Grand Rapids: Eerdmans, 1994), 2:386-96.

tion, an evangelical essential though one not indispensable for salvation. He is unashamed to speak of Mary as "the mother of God," affirming the christological rationale for the same. He gives respectful attention to Roman Catholic and Orthodox teaching on the privileges of Mary, but measures Mariological claims by Scripture, finding a place for Mary only "on this side" of the God-world divide. Mary, whom Scripture describes as "full of grace," is a unique model of holiness and companion in redemption, always an "exemplar of faith" but never an "object of faith."

The catholic sensibility, so well illustrated here by Bloesch's attention to Mary, could be pressed further, however, in the direction of much Roman Catholic theology today by seeing through Mary's song (Luke 1:46-55) that God has "brought down the powerful from their thrones, and lifted up the lowly," giving thereby a mandate for solidarity with the lowly in their struggle for justice.

On the other hand, an *evangelical* catholicity and Reformed sensibility in the Mercersburg tradition would question Bloesch's proposal that we "may perhaps in our prayers" ask for the intercession of Mary and the saints, however that request for the intercession is surrounded by qualifications that "their prayers are effectual only when united with those of Jesus Christ."[75] The recovery of a biblical doctrine of the communion of saints in the Mercersburg tradition does not "go to them"[76] but rather prays *with* them. This is more faithful to Bloesch's own stated intention that Mary is "companion in redemption."

Inclusive Language

Inclusive language has been a major question for Bloesch, current proposals illustrating the cultural captivity of modern theology. He is one of the first twentieth-century theologians to have given sustained attention to the subject and to have discerned its theological minefields. The topic with special reference to its bearing on Christology deserves, therefore, extended treatment.

Bloesch is right in challenging proposals that undercut basic Christian teaching about the Trinity and the person of Christ, ones that repeat the

75. Bloesch, *Jesus Christ*, p. 118.
76. Bloesch, *Jesus Christ*, p. 118.

reductionisms rejected by the church in the ancient christological contro-versies. He sees (a) the docetic premise in the elimination of the maleness of Jesus both conceptually and pronominally, (b) the Nestorian separation of the natures by rejecting the language of "Son," and (c) Arianism, subor-dinationism, and reduction of the Trinity to a functional status in substi-tuting "Creator, Redeemer, and Sanctifier" or "God, Christ, and the Spirit" for the universal trinitarian formula of Father, Son, and Holy Spirit.

Along with his polemic against ideological feminism, but not often ac-knowledged by either his critics or his supporters, is the challenge he early mounted to "patriarchalism," his assertion that "God is not male" and his suggestion that "it might . . . be permissible on occasion to address the deity in terms such as 'Holy Mother, Wisdom of God' or 'Wisdom of God, our Mother,' since such usage has some biblical support."[77] On the language for God as it pertains to the person of Christ, Bloesch draws on Barth's linkage of revelation with "the language of Zion."[78] Living and writing before the current inclusivist proposals, Barth's language practice is traditional in all respects, generically masculine for God as well as human beings. However, (1) Barth's teaching about "the pre-existence of Jesus Christ" (which Bloesch appropriates and develops in his own way in *Jesus Christ*) and (2) Barth's view of the non-applicability of our human understanding of "father" to God as Father (and son to Son) have import for the language is-sue, reflecting the Reformed accent on the divine sovereignty:

> No human father is the creator of his child, the controller of its des-tiny, or its savior from sin, guilt, and death. No human father is by his word the source of its temporal life. In this proper, true, and primary sense God — and He alone — is Father.[79]

Bloesch here quotes Barth, rightly commenting that "the prophets and apostles did not impose upon God a conception drawn from their patriar-chal society, but they received from God through his revelation the true and original meaning of fatherhood."[80]

The christocentric-cum-sovereignty note appearing here means that only God will define what *Father* means and that we thereby look to Jesus

---

77. Bloesch, *Is the Bible Sexist?* pp. 72, 73.
78. Bloesch, *Battle for the Trinity*, p. 23 and passim.
79. Barth, quoted in Bloesch, *Is the Bible Sexist?* p. 77.
80. Bloesch, *Is the Bible Sexist?* p. 77.

Christ for that disclosure. Yet in the inclusive language dispute Bloesch contends that *Father* is used in Scripture and Christian faith to describe God because it conveys the masculine qualities of "power, initiative and superordination."[81] This argument for masculine usage is inconsistent with the Barth/Bloesch veto on attributing masculine human qualities to God the Father (or Son) instead of looking to Christ for definition of our analogies. It invites the Feuerbachian critique deployed by Barth against a liberal religion that projects onto deity our values. Here Bloesch seems to be closer to *analogia entis* than Barth's *analogia fidei,* the catholic thereby edging aside the Reformed tradition.

A Barthian case, however, can be made for Bloesch's retention of "Son," trinitarian language, and the use of the *he* pronoun for the person. The pre-existence of Jesus means that a male figure is the Elect of God and thus, based on the unity of the human and divine natures, *only* "the Son" as well as "the only Son" in the trinitarian family. Based on that same unity *he* is the proper pronoun for the person of Christ in both natures.

Why God chose a male incarnation is quite another matter, one arguably related to the primal human sin of *hubris,* manifest in the history of the human race in the abuse of power by history's dominant patriarchal societies. This masculine tendency toward the sin of *superbia* is radically challenged in the male Jesus. The meanings of *Son* and *he* have to do with the transvaluation of human values on the cross. Thus following Barth, we define *Son* as we do *Father,* not from the masculine attributes of power, initiative, and superordination but from the victory won on Calvary by the divine vulnerability.

Ecclesial Implications

With regard to the ecclesial implications of Christology, Bloesch's views on the sacraments have affinities with *the* Reformed Mercersburg theology, as in his affirmation of a baptismal grace that requires the response of faith in contrast to "catholic" views of baptismal regeneration.[82] However, Mercersburg's evangelical catholicity connects the doctrine of the incarnation to ecclesiology in such a manner (contra the too-simple "church as the

---

81. Bloesch, *Is the Bible Sexist?* p. 72.
82. Bloesch, *Jesus Christ,* pp. 188-89.

continuation of the incarnation" as in the Oxford movement) that the sectarian tendencies of both frontier and latter-day evangelicalism are called
into question. Here may lie the difference, institutionally, between an
evangelical separatist tendency in the current church struggle based on a
sect-type ecclesiology, and an ecumenical strategy of internal reform based
on a church-type ecclesiology.[83]

Application

In all his christological-cum-soteriological writings Bloesch makes a
strong Reformation witness to the centrality of justification by grace
through faith. He has faithfully resisted the pervasive works-righteousness
of American culture and the accommodationist theologies of modernity
and postmodernity. Evangelical and Reformed commitments are clearly at
work here.

All three self-identifications (evangelical, Reformed, and catholic)
manifest themselves in Bloesch's stress on sanctification. From the beginning Bloesch has insisted that "the fruit is organically related to the root."[84]
A biblical understanding of personal salvation views grace to be "imparted" as well as "imputed." Such is the insistence of the Reformed tradition in its long encounter with Lutheran theology.[85] Sanctification is *also*
an evangelical emphasis and a catholic accent. We are in Bloesch's debt for
his stewardship of all three traditions.

Justification cum sanctification, further, is lodged within the *ordo
salutis*. Here again Bloesch draws on his Reformed heritage to good purpose. While he has criticized most forms of narrative theology, a case could
be made that the *ordo* itself is a version of it: a macro-story beginning with
the protological electing love of God, proceeding into time through the
general call to the application of the benefits of Christ to the believer who
lives out the stages of a personal story (regeneration, justification, sanctifi-

83. Thus the difference in relations to the UCC between the two neo-confessional movements in the UCC, the Biblical Witness Fellowship and Confessing Christ.

84. Bloesch, *Christian Life*, p. 30.

85. Continuing to this day as in the North American Lutheran-Reformed dialogue, with
the consummation of "full communion" in 1997. See Keith F. Nickle and Timothy F. Lull,
eds., *A Common Calling: The Witness of Our Reformation Churches in North America Today*
(Minneapolis: Augsburg, 1993).

cation, adoption, perseverance), a narrative that moves finally to eschato-logical glorification.

While Bloesch gives sanctification its due, he understands also the persistence of sin in the pilgrimage of the believer. Reformed sobriety is here at work, but just as much so are the *simul iustus et peccator* of his Lutheran lineage and his debt to Reinhold Niebuhr. In this respect, the often too-exuberant expectations of the evangelical born-again experience are qualified by the realism of the magisterial Reformation.

A critical contribution Bloesch makes to contemporary theology in this soteriological locus emerges in his exchange with the views of Karl Barth and also in his debate with varieties of contemporary pluralist theology and some evangelical theologians similarly affected by today's religious pluralism. Bloesch gives a strong witness to the salvific weight of justifying faith. He is critical of Barth's construal of faith as *noetic* but not *ontic*. The hundreds of references in the New Testament to the inseparability of the act of faith from personal salvation call radically into question its delimitation to the status only of knowledge of a saving relationship previously established.

Barth's idiosyncratic view on this subject reflects a comparable refusal to associate God and/or grace unambiguously with one or another of the traditional media of the saving work of Christ to which they have been linked: church, sacraments, Scripture, Christian ethics, the covenant with Noah, and so on. In these latter cases, a Barthian actualism calculated to protect the divine sovereignty allows the medium to become ever and again only an *occasion* for grace as determined by the freedom of God, a discontinuity that disallows the promise of Christ to be always with the church: a continuing real presence in Word and sacraments, Scripture's trustworthiness a constant based on authorial inspiration, an ethics that affirms universally accessible moral norms and the reality of a general revelation.[86] In the matter of salvation by grace through faith, the freedom of God to be *for us* savingly in the once-happenedness of Jesus Christ and free *from* us otherwise precludes any lasting *state* of personal salvation by grace through faith. Bloesch, for all the influence of Barth, will not let go of this evangelical essential, and rightly takes Barth to task for his omission.

At another point, however, Barth is a corrective to Bloesch's view of the ultimate destiny of those without faith. Bloesch speaks in Barthian terms

---

86. A critique developed in Fackre, *The Doctrine of Revelation: A Narrative Interpretation* (Grand Rapids: Eerdmans, 1997), pp. 137-48 and passim.

of a mercy that is boundless and our need and right to "hope and pray" for them. For Barth, reflecting here the Reformed accent on the divine sovereignty, this means the freedom of God to overturn even the most determined resistance (or ignorance) of those without faith. While a universal homecoming *cannot* be an *article of faith* (universalism) — given the freedom of God to determine what God will ultimately do — it *can* be an *article of hope,*

> for there is no good reason why we should forbid ourselves, or be forbidden, openness to the possibility that in the reality of God and man in Jesus Christ there is contained much more than we might expect and therefore the supremely unexpected withdrawal of that final threat. . . . If we are certainly forbidden to count on this as though we had a claim to it . . . we are surely commanded the more definitely to hope and pray for it . . . to hope and pray cautiously and yet distinctly that, in spite of everything which may seem quite conclusively to proclaim the opposite, his compassion should not fail, and that in accordance with his mercy which is "new every morning," He "will not cast off forever" (Lam 3:22f., 31).[87]

This is a larger hope and a greater emphasis on the freedom of God than found in Bloesch's view, perhaps a reflection again of the need for the Reformed accent to be given its full due.[88]

There is another way to honor three of Bloesch's points in this discussion: the crucial role of the decision of faith, the reality of hell, and the boundless mercy of God. (1) Following the Reformed traditions of the Mercersburg theology and the New England Congregationalist "Andover Theory" (each exegeting 1 Peter 3–4 and the descent to the place of the dead in the Apostles' Creed), the barrier of death is breached by the Hound of Heaven, who pursues those who have not heard or heard aright. (2) For those without faith and obedience, hell is real and lasting. (3) The bound-

---

87. Karl Barth, *Church Dogmatics*, IV/3, first part, pp. 477-78.

88. At one point Bloesch seems to have the passage cited above in mind when he says he "does not share his [Barth's] expectation of a universal final salvation" (Bloesch, *Jesus Is Victor*, p. 118). However, there is an important distinction between "expectation" and "hope." The former is an uncharacteristically Barthian assumption of our penetration of God's freedom, and the latter an acknowledgment of that freedom, but with attention to evidences granted of what that might be in God's freedom for us in Jesus Christ.

less mercy of God through even the pains of hell is a rehabilitating love whose fires can purge our worst sin (1 Cor. 3:13-15); hell is lasting but not everlasting. That such fires will cleanse all is, as Barth insists, not an article of faith but rather an article of hope that God "will not cast off forever."

Conclusion

Donald Bloesch has honed a Christology that could make a major contribution to the renewal of the church and the revitalization of Christian theology. Its uniqueness lies in the bringing together of evangelical, Reformed, and catholic traditions. However differently they might be configured as indicated in the previous commentary, these are charisms integral to the body of Christ and to the body of Christian teaching about the person and work of Jesus Christ. Would that the church reformed and the church catholic receive the gifts so offered with the same welcome extended by the evangelical community! May the conversation carried on in this chapter, and in the book in which it appears, work to that end.

CHAPTER 9

Christology in Ecumenical Perspective

What would a *Reformed* signature on the 1999 Lutheran–Roman Catholic "Joint Declaration on the Doctrine of Justification" do for relations in Northern Ireland? Or, if consummated earlier, what would have been its effect in Puritan New England upon the arrival of immigrant Catholic folk? Or, later, for Protestant-Catholic collegiality in the South African struggle where Reformed churches both contributed to, yet also resisted, apartheid? In the same vein, has the Joint Declaration had any effect so far in lands where Catholic and Lutheran populations have had a history of hostility? Or where these two traditions are now enjoined to make "this common understanding of justification . . . bear fruit in the life and teaching of the churches," and thus their mission in the world?[1] Such questions presume the socio-political as well as the ecclesial import of this document, its potential role in healing rifts in the wider community as well as within the church. Reformed Christianity is by nature *world-formative*, as Nicholas Wolterstorff has described it,[2] approaching doctrine with an

---

1. The Lutheran Federation and the Roman Catholic Church, *Joint Declaration on the Doctrine of Justification*, English-Language Edition (Grand Rapids: Eerdmans, 2000), section 5, para. 43, p. 27; hereafter *JDDJ*.

2. Nicholas Wolterstorff, *Until Justice and Peace Embrace* (Grand Rapids: Eerdmans, 1983), pp. 3-22.

eye to its worldly consequences. Thus justification is inseparable from sanctification, the latter touching society as well as souls.

But just what is "*the* Reformed perspective"? In a current volume, thirty Reformed theologians opine about the future of their tradition, giving a bewildering variety of views as to what constitutes Reformed theology.[3] From this we might wonder if there is such a thing as "the" Reformed perspective. Indeed, the greatest Reformed theologian of modern times, Karl Barth, remarked that, in spite of all our many catechisms and credos, we have "*no* Augsburg Confession, *no* Formula of Concord . . . which might later, like the Lutheran, come to possess the odor of sanctity. . . . It *may* be our doctrinal task to make a careful revision of the theology of Geneva or the Heidelberg Catechism or the Synod of Dort. . . ."[4] This commitment to reinterrogate our own tradition is illustrated by the plethora of new confessions, especially in the growing Reformed churches of Asia and Africa.[5] If there is such diversity, does the Reformed tradition have the kind of coherence that would enable it to sign something like a "joint declaration"?

The Reformed tradition does have an identity, one marked by two distinguishing characteristics, the aforementioned accent on *sanctification* with its strong social import, and a second, a focus on the divine *sovereignty*. The latter, in fact, accounts for the internal diversity within its unity. The emphasis on the glory of God, the freedom of God, means that the divine majesty forbids the domestication of deity in any human forms or formulations, that all are subject to re-form. So the tradition's very name, and its battle cry, *ecclesia reformata et semper reformanda!* As such, this second defining characteristic will prompt a second set of queries. For one, on general matters, does the Joint Declaration take into sufficient account that the sovereign "Lord has more truth and light yet to break forth from his holy Word" (the words of Reformed pastor of the Pilgrims, John Robinson, as he sent the *Mayflower* on its way)? And on the specifics of justification, what of the aptness of Barth's concern that justification can be tied so closely to "the question of the individual experience of grace . . . Lu-

3. David Willis and Michael Welker, eds., *Toward the Future of Reformed Theology: Tasks, Topics, Traditions* (Grand Rapids: Eerdmans, 1999).

4. Karl Barth, *The Word of God and the Word of Man,* trans. Douglas Horton (Boston: The Pilgrim Press, 1928), pp. 229, 230.

5. Discussed and documented in the essay of Eberhard Busch, "The Closeness of the Distant: Reformed Confessions after 1945," in Willis and Welker, eds., *Toward the Future of Reformed Theology,* pp. 512-31.

ther's well-known question in the cloister . . . ," the "subjective appropriation of salvation," that the "objective demonstration of divine grace" by the sovereign God in the Person and Work of Christ is obscured?[6]

But turn-about is fair play. It must be asked of the Reformed: Have your two defining characteristics created their own problems — the stress on sanctification producing activist churches with little doctrinal substance, and the accent on sovereignty so distancing God from the givens — ecclesial and doctrinal — that your churches capitulate ever and again to the Zeitgeist? These are fair questions, for they discern a temptation in Reformed teaching to allow its accents to become a full-blown ideology.[7] When the Reformed *emphases* become the *sum and substance* of the Reformed tradition, rather than a *perspective on* the biblical and classical sum and substance of faith, its tradition is in crisis. Interestingly, in a second new book on the Reformed family, ecumenist Lukas Vischer offers a counterpoint to charges of Reformed incoherence by pinpointing both its common doctrinal substance grounded in Scripture and the classical tradition, and the distinguishing perspectives identified as sanctification and sovereignty.[8]

I was made very aware of the defining marks of sovereignty and sanctification during twelve years in the recent U.S. Lutheran-Reformed dialogue. There the Lutheran *finitum capax infiniti* kept meeting the Reformed *finitum non capax infiniti* — Christ as "haveable" in Dietrich Bonhoeffer's word, the Lutheran *solidarity* of Christ *in, with,* and *under,* encountering the Reformed *sovereignty* of Christ *over,* Christ as "unhaveable."[9] And in the second instance, the Lutheran stress on the persistence of sin in soul and society, *simul iustus et peccator,* kept confronting the Reformed *sanctificatio,* the possibility of advance in the same.[10] While

---

6. Karl Barth, *Church Dogmatics,* IV/1, trans. Geoffrey Bromiley (Edinburgh: T. & T. Clark, 1956), pp. 150, 149.

7. Of course, a temptation that attends every tradition.

8. Lukas Vischer, "The Reformed Tradition and Its Multiple Facets," in *The Reformed Family Worldwide: A Survey of Reformed Churches, Theological Schools and International Organizations,* ed. Jean-Jacques Bauswein and Lukas Vischer (Grand Rapids: Eerdmans, 1999). See esp. "The Reformed Heritage," pp. 26-33.

9. In Bonhoeffer's early critique of Karl Barth's *incapax, Act and Being,* trans. Bernard Noble (New York: Harper & Bros., 1961), pp. 90-91.

10. See Keith F. Nickle and Timothy F. Lull, eds., *A Common Calling: The Witness of Our Reformation Churches in North America Today* (Minneapolis: Augsburg, 1993), pp. 35-55 and passim. Also, Gabriel Fackre and Michael Root, *Affirmations and Admonitions* (Grand Rapids: Eerdmans, 1998), pp. 1-43.

these differences proved church-dividing for centuries, when relocated in a new context of "mutual affirmation" regarding common articles of fundamental faith, they came to be understood as occasions for mutual teachability, or as it was phrased in the dialogue, "mutual admonition," eventuating in a full communion accord.

From all the foregoing it can be seen that the formula developed in that dialogue, "mutual affirmation and mutual admonition," might prove illuminating in evaluating the Joint Declaration, and I shall use it in my Reformed commentary. Ecumenist Harding Meyer, commending its appearance in the U.S. Lutheran-Reformed dialogue, noted that in it "a clearly *positive function* is being attributed to the differences, the function of mutual admonition, or mutual correction, of being 'no trespassing signs.'"[11] Of course, the Joint Declaration and its predecessor texts are no strangers to these twins, albeit admonishments described in the language of "concerns," "emphases," and "salutary warnings."[12] Finally, differences, construed as both gifts and admonitions, have their charter in Paul's counsel to the diverse parties in the Corinthian congregation to consider each as a charism integral to the body of Christ, but, standing alone, as an awkward substitute for the fullness of its form (1 Cor. 12). Thus "the eye cannot say to the hand, 'I have no need of you . . .'" (1 Cor. 12:21).

We turn to a Reformed reading of biblical and classical understandings of justification, and then to its implications for the Joint Declaration.

The Centrality of Justification in the Reformed Tradition

The doctrine of justification is a fundamental teaching of the Reformed tradition. Calvin declared it to be "the principal ground on which religion

---

11. Harding Meyer, "A Common Calling in Relation to International Agreements," *Ecumenical Trends* 23, no. 8 (September 1994): 4/116-5/117.

12. As in Karl Lehmann and Wolfhart Pannenberg, eds., *The Condemnations of the Reformation Era: Do They Still Divide?* trans. Margaret Kohl (Minneapolis: Augsburg Fortress, 1990), pp. 38, 40, 52, 68-69. The *JDDJ* cites approvingly the phrase from the foregoing — "salutary warnings" — as the continuing function of the sixteenth-century condemnations (sec. 5, par. 43). For an attack on the idea of differences as "emphases" and "concerns," see Gerhard Forde, "What Finally to Do about the (Counter-) Reformation Condemnations," *The Lutheran Quarterly* 11 (1997): 3-16.

must be supported," expounding it at length in his *Institutes of the Christian Religion,* with the Reformed Confessions and classical Reformed theologians following suit.[13] It has remained central in twentieth-century Lutheran-Reformed dialogues, as in the words of the North American 1983 accord, "Invitation to Action," influenced by the 1973 European Leuenberg Agreement:[14]

> Both Lutheran and Reformed traditions confess [the] gospel in the language of justification by grace alone through faith alone. This doctrine was the central theological rediscovery of the Reformation; it was proclaimed by Martin Luther and by John Calvin and their respective followers.[15]

The Reformed voice on justification has been heard in some of the ecumenical dialogues with the Roman Catholic Church, as in a "common confession of faith" in the joint ecclesiological inquiry, *Toward a Common Understanding of the Church,* where Catholic and Reformed theologians were able to say together:

> Because we believe in Christ, the one Mediator between God and humankind, we believe we are justified by the grace which comes from him by means of faith which is a living and life-giving faith. We rec-

---

13. John Calvin, *Institutes of the Christian Religion,* Book III, Chapter XI, par. 1, trans. Henry Beveridge (Grand Rapids: Eerdmans, 1957), vol. 2, pp. 25-26. In his study of justification and the Reformed Confessions, G. C. Berkouwer observes, "A single theme plays through all three documents, the Belgic Confession, the Heidelberg Catechism, and the Canons of Dort, the theme of *sola fide.*" "Justification by Faith," in *Major Themes in the Reformed Tradition,* ed. Donald McKim (Grand Rapids: Eerdmans, 1992), p. 136. See also *The Second Helvetic Confession,* XV, XVI, and Heinrich Heppe summarizing Reformed teaching in his compendium, *Reformed Dogmatics,* trans. G. T. Thompson (Grand Rapids: Baker, 1978), p. 543: "The whole evangelical doctrine of salvation stands or falls with the doctrine of justification as being the inmost core of the doctrine of redemption."

14. Now more than European in its ninety national churches, including five from South America. See *Die Kirche Jesu Christi: Der reformatorische Beitrag zum ökumenischen Dialog über die kirchliche Einheit* (Frankfurt am Main: Verlag Otto Lembeck, 1995).

15. "Joint Statement on Justification," in *Invitation to Action: The Lutheran-Reformed Dialogue III, 1981-1983,* ed. James E. Andrews and Joseph A. Burgess (Minneapolis: Fortress Press, 1984), p. 9. A section from the Leuenberg Agreement, reflecting this consensus, "The Message of Justification as the Message of the Free Grace of God," was incorporated into the 1997 U.S. Lutheran-Reformed "Formula of Agreement."

ognize that our justification is a totally gratuitous work accomplished by God in Christ.[16]

Representatives from Reformed churches also took part in working parties that contributed to the Ecumenical Study Group whose reports concluded that the condemnations of the sixteenth century no longer apply to the present partners, and some Reformed bodies have made response to it.[17] For all that, the Yale consultation on the Joint Declaration in which this paper is being delivered is a unique venture by its inclusion of both Reformed and Anglican responses to the historic Lutheran-Catholic agreement, and is a model for larger ecumenical dialogue and witness.[18]

Yet we must deal with caveats about justification coming from some Reformed theologians who have questioned its centrality. Not *sola fide* but *soli Deo gloria* is the Reformed tradition's organizing principle, they say — not the anthropocentric questions of *our* faith or *our* works but the theocentric will and way of the sovereign God. Others have asserted that Calvin was really the "theologian of sanctification," not a theologian of justification. And recently Jürgen Moltmann has written critically about the Joint Declaration, holding that the justice of God in the face of the sufferings of the world is the commanding question today, not the justification of the sinner *coram Deo*.[19]

G. C. Berkouwer has demonstrated that the *sola-soli* juxtaposition is a misunderstanding of the Reformed view,[20] and Barth has rightly chal-

---

16. "Our Common Confession of Faith," *Towards a Common Understanding of the Church: Reformed/Roman Catholic International Dialogue, Second Phase* (Geneva: World Alliance of Reformed Churches, 1991), p. 29. Note too the commentary on it and other Roman Catholic–Reformed conversations in Martien E. Brinkman and Henk Witte, eds., *From Roots to Fruits: Protestants and Catholics Toward a Common Understanding of the Church* (Geneva: World Alliance of Reformed Churches, 1998).

17. Lehmann and Pannenberg, eds., *The Condemnations of the Reformation Era: Do They Still Divide?* p. x, allude to that participation. The Arnoldshain Conference in Germany that includes Reformed Churches made a response to the Joint Declaration.

18. A regional New England consultation modeled on this one, cooperatively planned by Roman Catholic, Lutheran, Reformed, and Episcopal ecumenists, took place on April 10, 2000, in Acton, Massachusetts.

19. "*Bemerkungen zur 'Gemeinsamen Erklärung zur Rechtfertigungslehre' (GER) und zur 'Gemeinsamen offiziellen Feststellung' (GOF).*"

20. See the discussion and rejection of this in G. C. Berkouwer, "Justification by Faith," in McKim, ed., *Major Themes in the Reformed Tradition*, pp. 140-41.

lenged the caricature of Calvin as only a theologian of sanctification.[21] I will try to show later what Moltmann has missed in the Joint Declaration. Nevertheless, as can be easily seen, embedded in these judgments *are* the defining characteristics of "sovereignty" and "sanctification," but used to exclude the centrality of justification rather than as a Reformed perspective interpreting it.

Now to the classical view of justification found in Reformed confessions and traditions and in passages from John Calvin in his *Institutes of the Christian Religion*.

Justification Encompassed: The Reformed View

In a key section of the *Institutes* Calvin develops his understanding of justification in conjunction with John 3:16: "For God so loved the world that he gave his only Son, that everyone who believes in him may not perish but have eternal life." His use and exposition of this verse is significant because it presses justification back to its origins in the being and actions of the triune God as they address the fundamental challenge of the world's fall. As such, it reflects the characteristic Reformed accent on the divine sovereignty. Justification is conceived in macrocosmic as well as microcosmic terms. I shall call this justification *writ large*, the "objective" trinitarian and christological foundations of justification *writ small*, its "subjective" reception by faith.[22]

Driving justification back to its source in the sovereign will and way of God explains why "election" has been a constant in the Reformed tradition. Indeed, the discussion of justification in the *Institutes*, the traditional Reformed confessions, and classic Reformed theologians, is set in the context of predestination, an expression of the Reformed focus on the divine sovereignty. Given both the contributions and the pitfalls of this latter preoccupation, we shall return to it as an occasion for some "mutual admonitions" between the Reformed and other Christian traditions. But my point

21. So Barth's observation and refutation in *Church Dogmatics*, IV/2, trans. G. W. Bromiley (Edinburgh: T. & T. Clark, 1958), pp. 509-10. Interestingly, he earlier assigned the contributions of Calvin to the royal office of sanctification and Luther to the priestly office of justification. *Church Dogmatics*, IV/1, pp. 145-46.

22. As in John Murray, *Redemption Accomplished and Applied* (Grand Rapids: Eerdmans, 1955, 1978).

here is that the Reformed perspective on justification, shaped by its accent on the divine sovereignty, puts to the fore the will and way of the triune God as manifest in Christ. This theocentric, rather than anthropocentric, reading is nicely illustrated by Calvin's frequent counsel on matters of election regarding the assurance of salvation, urging attention not to the state of our faith, weak and ambiguous as it always is, but to the trustworthiness of the divine deed and promise.[23] For him Jesus Christ is the "mirror" in which we look for that assurance, an assertion not unlike that of Luther's allusion to Christ as the "Book of Life" that makes for the same confidence, a theme echoed, in fact, in the Joint Declaration itself.[24]

This "encompassing view" of justification might be called a *narrative* interpretation of the doctrine, as Markus Barth does in his biblical study, *Justification*.[25] Comparing it to "the liturgies of the Eastern Church and the passion plays of the Western Church," he traces it from the electing decision of God, through the Person and Work of Christ that engage the rebel world, to personal faith busy in love, and finally to the eschatological homecoming, "five days in the process of justification. . . ."[26]

In a chapter "The Beginning of Justification," Calvin takes the doctrine on its "writ large" to "writ small" journey, the grand narrative of John 3:16, albeit stated in the causal categories of his time.

> The efficient cause of our eternal salvation the Scripture uniformly proclaims to be the mercy and free love of the heavenly Father toward us; the material cause to be Christ, with the obedience by which he purchased righteousness for us; and what can be the formal or instrumental cause but faith? John includes the three in one sentence when he says, "God so loved the world, that he gave his only begotten Son, that whosoever believeth in him should not perish but have everlasting life" (John iii.16).[27]

23. John Hesselink traces such out in Calvin's catechism, and throughout the *Institutes*. See I. John Hesselink, *Calvin's First Catechism: A Commentary* (Louisville: Westminster John Knox, 1997), pp. 96-98.

24. Calvin, *Institutes of the Christian Religion*, Book II, Chapter XXIV, par. 5. See the reference to the Book of Life in *The Formula of Concord*, Art. 11, Sect. 2. And in the *JDDJ* all the paragraphs on assurance, in 4.6, pp. 34-36.

25. Markus Barth, *Justification: Pauline Texts Interpreted in the Light of Old and New Testaments* (Grand Rapids: Eerdmans, 1971).

26. Markus Barth, *Justification*, p. 21.

27. John Calvin, *Institutes of the Christian Religion*, Book III, Chapter XIV, par. 17 (vol. 2,

He adds that Paul gathers up the three in his own formulas in both Romans and Ephesians.[28] And Calvin describes justification elsewhere in explicitly trinitarian terms:

> The efficient cause of our salvation is placed in the love of the Father; the material cause in the obedience of the Son; the instrumental cause in the illumination of the Spirit, that is in faith. . . .[29]

Calvin's wide-ranging view was carried forward in traditional Reformed teaching where the objective and subjective are brought together, as in the 1559 French Confession of Faith which declares that "on the cross we are reconciled to God and justified before him" and then "made partakers of this justification by faith alone,"[30] but done so increasingly in a decretal context, as in the distinction between "the decree of justification" and "justification . . . made in this life," yet always entailing the narrative of the electing Father, the accomplishing Son, and the *applicatio salutis* by the work of the Holy Spirit.[31]

For all the Reformed scholasticism that pressed justification in a supralapsarian direction with its elect "us" and reprobate "them," another Reformed theologian was to come along who gave the same priority to election, and even double predestination, but took these things in quite a different direction. Thus Karl Barth speaks of

> a divine decision and action into which the whole of the human race is gathered up in the judgment rendered on the cross, the verdict in Jesus Christ by which man is justified. This justifying sentence of God is His decision in which man's being as the subject of that act [of human pride] is repudiated, his responsibility for that act, his guilt is pardoned, canceled and removed. . . . Justification definitely means the sentence executed and revealed in Jesus Christ and His death and

---

p. 85). He includes a fourth, citing Paul, a "final cause" being the demonstration of the divine righteousness.

28. Calvin, *Institutes*, vol. 2, pp. 86-87.

29. Calvin, *Institutes*, vol. 2, p. 88. See also Book II, Chapter XVII, where John 3:16 is exegeted and causal language deployed.

30. "The French Confession of Faith, 1559," in *Reformed Confessions of the Sixteenth Century*, ed. Arthur C. Cochrane (Philadelphia: Westminster Press, 1966), pp. 150, 151.

31. See Heppe, *Reformed Dogmatics*, p. 557 and passim.

resurrection, the No and Yes with which God vindicates Himself in relation to covenant-breaking man. . . .[32]

True to the Reformed stress on the divine sovereignty, this verdict is rendered

certainly on behalf of man, but primarily for His [God's] own sake, to assert His honor and to maintain His glory against him.[33]

The worthy stress on the *objective* dimension of justification found in both the traditional Calvinist and contemporary Barthian views does have its downside. It can become so dominant that it threatens the importance of the *subjective,* issuing in the former in a hyper-Calvinist double predestination in which the significance of the decision of faith erodes, or in the latter in which justifying faith becomes the knowledge given to some of the justification of all, rather than the graced medium through which the baptized believer is justified before God. We shall return to this later when considering the admonitions the Reformed need to hear from others. For now, let it be noted that the defining characteristic of Reformed teaching on justification is to place the microcosmic "for me" against the background of the macrocosmic "for the world." Justification in the Reformed tradition begins in the sovereign purposes of the Father, is accomplished in the saving Person and Work of the Son, and is brought through the church to persons by the Holy Spirit's gift of faith and its sanctifying consequences. The Leuenberg Agreement on justification sets forth this wide-ranging view:

The true understanding of the gospel was expressed by the fathers of the Reformation in the doctrine of justification. In this message, Je-

32. Barth, *Church Dogmatics,* IV/1, pp. 145, 96. See also how Eberhard Jüngel has incorporated this aspect into his reading of justification, a factor that may have contributed to his initial questioning and later endorsement of the Joint Declaration. Eberhard Jüngel, "On the Doctrine of Justification," *International Journal of Systematic Theology* 1, no. 1 (1999): 25: "The centre of Christian proclamation is that the history of Jesus Christ is not a private affair, but that, in that history, God's history with the whole of humanity takes place, and that in this one, unique history there occurs a liberating change of direction in the deadly fate of sin-dominated humanity. . . ." See also his "Kardinale Probleme," *Stimmen der Zeit* 11 (November 1999): 727-35.

33. Barth, *Church Dogmatics,* IV/1, p. 98.

sus Christ is acknowledged as the one in whom God became [human] and bound himself to [humanity]; as the crucified and risen one who took God's judgment upon himself and in so doing demonstrated God's love to sinners. . . . Through his word, God by His Holy Spirit calls all . . . to repent and believe, and assures the believing sinner of his righteousness in Jesus Christ. Whoever puts his trust in the gospel is justified in God's sight for the sake of Jesus Christ and is set free from the accusation of the law. In daily repentance and renewal he lives within the fellowship in praise of God and in the service of others. . . .[34]

In passing, it is worth noting that the Reformed impulse found here to treat doctrine "holistically" recurs in other loci. For example, Calvin's understanding of the Atonement, while centering on the cross, relates this priestly ministry of vicarious suffering and death to the prophetic ministry of life and teachings and royal ministry of victory announced and effected in the resurrection, as in his well-known formulation of the *munus triplex*.[35] R. S. Franks argues that this encompassing understanding of the Atonement is a major contribution of the Reformed tradition to the history of Christian thought.[36]

Affirmations

Justification in Its Fullness

We took note of how in the *Institutes* John 3:16 is the New Testament platform for a narrative view of justification. Interestingly, the *JDDJ* places that *same* text at the head of its paragraphs of biblical documentation. But more significantly, it treats the doctrine in the encompassing framework implied by this text, paralleling Calvin's own interpretation. The key initial state-

---

34. "The Message of Justification as the Message of the Free Grace of God," *Leuenberg Agreement*, II/6/1, in *Invitation to Action*, p. 67.

35. Calvin, *Institutes*, Book II, Chapter XV (vol. 1, pp. 425-32ff.).

36. Robert S. Franks, *The Work of Christ: A Historical Study of Christian Doctrine* (London: Thomas Nelson, 1962), pp. 333-51. Its ecumenical import can be seen in the use made of the threefold office in the Decree on the Apostolate of the Laity. *The Documents of Vatican II*, ed. Walter Abbott, S.J. (New York: Guild Press, 1966), pp. 491-95.

ment of "The Common Understanding of Justification," echoing in places the language of John 3:16, sets forth this long and deep view of the doctrine:

In faith we together hold the conviction that justification is the work of the triune God. The Father sent his Son into the world to save sinners. The foundation and presupposition of justification is the incarnation, death and resurrection of Christ. Justification thus means that Christ himself is our righteousness, in which we share through the Holy Spirit in accord with the will of the Father. Together we confess: by grace alone, in faith in Christ's saving work and not because of any merit on our part, we are accepted by God and receive the Holy Spirit, who renews our hearts while equipping and calling us to good works.[37]

This is a construal of the doctrine as justification writ *both* large and small, very similar to classical and current Reformed understandings. Its narrative begins with the trinitarian-christological "foundation and presupposition," the "work of the triune God" as the mercy-filled mission of the Father in sending the Son whose "incarnation, death and resurrection" overcame the world's rebellion and brought reconciliation, and moves to the work of the Holy Spirit making it available to us by grace in a faith that both "equips and calls . . . to good works."

Justification Writ Large: A "Meta-Principle" and Criterion?

Our discernment here of the difference between the "large" and "small" aspects of justification and their interrelations may shed light on what has been described in the U.S. dialogue variously as the "meta-linguistic," "meta-theological," or "meta-methodological" principle necessary to "judge all theological formulations . . . or all theologies."[38] It also has implications for the assertion of justification as "an indispensable criterion, which constantly serves to orient all the teaching and practice of our churches to Christ" (3/18). And, possibly, for the reference to the Catholic commitment to "several criteria."

---

37. *JDDJ*, sec. 3, par. 15.

38. So summarized by George Tavard in *Justification: An Ecumenical Study* (New York: Paulist Press, 1983), p. 62.

Through these Reformed spectacles, it appears that both the meta-principle and the indispensable criterion have to do with "justification writ large." The redemption of the world by the triune God, the justification of the godless, is by grace alone, not by any human work. The "trust" that this is so has to do with "redemption accomplished" in Christ by the triune God, a norm by which all other claims to ultimacy must be measured. Touching the question of *why* the world is saved from sin, evil, and death, and *who* does it, there is one answer only: out of the love of the Father and in the deed of the Son, a divine purpose and action that alone warrants our faith, and a disavowal of trust in any other way of salvation.

If this reading is correct, the parallel of the heart of this to the 1934 Barmen Declaration is striking, as in the latter's key sentence:

> Jesus Christ, as he is attested for us in Holy Scripture is the one Word of God which we have to hear and which we have to trust and obey in life and in death.

Indeed, the Joint Declaration without the language of "criterion" says something very close to Barmen:

> Lutherans and Catholics share the goal of confessing Christ, who is to be trusted above all things as the one Mediator (1 Timothy 2:5-6). . . .[39]

This christocentricity, rooted in the Trinity, is a criteriological commitment in the face of claims to another Word, another Mediator, and thus a determinative "focus" (George Tavard) of any joint understanding of justification, and in that sense a standard for all theological formulations and proposals. All this sounds, functionally, if not formally, very much like "the article by which the church stands or falls." The conclusions of both the U.S. and European dialogues give further confirmation to its normative role. Noting the "new insights" that make today's convergences possible, the German dialogue cites and interprets the U.S. dialogue:

> . . . the barricades can be torn down only if we remain unswervingly on the Christological foundation expressed — with particular reference to the doctrine of justification — in the Lutheran-Catholic dialogue that took place in the United States: "Christ and his gospel are

---

39. *JDDJ*, 3/18.

the source, center and norm of Christian life, individual and corporate, in church and world. Christians have no other basis for eternal life and hope of final salvation than God's free gift in Jesus Christ, extended to them in the Holy Spirit."[40]

Given the christological focus of these remarks, this assertion of Barth's is interesting:

The *articulus stantis et cadentis ecclesiae* is not the doctrine of justification as such, but its basis and culmination: the confession of Jesus Christ in whom are hid all the treasures of wisdom and knowledge (Col. 2:3); the knowledge of His being and activity for us and to us and with us. It could probably be shown that this was also the opinion of Luther. . . . Christ . . . the centre, the starting point and the finishing point. . . .[41]

There is an echo here of the First Helvetic Confession of 1536, which declares that

the most sublime and principal article and the one that should be expressly set forth in every sermon . . . should be that we are preserved and saved solely by the mercy of God and the merit of Christ.[42]

Indeed, it's interesting that "Luther expressed his warm approval" of this Reformed Confession.[43]

For Barth, Jesus Christ occupies that privileged place, as in the Barmen Declaration he helped to draft. Yet "Christ" as the "one Word of God" who calls us to trust and obey is inseparable from the triune God and thus bespeaks "justification writ large."

Do Barth's reservations about what constitutes the article by which the church stands or falls shed some light on the Roman Catholic reluctance to

---

40. "Justification," in Lehmann and Pannenberg, eds., *The Condemnations of the Reformation Era: Do They Still Divide?* p. 36. The quotation is from *Justification by Faith: Lutherans and Catholics in Dialogue*, VII, ed. H. G. Anderson, T. Austin Murphy, Joseph A. Burgess (Minneapolis: Augsburg, 1985), "Common Statement," p. 71.

41. Barth, *Church Dogmatics*, IV/1, pp. 527-29.

42. "The First Helvetic Confession of 1536," in Cochrane, ed., *Reformed Confessions of the Sixteenth Century*, p. 104.

43. "The First Helvetic Confession of 1536," p. 98, editor Arthur Cochrane's comment.

make justification by faith the *sole* criterion for orienting all teaching and practice? Pannenberg, a not-infrequent critic of Barth, appears to be open also to other criteria. He suggests that "the unity in substance of the Son with the Father, . . . in a way similar to the doctrine of justification, orients the whole teaching and *praxis* of the Church . . ." might be what the Roman Catholic caveat legitimately had in mind.[44] But the trinitarian-christological grounding of justification cited in the *JDDL* — and in Barth's own christocentricity — presumes just that unity. Thus justification writ large, so understood, appears to be indispensable and unique as a standard for orienting all teaching and practice, for all parties concerned.

Yet surely there is another reservation Roman Catholics have about asserting justification as the sole criterion. Walter Kasper, Carl Peter, and Avery Dulles in their comments all press a question yet to be fully addressed in ecumenical dialogue: the place of the church vis-à-vis justification.[45] Does this reservation indicate that there is another *question* to be faced along with the one addressed by justification? Not *why* and *by* whom the reconciling work is done, but *how* the faith that receives the decision and deed of the triune God is mediated to us?

Walter Kasper's suggestion is intriguing: the way through may be to learn from the Eastern Church's stress on pneumatology, its insight that "the church does not control salvation, but it can and must pray with authority for the Spirit of Jesus Christ who mediates salvation, and it can be certain this prayer is heard on the basis of the promise made by Jesus Christ."[46] Intriguing especially for Reformed ears, for as Paul Fries has argued, "the Reformed ethos is to be explained not through its Christology as such, but through its unique conjoining of the doctrines of Christ and the Spirit."[47] The Reformed stress on the place of the Holy Spirit is directly

---

44. Wolfhart Pannenberg, "New Consensuses, Defused Conflicts, Protestant Anxieties," slightly abridged translation, 1999, of article in *Idea* 2.2 (1998); reprinted in "epd. Dokumentation" 11/98.

45. See Walter Kasper, "Basic Consensus and Church Fellowship," in *In Search of Christian Unity: Basic Consensus/Basic Differences*, ed. Joseph Burgess (Minneapolis: Augsburg Fortress, 1991), esp. pp. 34-39; Carl Peter, "Justification by Faith and the Need of Another Critical Principle," in Anderson, Murphy, and Burgess, eds., *Justification by Faith*, pp. 304-15; Avery Dulles, "Two Languages of Salvation," *First Things* 98 (December 1999): 25-30.

46. Kasper, "Basic Consensus and Church Fellowship," p. 39.

47. Paul Fries, "Fundamental Consensus and Church Fellowship: A Reformed Perspective," in Burgess, ed., *In Search of Christian Unity*, pp. 157-58.

related to its defining characteristic of *sovereignty*. A gracious divine majesty requires the work of the Holy Spirit to bring its benefits to us. As Fries says about Reformed teaching,

> The Spirit is the divine intermediary between the ascended Christ and the Christian community, working not only in the hearts of the faithful, but also through the offices and orders of the church. The real presence of the flesh and blood of Christ in the Lord's Supper is the work of the Spirit, but so is the discipline exercised by the elder.[48]

Pneumatology gives the Reformed tradition its churchly character, as reflected in its stress on discipline, orders, and offices, on the one hand, and its sacramental teaching, on the other.[49] Reformed ecclesiology has tended to stress one or the other of these, in the first case putting to the fore a view of the church as the "visible saints," as in its Congregational expressions, or in the second an "evangelical catholic" view as in its Mercersburg theology.[50] In both cases, the Holy Spirit brings Christ to us through the visible church. If there is an article by which the church stands or falls, such must presuppose an article on the church itself that comes under the justification criterion. Of course, because Christ is Lord of the church, its givens are always accountable to him as the one Word the church always must trust and obey.

Whether it be Barth's assertion of that one Word as the higher article, or the Reformed stress on the church of the Holy Spirit, there is a readiness here to probe further the meaning of "other criteria." Surely, "the mercy of

48. Fries, "Fundamental Consensus and Church Fellowship," p. 158.

49. Also on the high profile it gives to Israel as visible people of the covenant. There is an extensive current Reformed literature on anti-supersessionism, the latter discussed in Chapter 4.

50. On the former, see Alan P. F. Sell, *Saints Visible, Orderly and Catholic: The Congregational Idea of the Church* (Allison Park, Pa.: Pickwick Press, 1986), and on the latter the literature on the Mercersburg movement, the school of thought associated with the nineteenth-century Reformed seminary in Mercersburg, Pennsylvania, its theologians, John Williamson Nevin and Philip Schaff, and the journal *The Mercersburg Review*. This "evangelical catholic" wing of the Reformed tradition is still alive and well through its *New Mercersburg Review* and Mercersburg Society. For some of the original writings, see Charles Yrigoyen Jr. and George H. Bricker, *Catholic and Reformed: Selected Theological Writings of John Williamson Nevin* (Pittsburgh: Pickwick Press, 1978), and Yrigoyen and Bricker, *Reformed and Catholic: Selected Historical and Theological Writings of Philip Schaff* (Pittsburgh: Pickwick Press, 1979).

God and the merit of Christ" — justification writ large — qualifies as a "most sublime article" (First Helvetic Confession). And its trinitarian premise cannot be without an article on the holy catholic church that stands or falls by the justifying Word, no head without the body, no Son of the Father without the Holy Spirit.

Justification Writ Small

How do we get from justification writ large to the same writ small, to the *pro me* aspect of justification? The *JDDJ* answers in various ways, but with a common refrain:

By grace alone, in faith in Christ's saving work . . . we are accepted by God and receive the Holy Spirit who renews our hearts while equipping and calling us to good works (sec. 3, par. 15); through Christ alone when we receive this salvation in faith . . . God's gift through the Holy Spirit who works through Word and Sacrament . . . and who leads believers into the renewal of life . . . (3/16); When persons come by faith to share in Christ, God no longer imputes to them their sin and through the Holy Spirit effects in them an active love (4.2/22); We confess together that sinners are justified by faith in the saving act of God in Christ. . . . They place their trust in God's gracious promise by justifying faith, which includes hope in God and love for him (4.3/25).

In carefully worded sentences it moves narratively from "God's gracious promise" and "Christ's saving work" to the Holy Spirit's gift of faith and the renewal of life. What is said here *together* is: (1) "justifying faith" is "trust" in the "promise"; (2) this faith that justifies cannot be what it is without "hope and love," or, otherwise stated, without genuine "renewal" and thus "the equipping and calling to good works"; (3) throughout, all is by grace alone, excluding any human merit. Whatever other questions are involved — the naming of sin ruled by grace, the language and location of merit, the assurance of salvation — a consensus is asserted on these three points of subjective soteriology.

To these affirmations, there can only be a joyful Reformed "Amen." Here is an "inclusive" understanding of justification received. Justifying faith is the receptor of Christ's saving work, but such is what it is only if that faith is busy in love. Justification is distinct from, but also inseparable from, sanctification (4.2/22), language identical to Calvin's and that of the

Westminster Larger Catechism.[51] Conjoined are the "declaration of for-giveness" and "the renewal of life," or in Reformed lingo "regeneration." And like the Reformed accent on the divine sovereignty, grace is all the way down from justification's "beginning" to its ending, as "all persons depend completely on the saving grace of God for their salvation" (4.1/19).

Yes, an agreement on three basics, but . . . and it is a big "but." The European dialogue, after making all the contextual, historical, and biblical qualifications that soften the sixteenth-century polarization, declares that there is "evidently a clear difference."[52] It has to do with how the saving work of Christ is applied — by imputation or impartation, by forensic declaration or by "a 'quality' intrinsically 'adhering' to the soul."[53] And from this difference follow all the related divergences on concupiscence and the *simul,* merit, the place of works, law and gospel.

What is at the root of this difference? Here are some Reformed speculations. Is it because for Luther, justification was a question of how the self, coming before God only with its incurved soul, must depend for salvation on Christ alone and grace alone as received by faith alone? But for the Catholic Church spread throughout the world with its corporate sense of responsibility for that realm, was it, and is it, a question of how the baptized live out their faith so it might shape that world? Hence its insistence that Christ alone and grace alone empower faith to respond to that mandate? Given their concerns and even their locations, one kind of question faces "up," the other "out"? One accents pardon and the other power? One imputation, the other impartation? One *coram Deo,* the other *coram mundo?* One gravitates to Paul and the other to James? And in a body with all its parts, how can there not be a charism to steward each kind of question and each answer? When fear descends that one's own body part could be amputated, a "salutary warning" is given. And with it also imperial claims may be made that assault other body parts.

The condemnations of the sixteenth century based on this difference, and

---

51. "Although sanctification be inseparably joined with justification, yet they differ, in that God in justification imputeth the righteousness of Christ; in sanctification, his Spirit infuseth grace, and enableth to the exercise thereof; in the former sin is pardoned; in the other, it is subdued . . . ," *Westminster Larger Catechism,* Q. 77.

52. Lehmann and Pannenberg, *The Condemnations of the Reformation Era: Do They Still Divide?* p. 47.

53. Lehmann and Pannenberg, *The Condemnations of the Reformation Era: Do They Still Divide?* p. 47

in the hour's polemics inclined to assert one's charism as definitive, are, by the October signing, now deemed inapplicable to the present partners. Why so? Is it because of fresh insights from biblical and historical studies, and theological clarification of ambiguities and misrepresentations? Surely these are important. But my Reformed spectacles discern another possible factor. The differences are livable and even mutually teachable now, because the focus has shifted to the trinitarian-christological dimension of justification. This sounds like the conclusion in the U.S. dialogue, italicized there for emphasis:

> *Our hope of justification and salvation rests in Christ Jesus and on the gospel whereby the good news of God's merciful action in Christ is made known; we do not place our ultimate trust in anything other than God's promise and saving work in Christ.*[54]

The statement goes on to acknowledge remaining differences on justification by faith but questions whether they need be church-dividing given the mandate to "proclaim together the one, undivided gospel of God's saving mercy in Jesus Christ."[55]

It appears here and in the *JDDJ* that "faith" or "trust" is used in two different ways. When reference is made to "justification and salvation" writ large, we have to do with a *corporate* faith *that* "God's promise and saving work in Christ" are true. Justification writ small entails a saving *personal* faith *in* Christ. The former is juxtaposed to the belief that the world is saved by its own works. The latter stands against the belief that the self can be justified before God by its own works. In the latter are entailed Roman Catholic–Reformation differences on the relation of forensic and infused righteousness. But their tolerability, and perhaps even their mutual teachability, are made possible by a stated ultimate trust in "the one, undivided gospel of God's saving mercy in Jesus Christ."

In a time in which Jesus Christ, the Mediator, this "one Word we have to trust and obey," must be boldly declared, divided Christians find each other so they might speak it with one voice and live it out together.[56] I believe the

---

54. "Common Statement, Introduction," in Anderson, Murphy, and Burgess, eds., *Justification by Faith*, p. 16.

55. "Common Statement, Introduction," p. 16.

56. A conclusion to which Avery Dulles seems to come, after raising questions about how much reconciliation of views was in fact achieved by the *JDDJ*, "Two Languages of Salvation: The Lutheran-Catholic Joint Declaration," pp. 29-30.

"joint declaration" of that trinitarian-christological root of justification made it possible to view the differences on justification writ small in a new light. It created an atmosphere in which each partner can be open to the charism of the other. Such agreement also enables us to see that in the polemics of the past, each was right in what it affirmed and wrong in what its extreme formulations denied. Yet the mutual condemnations continue to carry with them "concerns" and "salutary warnings" about reductionist temptations. Hence the "no trespassing signs," the readiness to receive and willingness to give admonitions. What then of a Reformed giving *and* receiving of them?

Admonitions

To Roman Catholic and Lutheran Together

The Theocentric and Anthropocentric

If the achievement of the *JDDJ* is related to its grounding of the doctrine in justification writ large, then this "theocentric" reading should not be obscured by an anthropocentric reductionism. That is, a sole focus on the *pro me* of justification — whether justification is received by faith alone, or by faith, hope, and love, whether by imputation or impartation — will miss the big picture of justification. Whatever criticisms we might have of Karl Barth's theology, his reinterpretation of justification did bring again to the fore its trinitarian-christological grounding, and may well even have played some background role in the new consensus.[57] Let us keep our ecumenical eyes on the ultimate source and center of justification in the sovereign freedom and mercy of God manifest in the Person and Work of Jesus Christ. In the light of its own periodic drifts into anthropocentricity, this is a Reformed self-admonition as well as one to its partners.

57. The possibility of this is suggested by Barth's commendation of Hans Küng's study *Justification: The Doctrine of Karl Barth and a Catholic Reflection,* trans. Thomas Collins, Edmund E. Tolk, and David Granskou, with a letter by Karl Barth (New York: Thomas Nelson, 1964), pp. xix-xxii. However, there is a misreading of Barth by Küng traced in detail by Alister McGrath in "Justification: Barth, Trent and Küng," *The Scottish Journal of Theology* 34 (1981): 517-29. Nevertheless, Küng's discernment of the "objective" dimension in Barth as "the primary and decisive aspect of the theology of justification" (72) is correct and the point at hand. See also Eberhard Busch's essay written against the background of the current discussion of the *JDDJ,* "Karl Barth's Doctrine of Justification," typescript, 1999.

Baptism

A refrain in the *JDDJ* is the linkage of justification and baptism.[58] The biblical witness and ecumenical consensus expressed in the Lima document of the World Council of Churches, "BEM,"[59] is reinforced and interpreted in accord with a common Catholic and Lutheran stress on the "solidarity" of Christ with givens, in this case in the firm linkage of baptism and justification. A Reformed admonition based on its "sovereignty" accent points to the dangers of allowing this "haveability" to slide into a domestication of grace that precludes both the freedom of God and the response of faith. Yes, the promise of the divine Presence in the sacramental means of grace is trustworthy, but its efficacy is inextricable from the response of faith. Thus as BEM states it, "The necessity of faith for the reception of the salvation embodied and set forth in baptism is acknowledged by all churches."[60] Surely this is a further area of inquiry, one where mutual admonition is in order, for a sovereignty that separates baptism from justifying grace by an abstract doctrine of predestination or universalism on the one hand, or by an anti-sacramental memorialism on the other, is as reductionist as a haveability emphasis that takes grace captive in our means or excludes the place of personal faith by a too-narrow *ex opere operato* interpretation.

The Public Import of Justification

The Reformed accents on both sovereignty and sanctification press the question of the implications of any agreement on justification for public issues. Why not more about this in the Joint Declaration? Surely this undeveloped theme must be taken up in subsequent exploration of the agreement. Here Moltmann is right in his judgment that "we need a common doctrine of righteousness-justice-justification for the 21st century."[61]

The warrants for this are found in the view of justification writ both large and small in the document itself. As seen through Reformed eyes, the redemption of the world through the will of the Father and obedience of

58. *JDDJ*, 4.4, 28-30.

59. As in "The Meaning of Baptism," *Baptism, Eucharist and Ministry* (Geneva: World Council of Churches, 1982), pp. 2-4.

60. *Baptism, Eucharist and Ministry*, p. 3.

61. Jürgen Moltmann, "*Bemerkungen zur 'Gemeinsamen Erklärung zur Rechtfertigungslehre' (GER) und zur 'Gemeinsamen offiziellen Feststellung' (GOF)*," p. 2.

the Son — the trinitarian-christological justification writ large — is inseparable from *sanctification* writ large. As well as being declared forgiven by
the act of God in Christ, the world has been given both the gift and the call
to holiness.[62] Divine sovereignty over the public sector has been worked
out in the Reformed tradition in terms of the royal office of Christ within
the *munus triplex*. The victory of Christ over the powers and principalities
extends his rules over the counting house and voting booth as well as the
soul and the church, calling the public world to accountability and render-
ing possible its transformation.[63]

The grounds for public witness lie in sanctification writ small as well as
large. As the objective sanctification of the world provides the range of concern and hope, the impulse and mandate in the Christian life come from
the inseparability of justification and sanctification *pro me*. The personal
justification of the sinner is inseparable from a personal sanctification that
issues in public witness to the rule of Christ over the political, social, and
economic principalities and powers, one implemented by the church as well
as persons in the struggles for social change. Thus a Reformed reading of
justification will press for its "world-formative" outworking.

To the Lutheran Tradition

Lutheran-Reformed differences emerged early in Reformation history, especially so in christological and eucharistic controversies, rooted in the respective *capax* and *non capax* accents, Lutheran "solidarity" and Reformed
"sovereignty."[64] In the specifics of justification, the Reformed stress on the
divine sovereignty moves naturally, via its focus on election, to "justification writ large," and in so doing challenges any Lutheran preoccupation
with the *pro me*, as noted by Barth.[65] From Luther's anxiety and quest for

---

62. Developed by Barth in IV/2 as the exaltation of the Son, and the transformation of
the world *de iure*.

63. A theme explored by W. A. Visser 't Hooft in *The Kingship of Christ* (New York:
Harper & Brothers, 1948) and expressed with power during World War II by Karl Barth in
his *Letter to Great Britain from Switzerland* (London: Sheldon Press, 1941), pp. 9-11ff.

64. See Fackre and Root, *Affirmations and Admonitions*, pp. 1-43, and Gabriel Fackre,
"What the Lutherans and Reformed Can Learn from One Another," *The Christian Century*
114, no. 18 (June 4-11, 1997): 558-61.

65. Barth, *Church Dogmatics*, IV/1, p. 150.

assurance, through Lutheran pietism to modern existentialisms from Kierkegaard to Bultmann, the subjective dimension of justification has bulked large, threatening to obscure its objective trinitarian-christological foundations, ones critical to the agreement reached in the *JDDJ*.

Sanctification, the other Reformed accent, is acknowledged as well in the Lutheran tradition. However, fears of works-righteousness and ambivalence toward, or rejection of, the third use of the law, have so surrounded it with qualifications that the stress on believers' persistence in sin (the Lutheran *simul*) can obscure the possibilities of growth in grace and can counsel retreat into an apolitical "interiorization of piety." Here the Reformed tradition joins the Roman Catholic in a history of insistence on the inextricability of sanctification and justification, as well as a stress on the political mandates and possibilities of sanctification.[66] Yet, for all the kinship between Reformed stress on the regenerate life and the Catholic accent on the renewed life, serious differences continue. Hence, some Reformed admonitions to the other partner.

To the Catholic Tradition

Reformed join Lutherans in the emphasis on the radical character of the fall. Nothing in us warrants or contributes to the sinner's salvation. Hence the shared Reformation commitment to the *sola fide*. And with it the common suspicion that a Roman Catholic theology of infused righteousness invites human capacities into an equation that has room only for the divine pardon received by faith. The stress on the empowering grace of sanctification which the Reformed tradition shares with the Roman Catholic, is located, therefore, as sequential to justification, not coterminous with it as in the latter.

The same determination to give the sovereign God, rather than ourselves, all that is due, is at work in Reformed wariness about inordinate claims for human institutions as well as persons. The church is such an in-

---

66. Indeed, Calvin uses the language of "reward" alluded to in the *JDDJ*'s "Catholic understanding" of good works, declaring that "the faithful are rewarded with the promises which God gave in his law to the cultivators of righteousness and holiness," surrounding it, however, with the "threefold" qualification that works have nothing to do with justification which comes by faith alone, they are God's own gift being so honored, and their manifest pollutions are pardoned (*Institutes*, Book III, Chapter 17, 3 [vol. 2, p. 106]).

stitution. While different from all others, being the body of Christ, divine as well as human and steward of the means of saving grace, it is not the unqualified extension of the Incarnation. Further, no organ constitutes the whole body, each being a part awaiting final wholeness and healing. Hence Reformed cautions about delimiting the promises of God to any part of the household of faith. Given its finitude and flaws, the church on earth is always *ecclesia reformata et semper reformanda.*

A Reformation–Roman Catholic dialogue on this latter point could be facilitated by attention to Reinhold Niebuhr's political theology, appreciated as it is by Roman Catholic theologians. Shaped as he was by a combined Reformed-Lutheran lineage, Niebuhr carries this Reformation realism into the realm of social history, documenting the corruptibility of every advance, critiquing the utopian claims of movements of social change and arguing for self-criticism within institutions of power, including the church.[67] He makes his case for this realism on the basis not only of "special revelation" but from introspection and historical inquiry. Here the Reformed doctrine of common grace and Roman Catholic natural theology and natural law, though different in their assessment of the depth of the fall, are in hailing distance regarding the possibilities of universal moral reasoning.[68]

And, a final admonition, one earlier noted. The Reformed stress on the divine sovereignty reminds Catholics as well as Lutherans of the limitations of a too-exclusively anthropological reading of justification, with the *pro me* preoccupation neglecting its *soli Deo gloria* source and center.

To the Reformed — from Lutherans and Roman Catholics

What happens when Reformed "sovereignty" takes charge of the doctrine of justification, rather than being a perspective on it? The answer is in the history of Reformed thought on predestination. From Calvin forward, the sound impulse to ground justification in the eternal purposes of God has been accompanied by a speculative leap into the workings of the divine mind

---

67. See *The Nature and Destiny of Man*, vols. 1 and 2 (New York: Charles Scribner's Sons, 1968), passim, and Gabriel Fackre, *The Promise of Reinhold Niebuhr* (Lanham, Md.: University Press of America, 1994).

68. The role of common grace and the "covenant with Noah" — "general revelation" — vis-à-vis special revelation is discussed in Fackre, *The Doctrine of Revelation* (Grand Rapids: Eerdmans, 1977), pp. 37-178.

as to who is elect and who is reprobate. Thus sovereignty cum justification eventuates in theories of double predestination, controversies as to whether such is supralapsarian, infralapsarian, or sublapsarian and the like.[69] All this with a painful history of internal disputes in which one reductionism matches another, from the Dutch Arminians forward. In the same Reformed stream appears the twentieth-century Karl Barth with his new reading of the sovereign purposes of God, Christ being both elect and reprobate, with all of humanity in the Son's humiliation and exaltation. But then comes the lingering suspicion here of a structural universalism, however disavowed.[70] In all cases a single-minded stress on the divine sovereignty seems to be at work.

The admonitory corrective from other traditions comes in various ways. Lutherans have treated election as the existential testimony of the believer to the surety of election rather than a speculative theory on the source of belief and unbelief.[71] And Catholics have been concerned to assert the call for personal responsibility. These are legitimate admonitions. They counsel us to read "predestination" as the confidence that God shall be "all and in all" without the speculative details. And to be wary of "the tendency to 'explain' the doctrine by pressing the logical implications of the divine sovereignty,"[72] erasing thereby personal responsibility. Wiser, argues Reformed theologian Paul Jewett, to assert *both* a pure electing grace *and* human responsibility, and understand that as a "paradox" this may be explored but can never be explained.[73]

And admonitions are in order as well concerning aspects of Reformed thinking on sanctification. Certainly, the Lutheran stress on the *simul* must be clearly heard, reminding the Reformed tradition of its own professed realism about continuing sin, one too often overwhelmed by its stress on growth in the sanctified life. Again, Reinhold Niebuhr made the point tell-

---

69. For a comparison of the three, see Paul K. Jewett, *Election and Predestination* (Grand Rapids: Eerdmans, 1985), pp. 83-105.

70. On the disavowal, see Karl Barth, *Church Dogmatics*, IV/3, first part, pp. 477-78.

71. See this observation in the North American Lutheran-Reformed dialogue, *A Common Calling*, pp. 54-55.

72. Jewett, *Election and Predestination*, p. 78.

73. Jewett, *Election and Predestination* (New York: G. & C. & H. Carvill, 1830), pp. 92, 106-9, 113-14, 136-39. See also Donald Baillie on "the paradox of grace," in *God Was in Christ: An Essay on Incarnation and Atonement* (New York: Charles Scribner's Sons, 1948), pp. 114-18. So too Jonathan Edwards on "efficacious grace" in "Miscellaneous Remarks," *Works*, vol. 7, pp. iv, 48.

ingly vis-à-vis the Reformed tradition's exuberant historical expectations and theocratic pretensions when it too quickly transferred the confidences in personal growth to the public arena. Sin persists at every stage of historical advance, and we should be soberly aware of the hubris that plagues the most "righteous" social, economic, and political causes.

While the Roman Catholic tradition also finds a large place for sanctification and growth, personal and public, its ecclesial lens discerns another dimension of holiness not limited to personal or social performance. Thus the "holy" church of the creeds has to do with a conferred status, not an achieved one, a warning to Reformed tendencies, with their legitimate emphasis on discipline, not to reduce the church to the morally and spiritually "pure." The Reformed tradition needs an enlargement of its concept of the church when it limits it to the "visible saints," for holiness finally roots, as it should know from its own accent on sovereignty, not in our performances but in God's purposes.[74] Indeed, it has not been without this emphasis on the objectivity of Christ's ecclesial grace, as in the "Mercersburg theology," a sacramental and liturgical movement in nineteenth- and twentieth-century Reformed churches.[75]

Jürgen Moltmann's "remarks" on the *JDDJ* bring together both the strengths and weaknesses of the Reformed focus on sovereignty and sanctification. While rightly urging the development of a new dimension of the doctrine for a new age (thus the characteristic Reformed stress on a contextualizing *semper reformanda* under the divine sovereignty), and pressing the justice import of justification (thus the characteristic Reformed stress on society's sanctification), he wrongly diminishes the personal problematic of sin as a creature of the medieval issue of penance, one to be relativized in order to move on to the twenty-first-century problematic of justice.[76] The sin in the heart of every human being is a perennial problem

---

74. Ironically, here is the Reformed tradition's own teaching of the divine sovereignty, muted in this case by its zealous partner, sanctification.

75. See the earlier references to Nevin and Schaff.

76. The industrial missioner Horst Symanowski formulated this point in the heyday of the secular theologies of the 1960s in oft-repeated words: In the sixteenth century, Luther lay awake at night asking "How can I find a gracious God?" Today we lie awake asking "How can we find a gracious neighbor?" Thus yesterday the problem was the alienation between the soul and God; today it is the estrangement between black and white, rich and poor, East and West, men and women, young and old. One of the lessons we should have learned since is the inseparability of the personal and the public.

entailing the perennial Word of justification to the sinner. Further, it is reality that will come back to haunt our efforts at social change, for sin persists in the champions of justice as well as its foes. If unacknowledged and unchecked, it leads to the arrogance and tyranny of the self-righteous cause and social system, as well as of the self-righteous soul.[77]

A final sobering recognition with its attendant admonition. It was Lutherans in dialogue with Roman Catholics who launched and sustained this conversation in a variety of national and international settings and finalized it in an official action, *not* the Reformed churches, or those of the left wing of the Reformation, or the Anglican communion, or any other Protestant heir. Why were the Reformed churches not more involved in this initiative? Did it take churches that cared deeply about classical doctrine? Surely the Roman communion does so care. And among Reformation colleagues, Lutherans over time have been the premier stewards of historic doctrine, associated, it can be argued, with its *capax*, the "haveability" of Christ in the givens, in this case its confessional lore (not to be altered — no 1540 *variata* version of the 1530 Augsburg Confession!). The Reformed *incapax* demands an ever-reforming church with its ever-updated creeds and confessions, but also has tempted us to allow the erosion of the historic doctrinal landmarks and celebrate diversity to the exclusion of unity. Thus our need for admonition from Lutherans and Catholics to attend to the solidarities in conjunction with the sovereignties.

Conclusion

"We intend to stay together." So declared the first assembly of the World Council of Churches in the bright early days of twentieth-century ecumenism.[78] Is the future of that "together" now in a new phase inseparable from those who have forged their own joint declaration? If so, may the Yale consultation's invitation to other communions to bring their charisms be a portent of things to come. And could an intention to "stay together" include the use of the Joint Declaration as a study document for parishes in

77. An uncritical naïveté about the corruptibility of the righteous cause to which my own Reformed tradition is regularly tempted, as acknowledged in Fackre, "What the Lutherans and Reformed Can Learn from One Another," pp. 558-61.

78. As a student I was present at the 1948 Amsterdam Assembly, hearing this earlier "joint declaration" read on its final day.

local communities, much like the post–Vatican II Living Room Dialogues? And out of that common study could there grow a common witness to the God whose love sent an only Son to reconcile the world? And could the new amity signaled by this agreement have an impact on old conflicts in nations as well as churches?

Whatever giant hurdles remain before a final life together of Christ's Church on earth, the Joint Declaration can be a landmark in mission as well as a step toward unity. May there be a "Yes" to all the previous questions. And with it a commitment to common study, proclamation, and action, testifying that Jesus Christ is the one Word of the Father whose Holy Spirit empowers us to trust and obey in life and in death.

PART V

CHRISTOLOGY IN PILGRIMAGE

CHAPTER 10

The Galilean Christ

I n the popular religious press, and in the mass media as well, "Christology" in the late twentieth century and early twenty-first often takes
form as the reportings of the "Jesus Seminar." With their color-coded
judgments on the authenticity of this or that Jesus text, as determined by
their tools of critical scholarship, a New Testament picture of Jesus
emerges. Better, a varied picture of Jesus takes shape. Whether it be that of
a wandering cynic philosopher, mystic, social reformer, vagabond sage,
etc., the picture points to a Galilean figure. What transpired in the walk
and talk on those paths, hills, and in its towns constitutes the Person and
Work of Christ. No Calvary cross or Easter crown here, given the overlay of
church dogma that participants believe obscures the historical Jesus.

In Volume 2 of this series, the critical sense of Scripture is given a place
in the work of theology. Its role, however, is ministerial not magisterial, of
the *bene esse* of biblical understanding — its well-being, not its being, as
such. When made arbiter of Christology, it distorts that servant role, dis-
placing the full, or "theological," sense of Scripture. For all that, the work
of the critical scholar as a resource in discerning the meaning of Christ can
be a gift to the church, especially as it pertains to the prophetic office of
Christ exercised in Galilean ministry. Therefore we locate it here.[1]

1. For a discussion of the varied senses of Scripture, see Gabriel Fackre, *The Christian*

In examining the role of critical scholarship in the field of systematics, both its strengths and its weaknesses, a look at how a systematic theologian actually deploys these tools will be instructive. No one has worked harder at that task in the late twentieth century than Edward Schillebeeckx. In two massive volumes, *Jesus* and *Christ,* and a running dialogue with critics and supporters that grew out of his project, Schillebeeckx has laid out his program in exhausting detail. The picture of Jesus that emerges is, as with the later Jesus Seminar, that of the Galilean, though with the marks of a figure that mirrors the "today" of his time rather than that of the later critics.[2] Also, Schillebeeckx's Roman Catholic ecclesial location impacts his presentation, as does that of various members in the Jesus Seminar, albeit explicitly in his case, but unacknowledged in others.[3] Thus this section on

---

Story: A Narrative Interpretation of Christian Doctrine, vol. 2: *Scripture in the Church for the World* (Grand Rapids: Eerdmans, 1978), and passim.

2. James Dunn has nicely summarized the "neo-liberal" quest for Jesus represented by the Jesus Seminar and its kin:

> The pictures which emerge are riveting: a Jesus who was "a Galilean deviant," "a free spirit," "the proverbial party animal," "a vagabond sage," "a simple sage," "a subversive sage," "the subverter of the everyday world around him" (Funk); Jesus as a liberation theologian; a Jesus almost completely shorn of kingdom of God language and Jewish concerns, emerging instead as a teacher of aphoristic wisdom heavily influenced by the Cynic philosophy of Hellenized Galilee; "a social gadfly, an irritant on the skin of conventional mores and values," a Cynic Jesus. Much more carefully delineating on his broad canvas and giving welcome renewed attention to the stories of Jesus' healings, Crossan nevertheless ends up with Jesus as "a peasant Jewish Cynic" calling for radical egalitarianism and proclaiming "the brokerless kingdom of God." Borg has developed a more richly rounded picture of Jesus . . . as "a teacher of a culturally subversive wisdom . . . who taught a subversive and alternative wisdom." This is not the nineteenth-century Liberal redivivus. But it is a Jesus stripped of the elements of (later) faith which modernity has found so problematic. Nor is it the kindly nineteenth-century Sunday School teacher who has thus been recovered. But it is a Jesus who could well be imagined in many a twentieth-century faculty staff room as an independent "loose cannon" academic, with his unsettling anecdotes, disturbing aphorisms, and provocative rhetoric. Consequently, the same question arises once again which proved so fatal to the nineteenth-century Liberal Jesus: whether this neo-Liberal Jesus is any less a construct and retrojection of late-twentieth-century ideals and aspirations than was the Liberal Jesus of late-nineteenth-century ideals and aspirations. (James D. G. Dunn, *Jesus Remembered* [Grand Rapids: Eerdmans, 2003], pp. 61-63)

3. A case could be made, for example, that the Lutheran heritage of Marcus Borg and the Roman Catholic–shaped John Dominic Crossan reflect their own reconstruction of the historical Jesus.

the Galilean Christ will be an engagement with the thought of Schillebeeckx.

The attention being given to the work of Edward Schillebeeckx by
both Roman Catholic and Protestant theologians is both a sign and a gift
of our present ecumenical environment. And, if surprise is a feature of
the grace of *oikoumenē*, testimonies are abundant to its presence here.
When have the heirs of Calvin and Luther been driven so implacably to
their Bibles to do systematic theology because a Roman Catholic has
urged them to do so?

The rumination that follows is the result of Schillebeeckx's impact on a
yearlong Theological Tabletalk inquiry at Andover Newton during which a
group of clergy, students, and faculty struggled weekly with *Jesus* and
Christ. That conversation sent me on a search for the organizing princi-
ple(s) of this outpouring of learning, exegesis, and argument. What are the
basic reference points, stated or implied, to which Schillebeeckx returns
time and again in making his case? What is the skeletal framework of this
massive body of thought? In a modest approach to the answer to these
questions, there is the identification of four bones in that body structure.
Further, some anatomical comments will be made about their strengths
and weaknesses. Already such investigations have gone on, but except for
reviews and occasional comments in such places as *Consensus in Theology?*[4] not much careful response and critique have come in North America
from non–Roman Catholic theologians.

We begin the search for key elements in the structure of Schillebeeckx's
thought by agreement with John Haughey: "The best access into his intensely fertile mind is the issue of experience as the medium of God's revelation. More particularly, Schillebeeckx focuses on Jesus' own experience
and the experience of Jesus' first followers, both as individuals and after his
death the primitive communities' experience of his presence."[5] But
Haughey does not go far enough. Inseparable from the christological and
ecclesial experiences is the universal "contrast experience." And there is another aspect of the matter to be reckoned with. Haughey puzzles over it:
"So crucial is the category of experience for him that the reader, at least

---

4. Leonard Swidler, ed., *Consensus in Theology? A Dialogue with Hans Küng and Edward
Schillebeeckx* (Philadelphia: Westminster Press, 1980) (also *Journal of Ecumenical Studies* 5,
no. 17 [Winter 1980]).

5. John C. Haughey, "Schillebeeckx's Christology," *Theology Today* 38 (July 1981): 201.

this reader, is led to wonder what Schillebeeckx's own experience of Christ is. When he approaches the question of modern experience, he slips into the innocuous term 'our' experience which gives more sociological and impersonal information than one wants after the emphasis on experience."[6] While traces of an answer to this charge are to be found in *Jesus* and *Christ,* the reader must go to the earlier sacramental reflections of Schillebeeckx for a fuller response. "'You have shown yourself to me, Christ, face to face,' says St. Ambrose: 'It is in your sacraments that I meet you.' . . . In the words of the Evangelist, 'Was not our heart burning within us whilst he spoke in the way?'"[7]

To understand the experiential matrix of Schillebeeckx's thought, we view it in the perspective of both the author's deep eucharistic piety and an earlier sacramentology, which anticipate many of the themes found in his christological research and argument.

The Contrast Experience

In Schillebeeckx's view there is a "universal experience" of negativity and positivity to which the Christian claim of salvation is correlated.[8] He returns repeatedly to this theme, identifying it in different ways and relating it to the disciples' "Easter experience," to Jesus' "Abba experience," to our own encounter with God as Christians, and to the claims for meaning and truth in other religions and movements in quest for human "well-being." The delineation of this experience is not so easy. For one thing, Schillebeeckx does not always use his basic terms in a consistent way. ("Contrast" sometimes means the disparity between hope and frustration; sometimes, the persistence of hope in the face of frustration.[9] "Negativity"

6. Haughey, "Schillebeeckx's Christology," pp. 201-2.

7. Edward Schillebeeckx, *Christ the Sacrament of the Encounter with God* (New York: Sheed & Ward, 1963), p. 222.

8. Edward Schillebeeckx, *The Understanding of Faith* (hereafter *Understanding*), trans. N. D. Smith (New York: Seabury Press, 1974), pp. 91ff. See the varied treatment of the theme in Edward Schillebeeckx, *Christ: The Experience of Jesus as Lord* (hereafter *Christ*), trans. John Bowden (New York: Seabury Press, 1980), pp. 36, 47, 201-3, 251-58, 278-79, 659-70, 723, 754-55, 818.

9. Edward Schillebeeckx, *Jesus: An Experiment in Christology* (hereafter *Jesus*), trans. Hubert Hoskins (New York: Seabury Press, 1979), pp. 19-20, 24, 593, 620-25. See also his *In-*

occasionally signifies the fact of suffering, evil, and death; at other times, the will to resist this anti-humanity.)[10] For another, not all the components are clearly identified and interrelated, nor does the richness of the idea get the attention it deserves in each of its frequent usages. Let us, then, try to answer Schillebeeckx's question, "What does the universal preunderstanding consist of . . . without which the Christian message cannot be universally valid?"[11] The elements of the universal contrast experience include: (1) the confrontation with the "datum of evil," (2) the sense that what is met in this datum is at cross-purposes with the way things are supposed to be, (3) elusive experiences of a positive sort, (4) a basic trust/hope that the last word on the way things are has not been spoken by the experiences of negativity, (5) an impulse to resist the powers of evil and their threat to our essential humanity, and (6) the emergence of a vision of wellbeing or salvation that promises another outcome, with its articulation in commensurate theory and practice. We examine each feature briefly.

The recurring theme in the characterization of negative experience is human misery. Calamities of persons and societies and the evils of history and nature beset us. Disaster and death militate against peace and life. As such, negativity imperils "the humanum." In William Wolf's typology of fundamental human questions — ignorance, sin, suffering, and death[12] — it is the third that constitutes Schillebeeckx's problematic. However often passing allusion may be made to the other three, the structure of his thought is built on the assumption that the enigma of human suffering constitutes the question to which a system of final meaning must address itself.[13]

The factuality of evil set within the contrast experience becomes theodicy, "Job's problem."[14] What is ought not to be. Negativity runs

---

terim Report on the Books Jesus *and* Christ (hereafter *Interim Report*) (New York: Crossroad, 1981), pp. 5-6; and his *Jesus Christ and Human Freedom* (New York: Herder & Herder, 1974), pp. 110-11.

10. *Jesus*, p. 24. See also *Understanding*, pp. 91-92.

11. *Understanding*, p. 91.

12. William Wolf, *No Cross, No Crown* (Garden City, N.Y.: Doubleday & Co., 1957), pp. 27-30.

13. Sin is integral to the "conversion vision" motifs to be subsequently examined but is not, finally, decisive in soteriological formulations. Ignorance and death are drawn into the category of evil.

14. *Jesus*, pp. 19, 24-25; see also *Understanding*, pp. 96-97.

counter to the deepest purposes; thus, there is a "contrast" in the very experience of evil.[15] This sense of contrast is not the creature of wishful thinking. There are warrants for it in yet another kind of universal human experience: "fragmentary," "fleeting" intuitions, "sporadic experiences of what 'makes sense.'"[16] They give us a glimpse of another possible outcome of our meeting with the data of evil, sharpening the feeling of the wrongness of negativity. More than that, they invite a hope that what *may* be so *might* be so: the purposes violated by negativity vindicated. Positive experiences provide grounds for trust. Again, we have to do with contrast, this time between the oppressive givens and another scenario. These "partly benign" encounters hint of deliverance and release.[17]

They do even more, declaring, "Resist!" There is something in the dynamics of hope juxtaposed to reality that evokes action toward the hope and grappling with the reality. The contrast experience declines "servility before the factual" (Bonhoeffer), contesting the hegemony of what is, a "critical negativity" or "negative dialectics."[18] Thus, encounter with evil, negativity's dissonance with ultimate purpose, its contradiction by a fleeting positivity, a tender trust in another possibility — all make for an explosive mix and its issue, resistance to the "No" of inhumanity.

Out of this coming together is also born a vision of well-being. Negativity and its contrast partner breed a dream of salvation, the righting of every wrong, the mending of every flaw. The fragmentary shall be whole, the fleeting permanent, ill-being transformed into well-being. At this point the variety of claimants to redemption, emancipation, happiness, and salvation make their entrance on the stage of our histories. The religious traditions know that wholeness can come only from a transcendent source.[19]

15. *Christ*, pp. 137-38.
16. *Jesus*, pp. 19, 24-25; *Understanding*, pp. 96-97.
17. *Jesus*, p. 20.
18. *Understanding*, pp. 91ff.
19. *Christ*, pp. 670-723. In addition to the configuration here delineated associated with "the contrast experience," Schillebeeckx uses the concept "negativity" also in another context, as the refractoriness of new experiences that challenge old assumptions (*Christ*, pp. 31, 40).

The Jesus Encounter

How does the particularity of a Good News that declares salvation to be in Jesus alone correlate with the universality of the contrast experience? That is our next question. Schillebeeckx's answer is "the Jesus encounter." This phrase is used here to cover three kinds of experiences: the "Easter experience" of the disciples, our own version of the same encounter, and Jesus' "Abba experience."

The Disciples' Easter Experience

The richness and diversity of Schillebeeckx's thoughts on this matter press us to do the same kind of methodical quest for his varied themes as we had to do in the analysis of the contrast experience. There are two sets of tracks, one that follows the spiritual journey of Mary Magdalene and the other women who experienced a manifestation of Jesus, and another in pursuit of the "official apostolic tradition" of Easter appearances. In both cases, Schillebeeckx is in search of something he believes lies behind the textual accounts of meetings with the crucified and risen Lord and the resurrection faith of the early community. "Unless anchored in this source-experience ('disclosure') the eschatological language is left in the air."[20]

Noting that there is weighty textual evidence for the case that the first Easter appearance was to Mary of Magdala — albeit in need of legitimation by "official" appearances to the apostles — Schillebeeckx speculates that she and the other women who shared the experience played an important part in getting "the whole Jesus affair . . . under way."[21] Hence, their version of the basic disclosure experience is to be included in any description of the Easter encounter of the first disciples.

A characterization of Mary Magdalene gives us a picture of Schillebeeckx's understanding of one kind of Jesus encounter. Mary was from

a small town on the west bank of the sea of Galilee, near the gay and frivolous capital city of Tiberias where Herod Antipas had his residence. Jesus apparently liberated this young woman and brought her

20. *Jesus*, pp. 345-46.
21. *Jesus*, p. 345.

to herself: she broke with her past. But the death of Jesus seemed at first to turn the life she had regained into a problem, until there came to her the loving assurance that the life regained was stronger than death. This Jesus lives. . . . Mary Magdalene may have played a part we do not know about in helping to convince the disciples that the new orientation of living which this Jesus had brought about in their lives has not been rendered meaningless by his death — quite the opposite. In these accounts of "private appearances" — a record of very intimate, personal religious experiences — the community recognizes its own experience. At a particular moment these people's mode of living received a jolt — likewise an intuition — that gave a definite orientation to their lives. In the radical change they undergo, experienced as something definitive, they apprehend Jesus as the One who lives. A specific here-and-now "lived" experience is thus given expression in eschatological language.[22]

What is going on here? The horizon of the contrast experience helps us to follow the trajectory of Schillebeeckx's thought. Mary's crushed expectations at the death of Jesus constitute an intense particularized form of the universal contrast experience. But the memories of the impact of Jesus on her life, as fortified and renewed in a post-crucifixion experience of "loving assurance" that his death could not defeat his promises, resulted in her conviction that "this Jesus lives." Thus the early "fragment" of liberating positivity, reborn in a decisive personal experience of assurance after Jesus' death, proved stronger than the negative empirical "datum of evil." A fundamental trust asserted itself, taking the form in the record of the community of a resurrection appearance of Jesus to Mary. As such, the Easter narratives about Jesus' encounter with the women are Christian code language for the conviction that "not history, but the benevolent One opposed to evil — God — has the last word."[23]

The route from assurance to "appearance" could be construed as the complete subjectivizing of the Easter claims of Christian faith. Schillebeeckx firmly denies this to be the case. His purpose is to carry the reader (the child of modernity who can understand the "Jesus affair" best when its human features are brought to the fore) along with him in the search for the secular underside of the Christian proclamation, with the

22. *Jesus*, pp. 344-45.
23. *Jesus*, p. 639.

help of critical scholarship. To take this tour does not preclude the belief that there is One on "the oilier side" of this human experience — the Jesus who is indeed alive beyond death. For Schillebeeckx, the faith in the "initiative" of the living Jesus can be made "reasonable" to the inquiring modern only by an exploration of its human underside (although never a rationally compelling one). Thus, there is an undoubted asseveration that the Source of my source experience is One who has transcended death: "Jesus himself stands at the source of what we are calling the 'Easter experience' of the disciples; at all events what we meet with here is an experience of grace."[24] That is not the same thing, of course, as an endorsement of the way the living Jesus comes to us in the textual accounts of appearance and their presupposition of a resurrection event. These, in Schillebeeckx's view, are the models of another day in which the ultimate trust of the Christian contrast experience and the grounds for it in the living Jesus receive ancient articulation. But more about this shortly,

In the longer treatment of the Easter experience in "the official tradition" of apostolic appearances, we find the Mary Magdalene contrast themes, but with a difference. They are developed around a "conversion vision" motif, and as such they introduce another aspect of the contrast problematic.

Acknowledging that we do not have any account of the source experiences of Peter and the Eleven, Schillebeeckx is convinced that there is such a matrix for their christological confession. (Indeed, this confession is made in very different models: the specific "crucified One has risen" that is assumed in the appearances, and alternative testimonies that do not necessarily presuppose this scenario including "the crucified One is the coming judge" [the *maranatha* Christology], and "the crucified One as miracle-worker [who] is actively present in his disciples.")[25] His aim is to retrieve the basic disclosure experience as best he can with the help of scholarship and reasonable inference. Once again the contrast experience hovers in the background as critical to his exposition.

The "datum of evil" (as suffering) with which we began is joined, in this second case, by the datum *of sin*. While the death of Jesus and, thus, the apparent refutation of eschatological expectations left Peter and the disciples in doubt and disarray, their *defection* adds another dimension to the experience of negativity. Because the disciples "let Jesus down" and in

24. *Jesus*, p. 392.
25. *Jesus*, p. 387.

panic fled at his crucifixion, their form of Easter experience is an about-face *(metanoia)* from this path of desertion to a decisive new "going after Jesus." For them the contrast begins as juxtaposition of their own profession of loyalty with their ignominious flight. But a redemptive contrast experience overcomes the destructive one, or better, a powerful new positive experience asserts its decisive influence, resolving the negativity of guilt, "a quite specific experience of grace and mercy, the result of which was that they were received back into a present fellowship with Jesus and confessed him to be their definitive salvation."[26] As with Mary Magdalene, this post-Golgotha encounter with Jesus is interpreted in the light of their earlier experience with the historical Jesus.

Repentance and reorientation to Jesus happened, Schillebeeckx believes, along the lines of the Jewish "conversion vision," an experience of gentile adherents to Judaism marked by the metaphors of blindness and sight, darkness and light, ignorance and enlightenment. He finds in the three accounts in Acts of Paul's Damascus Road conversion a clue to what that might have been, including a development within these accounts toward an authoritative appearance claim that put Paul in the ranks of apostolic Easter testimony. A special kind of Easter experience, characterized by repentance and forgiveness, and taking the form of a conversion vision, is asserted by Schillebeeckx to be at the root of the apostolic appearance tradition. Behind this Easter experience is a true "eschatological disclosure," one brought to being "by grace alone."[27] The consequence of this Jesus encounter was the reassembly of the apostolic community, the affirmation of his vindication by God, the taking up of the way and hope of Jesus, commitments expressed in the "arsenal of ideas" provided by the contemporary Jewish and Greek soteriological and eschatological models. A more careful scrutiny of the relationship of the experience to the model we shall reserve for our third major Schillebeeckxian motif.

Our Easter Experience

There is not much in Schillebeeckx's christological work about this third kind of contrast experience, as Haughey observes. However, it is clear that

26. *Jesus,* p. 381.
27. *Jesus,* p. 378.

Schillebeeckx believes that for Christians in any time and place there are both the possibility of and the necessity for an experience like that given to the first Christian community. Such an experience is possible because it is the same Jesus who comes to us. And the way he comes is the same. Since the accounts of a resurrected and transfigured body appearance are secondary models in which early Christians expressed their primary religious experience, our own experience is similar in kind to that of our spiritual forebears. It is different in form, housed in our own contemporary models; derivative in time; and different in degree, by virtue of the disciples' proximity to the historical figure of Jesus.

> In itself the Church's preaching of the resurrection is a gracious invitation and sovereign appeal to us to attain to this experience personally, each in our own life — in a different way for those on the Emmaus road, different again for Mary Magdalene, different too for Peter and the Eleven. There is not such a big difference between the way we are able, after Jesus' death, to come to faith in the crucified-and-risen One and the way in which the disciples of Jesus arrived at the same faith. Only we suffer from the crude and naive realism of what "appearance of Jesus" came to be in the later tradition, through unfamiliarity with the distinctive character of the Jewish-biblical way of speaking.[28]

Is it possible to say more about what Schillebeeckx might mean by this personal experience that is a response to "the Church's preaching of the resurrection"? A brief consideration of some of his earlier reflections on sacramental spirituality may illuminate this question. In Schillebeeckx's earlier writing, the invitation to a living relationship with Jesus comes primarily through the sacraments:

> Now how can we encounter the glorified Lord, who has withdrawn himself from our sight? . . . Christ makes his presence among us actively visible and tangible too, not directly through his own bodiliness, but by extending among us on earth in visible form the function of his bodily reality which is in heaven. This precisely is what the sacraments are: the earthly extension of the "body of the Lord." This is the Church.[29]

---

28. *Jesus*, p. 346.
29. Schillebeeckx, *Christ the Sacrament*, pp. 40, 41.

In the eucharist the relationship comes to its most intimate expression. As the personal relationship of the disciples was deepest in the table fellowship with Jesus, so our community with him is most profound in the encounter with his real presence in the eucharist.[30] This is, in particular, "the Catholic feeling," and this is why the magisterium has sought through efforts in dogmatic definition to protect and nurture this basic "datum of faith."[31]

Reinforcing the continuity of sacramental piety with the later christological themes is the use of existentialist and personalist motifs for reinterpreting the meaning of the sacraments in general and of the eucharist in particular. Seeking to translate today the sacramental vision formulated for another time in Aristotelian terms, Schillebeeckx speaks of sacramental grace as a personal meeting:

> The basic meaning [of the eucharist] can only be preserved for us in pure state if it is viewed from our present context of life and thus approached phenomenologically. . . . The specifically eucharistic "real presence" now . . . can be defined more precisely. . . . The basis of the entire eucharistic event is Christ's personal gift of himself to his fellow-men, and within this to the Father. . . . The Eucharist is the sacramental form of this event, Christ's giving of himself to the Father and to men.[32]

The parallel is striking between Schillebeeckx's later exploration of the centrality of an Easter experience that entails a real meeting with an eschatological Jesus — the disciples' encounter and ours — and this earlier focus on both the eucharistic real presence of the glorified humanity of Christ and its interpretation in terms of personal encounter. While the later Schillebeeckx would not confine the believers' encounter with Christ to the explicit sacramental life (neither does the earlier Schillebeeckx),[33] there is a continuity between earlier commitments to a eucharistic datum of faith which is "in the last resort, biblical,"[34] and the essence of our own Easter experience.

---

30. Edward Schillebeeckx, *The Eucharist*, trans. N. D. Smith (New York: Sheed & Ward, 1968), p. 123.

31. *The Eucharist*, pp. 60, 61.

32. *The Eucharist*, pp. 125-26, 137.

33. Schillebeeckx, *Christ the Sacrament*, pp. 197-216.

34. Schillebeeckx, *The Eucharist*, p. 51.

There is an interesting difference between the eucharistic reflections and the Easter inquiries. The contrast experience does not appear in the sacramental inquiry. That is no surprise. Schillebeeckx's sensitivity to the juxtaposition of negative and positive experiences is related to his own pilgrimage through recent decades of vision on a collision course with reality. The sacramental writing was done before the era of shattered dreams. History leaves its mark on our theological formulations.

Another difference between early and late ideas of encounter with Jesus is related to the significance Schillebeeckx places on the career of Jesus and, in this context, the role of Jesus' own personal encounter with God. "To put one's trust in Jesus is to ground oneself in what was named as the ground of Jesus' experience: the Father. It entails recognizing the authentic non-illusory reality of Jesus' *Abba* experience."[35] To this we now turn.

Jesus' Abba Experience

The Jesus encounter in its primordial expression is Jesus' own personal encounter with God in his "Abba experience." Schillebeeckx views this as the "source and secret of his being, message and manner of life."[36] While this experience is discussed in the context of the question of Jesus' uniqueness, the problematic of a "calamitous and pain-ridden history"[37] which we have identified in the other forms of the Jesus encounter lies at the heart of Jesus' own experience. Further, the graceful counter-evidence in his Abba experience is an intensification "in an original and personal way" that had its anticipations in "the religious life of the Jewish followers of Yahweh centuries before," and was, therefore, in continuity with "Israel's best moments of its experience of God."[38] Thus, we are talking here about a species of the genus, "contrast experience," albeit in its most definitive expression.

Drawing on the studies of Jeremias and B. van Iersel, Schillebeeckx argues that the term "Abba" as a form of address to God is unknown in rabbinic and late Jewish devotional literature.[39] It suggests an "unaffected simplicity" and a directness of relationship to God on the analogy of inti-

35. *Jesus*, p. 637.
36. *Jesus*, p. 256.
37. *Jesus*, p. 267.
38. *Jesus*, p. 268.
39. *Jesus*, p. 259.

mate family talk. For Jesus, this usage appears to be habitual. Schillebeeckx believes that his elemental trust in, and intercourse with, God constituted the grounds of Jesus' assurance about the solidarity of God with the human venture — and the resolution of the dilemma of negativity:

> In the calamitous and pain-ridden history within which Jesus stood it was impossible to find any grounds or indeed any reason at all which would serve to explain and make sense of the unqualified assurance of salvation that characterized his message. Such a hope expressed in a proclamation of the coming and already close salvation for men implied in God's rule . . . in Jesus is quite plainly rooted in a personal awareness of contrast; on the one hand the incorrigible irremediable history of man's suffering, a history of calamity, violence and injustice, of grinding, excruciating and oppressive enslavement; on the other hand Jesus' particular awareness of God, his Abba experience, his intercourse with God as the benevolent, solicitous one who is against evil, who will not admit the supremacy of evil and refuses to allow it the last word.[40]

Jesus' own experience and message were set in a historical context that lent itself to posing sharply the question of negativity. "For both Jew and Gentile Jesus' time was full to bursting with an assortment of hopes regarding some good thing to come. . . . The period of Jewish apocalyptic above all . . . was a 'story of blood and tears,' out of which the yearning grew: 'Enough is enough: the world must be changed — positively and radically changed!'"[41]

The juxtapositional feature of Jesus' contrast experience is reasserted in the mid-career of his ministry. Jesus knew failure in his proffer of salvation as eschatological envoy. The "fiasco in Galilee" began to strike home and had to be dealt with in his self-interpretation, especially so since it carried the portent of his final rejection and death. Touching the question of the validity of his Abba experience, it means that "Jesus himself was faced with the concrete task of reconciling the historical eventuality of his violent death with the assurance of his message of the approaching Kingdom of God."[42] At the very least this seems to have meant, according to

40. *Jesus,* p. 267.
41. *Jesus,* p. 20.
42. *Jesus,* p. 302.

Schillebeeckx, a firm "nevertheless" in the face of impending disaster: God could be counted on to vindicate the eschatological promises somehow. But more, the historical kernel of the Last Supper tradition suggested that Jesus willingly accepted his death as of a piece with his ministry in life and thus as having some soteriological meaning. Subsequently the New Testament interpretations of Jesus' death (the dramatic contrast, the "must" and soteriological views), therefore, all have possible grounds in Jesus' own self-understanding.[43] The form this confident acceptance took was the promise of continued fellowship with Jesus even after historical defeat and death. The trust born in the Abba experience cannot be undermined in this ultimate contrast test of the highest hopes in the worst of times.

In the three forms of the Jesus encounter there is a recurring motif: the universal human quandary about the evil that threatens the meaning of life finds a disclosure which give us an assurance "that you may not grieve as others who have no hope" (1 Thess. 4:13). "Human history without its successes, failures, illusions and disillusions — is surmounted by the living God. That is the heart of the Christian message."[44]

Experience and Interpretation

The question of what is abiding and what is transient in Christian proclamation is a lifelong concern for Schillebeeckx. For a sensitive theologian of a church living in the throes of twentieth-century aggiornamento it could not be otherwise. He ponders again and again how a contemporary believer can be both faithful to the ancient lore and an honest citizen of the modern world. For the Catholic theologian this entails respect for the formulations of Christian tradition, those within and beyond Scripture, and their intelligible and honorable reinterpretation in current modes of thought. This task of translation comes insistently to the fore in Schillebeeckx's christological work. Our third element in the structure of his thought, therefore, has to do with this problem. We have already begun to examine it under the rubric of the Jesus encounter, but the status of the *interpretation* of the disclosure experience has yet to be addressed.

The analysis of transubstantiation is suggestive of the method

43. *Jesus*, pp. 274-94.
44. *Jesus*, p. 639.

Schillebeeckx employs in relating experience to interpretation in Christology. We are confronted in the doctrine of transubstantiation with an earlier epoch's attempt to give expression in a then-meaningful Aristotelian substance-accident conceptuality to the "datum of faith," a datum constituted by both the biblical evidence and the experience of the universal church. In the Tridentine effort to do this, Schillebeeckx distinguishes three levels: (1) Foundational is the unthematic experience of faith itself, the awareness of a "eucharistic real presence" native to Catholic feeling, but also to be found in "the patristic intuition" of the Greek churches and anticipated in the "eucharistic desire" of churches in the Reformed tradition. (2) The fullness of this experience is inseparable from its lasting quality; expression is not faithful to experience if it does not honor the persistence of the Presence, which is "not simply at communion, but also before (after the liturgy of the consecration) and afterwards."[45] This means that not only Zwingli's memorialism but also Luther's consubstantiation view (which, for all of its realism, holds the eucharistic presence to be only *"in usu"*) is erosive of the datum of faith. To protect the latter, it is necessary to insist, following Thomas, on a *conversio*, a change of being, *trans-entatio*, at the consecration. We have here an "ontological" assertion, therefore, which is integral to the datum of faith.[46] (3) However, the way Thomas, and later Trent, gave more elaborate intellectual articulation to (a) the datum and (b) the ontological affirmation was through (c) the constructs of "natural philosophy," and that means the Aristotelian theory of substance and accidents. While Thomas treated these as parts of a "single vision," Schillebeeckx does not:

> [We] are at once confronted with the question as to whether the ontological can and must not be preserved even if the level of natural philosophy is no longer serviceable for us. . . . It is *a priori* quite conceivable that anyone who has to reject the specifically Aristotelian character of the doctrine of substance and accidents (we are after all, not bound by faith to an Aristotelian philosophy) may still be able to keep to an "ontological change," on the basis of which the answer to the question, "What *is* that?" after the consecration can no longer simply be "It is bread."[47]

45. Schillebeeckx, *The Eucharist*, p. 44.
46. *The Eucharist*, p. 63.
47. *The Eucharist*, p. 64.

Schillebeeckx then goes on to attempt to capture the datum of faith
(1) and the ontological affirmation of "conversion" (2) in formulations of
intersubjectivity (3) that he believes connect with contemporary sensibility.

There are some questions we shall ask about this scheme later, having
to do with its consistency. But for now we want to see if it sheds any light
on the sometimes confusingly overwritten treatment of the relation of experience to interpretation in the christological analogue. There appear to
be the same kind of levels in the latter as are found in the former:

(1) From the disciples' Jesus encounter to ours there is a common
Easter experience "below" the level of any specific theological articulation.
While it comes through a given framework of perception and conception,
and in turn is borne witness to in the images and idiom of a given time and
place, it is not dependent on them for its gratuitous life, whose source is finally the living Lord. (2) For all that, this "real presence" of the eschatological Jesus requires, even in its unthematic state, certain ontological assertions. Not any and every theological interpretation can be poured into this
experience. The authenticity of the experience is related to certain "core"
affirmations. Time and again Schillebeeckx draws our attention to these
ontological assertions that have the same decisive weight as the "change in
being" motifs in eucharistic theology. In an important passage they are
identified as "first-order assertions" in contrast to "second-order affirmations" (our "third level") that draw out the former in ever-new contexts
with their fitting models.[48] These first-order asseverations include: "our
belief that in Jesus God saves human beings"; our conviction that the rule
of God shall triumph over our "calamitous and pain-ridden history"; the
poor, the weak, the oppressed, and the outcasts as the special object of the
divine compassion and solidarity; our own call to a praxis in company
with God's action and vision in Jesus, the source and sustenance of the
hope in action in the Easter encounter with God to be found in the encounter with Jesus.

These themes are, of course, a summary of the meaning and message
of the historical Jesus. They constitute the working norm for any third-
level theological thematizations. Here is where the work of theology is
done in a given time and place. It begins at the earliest stage of Christian
proclamation, within the New Testament, as the different Christian communities of the first century seek to relate their vision of Jesus to the set-

---

48. *Jesus*, pp. 548-49; *Interim Report*, pp. 14-15.

ting in which they find themselves with its phantasmagoria of salvific expectations: messiah, eschatological prophet, son of man, son of God, Lord, Logos, etc. The appropriation of these culture-relative ideas — and their transformation in the process of appropriation according to particularities of the Jesus events — continues in the history of theological interpretation as new issues arise and new categories are provided.

In our own time and place it is incumbent upon us to express our experience and its ontological commitments to the meaning and message of Jesus in ways germane to, and intelligible in, the early twenty-first century. One key to contemporary theological interpretation for Schillebeeckx is the secular framework of modernity,[49] an assumption that persists through various phases of his writing in the past two decades. It is an important factor in an "experiment in Christology" that strives to uncover the humanity of Jesus and thus the humanity of faith itself to an era which he believes functions in essentially this-worldly terms. Another reference point for theological communication is the theme of emancipation or liberation.[50] Jesus' vision of the Reign of God and obedience to the eschatological prophet's call to "proclaim liberty to the captives" today means a faith and a church in solidarity with the forgotten and disenfranchised, a word of hope for them, an act of love toward them, and a struggle for justice with them. Enlarging the motif of emancipation to include the ills and cares of finitude, as well as the oppression of society, Schillebeeckx also calls for the liberation of the sorrowing from their fears, the lonely from their alienation, the sick and dying from their hopelessness.[51] In this idiom theological communication today preserves and renders articulate the core experiences, visions, and affirmations that in other contexts found expression in models of meaning appropriate to those settings.

The foregoing view of the relation of experience to interpretation functions in Schillebeeckx's treatment of the Easter experience and the eucharist and is given explicit statement in the early pages of *Christ*. Here it is argued that "there is no neutral given in experience, for alternative interpretations influence the very way in which we experience the world."[52] That is, even at

49. Edward Schillebeeckx, *God the Future of Man*, trans. N. D. Smith (New York: Sheed & Ward, 1968), pp. 53-116, 169-203.

50. *Human Freedom*, pp. 112-13; *Jesus*, pp. 35, 61; *Christ*, pp. 724-43.

51. *Human Freedom*, pp. 112-13; *Jesus*, p. 624; *Christ*, pp. 753, 756-62, 764-70, 790-801, 821-31.

52. *Christ*, p. 53.

its most rudimentary level, experience is inseparable from some kind of interpretation. "Experience is always interpreted experience."[53] This thesis is present operationally in the earlier assertion that there is no fully authentic eucharistic experience which does not include the conviction that the bread is different after the consecration, that we have to do with the lasting Real Presence — the abiding ontological affirmation that can express itself in varying philosophical formulations commensurate with the premises of one or another age (substance-accidents, intersubjectivity, etc.). It is also latent in the christological exposition in that the Easter experience, the disciples' and ours, cannot be had or expressed without the conviction that we have to do with the Real Presence of Jesus, the living reality of One who gives hope and calls us to love. Schillebeeckx's exegetical efforts are directed to giving substance to this ontological core of the Easter experience, just as his sacramental inquiries sought to identify the ontological assertion to which third-level intellectual models both point and are accountable. In the christological context, Schillebeeckx sees the early models of resurrection appearance, coming son of man, etc., as alternative ways of capturing the disciples' Easter experience. His own effort at reformulating in a modified liberation theology model is a way of giving expression to today's Easter experience.

However, two puzzles emerge for this writer in Schillebeeckx's discussion and application of these premises. One is found in a comment at the close of the argument in *Christ* on the inseparability of experience and interpretation:

> When the old concepts or interpretive elements no longer relate to new situations and when needs and necessities change, interpretive concepts also change. But the original experience persists through these changes: in their own different situations people still continue to experience God's salvation in Jesus. These changes do not themselves cause a crisis. As long as the basis of experience — experience of salvation in Jesus — remains, any possible crisis takes place above all on the level of conceptual interpretation.[54]

On the face of it, it would seem that the argument that interpretation is inseparable from experience, at least as it has functioned in the sacramental and christological inquiries, has been abandoned in the conclusion.

53. *Christ*, p. 31.
54. *Christ*, pp. 63-64.

Right here Schillebeeckx seems to be saying that experience is indeed separable from the ever-changing need for contextual reconceptualization. Sense can be made of the conclusion, however, if "experience" is understood to mean *second-level interpreted* experience, and packed into the phrase "experience of salvation in Jesus" are the native *ontological assertions* earlier identified. Thus, the changing "concepts or interpretative elements" refer to *third-level models* whose value lies in their communicative power in one cultural setting but not in another.

However, there is a more fundamental puzzle. It has to do with a possible clash of frameworks for understanding the relation of experience to interpretation. In our three-level analysis of both eucharistic and Easter experience, third-level reformulation (3) must be accountable to both the elemental encounter (1) and the ontological assertions (2) inseparable from it. The very enterprise of locating elements of the historical Jesus that can be found through the New Quest in order to test and formulate christological proposals presupposes identifiable level-two affirmations. But in Schillebeeckx's writing over the past several decades, both historicist and existentialist influences on his thought have prompted him to declare that we cannot retrieve the Christian message in its "pure state" or in "timeless" assertions. Our own historical contingency on the one hand and the inextricability of ancient confessions from their own social location on the other prevent such surgery.[55] What we may think to be either the "essence" of another age or all ages is, in fact, always colored by our own agendas.[56] Further, the very attempt to set aside our own agenda in the quest for essences removes us from that engaged stance in which faith happens. Authentic Christian conviction today is bound up with the real questions and categories of our time and place, as it was for the first Christian community: it strikes home only in engagement with contextual issues and idiom. And more, personal faith is never at arm's length from its subject; passion and personal encounter, not dispassion and impersonal observation, are integral to the Christian experience. Thus, both descriptively and normatively the search for an essential norm for christological confessions appears to be

55. *Jesus*, pp. 48-50; *Christ*, pp. 30ff., 53ff., 74ff.

56. *Jesus*, p. 53; *Interim Report*, Preface; Schillebeeckx, *God the Future of Man*, p. 8. In an astute review of *Christ* and *Interim Report*, John Galvin identifies the same kinds of ambiguity in Schillebeeckx's conception of the relation of experience to interpretation to which we have here pointed. He compares statements on pp. 63 and 292-93 in *Christ* that represent seemingly incompatible views (*Heythrop Journal* 23 [1982]: 78-82).

ruled out. The Christian experience cum interpretation is truth *for us* in the indicative and the imperative, and truth *for me.*

The indissolubility of experience and interpretation in this *second* train of thought appears to be rather different than the inseparability of experience and ontological assertion in the first one. In the latter case, the experience of Jesus cannot be had or understood unless it is in the posture of personal and social engagement. With regard to the role of interpretation, this means that the encounter with Jesus necessarily comes through, and is to be expressed in, conceptual models appropriate to a given time and place.[57] The premise of the relational view is that third-level models are integral to the experience of Jesus. One who has the encounter through the medium of the cultural model formed from the questions and visions of an era cannot help but express it in these contextual terms, and ought not try to do otherwise, for such would do violence to the existential unity of experience and (third-level) interpretation. In this view there is no room for second-level ontological affirmations. The relativity of Christian experience-interpretation, considered in both descriptive and normative ways, does not allow for them. Hence, we confront the enigma of the search by Schillebeeckx for interpretive second-level reference points in the historical Jesus in association with a theoretical rejection of them.

The Historical Jesus

The massive volumes *Jesus* and *Christ* are testimony to the importance of the bone, "the historical Jesus," in the skeletal structure of Schillebeeckx's current thought.

> If Christian faith is a faith in Jesus of Nazareth, in the sense that our attitude to him definitely settles our choice for or against God, that is to say in biblical terms, if it is a faith in Jesus of Nazareth, confessed as "Christ, the only begotten Son, our Lord," then faith-centered knowledge and confession of the faith are indeed bounded by our knowledge of the historical Jesus; and that knowledge . . . is bounded, that is, put in its place or kept within its proper bounds, by faith-directed interpretation.[58]

57. *Interim Report,* p. 8; *Christ,* pp. 31-40.
58. *Jesus,* pp. 70-71.

In this complex sentence, we find a connection between our first scenario on the relation of experience to interpretation and Schillebeeckx's attention to the life, teachings, religious experience, and death of Jesus. While faith-directed interpretation renders meaningful *to us* and *to me* the Jesus encounter, it must be accountable to what can be known about the Nazarene. And what can be known about Jesus must be sought for us today through the means of critical scholarship. But why is the historical Jesus as recoverable by the New Quest so decisive? There seem to be at least five reasons why this approach to Christology is a "question . . . of life or death for Christianity."[59]

The Christian religion is not ahistorical speculation or mystical flight from temporality. It is rooted in events. It claims that God came to us in human form. Therefore, believers must take seriously the figure in whom this entrance became manifest. That requires attention to "the memory of Jesus" embodied in the lore of the community. In a time when methods are available that can give clearer access to the figure behind the received memories of Scripture and tradition, every use should be made of them by those committed to the incarnational premises of Christian faith.[60]

The historical facts and features of Jesus are of special significance today because of the current interest in just these things. Radical activists, enthusiastic evangelicals, and the ordinary person in the street show an interest in the figure of Jesus. Much of this attraction has to do with the secular sensibilities of modernity. The culture of the West resonates to interpretations of Christianity that are made within the framework of its human-centered premises, ones that do not put a strain on its credulity on the one hand and address its wide-ranging human issues on the other. A christological confession that puts the human Jesus to the fore, therefore, makes sense to contemporaries.

Not only the demands of moderns who want human-scale warrant for their value choices, but the nature of ultimate truth itself requires the Christian community to state its case by the appeal to public evidence. "Mystification," "fide-ism," "ideology," and "dogmatic authority" are not the way to truth.[61] While it is not possible or proper for faith to offer air-

59. *Jesus*, p. 70.

60. Various testimonies to the importance of historical recovery are found in *Jesus*, pp. 22, 54, 65, 69, 73-76, 601, 635; *Christ*, pp. 639-40; *Human Freedom*, pp. 111-12; *Interim Report*, pp. 8, 25-28.

61. *Jesus*, pp. 602, 604-5.

tight arguments and thus turn itself into rationalism, it is possible and proper for faith to show its reasonableness.[62] Tools of modern critical exegesis serve this purpose. Their use demonstrates that Christianity is not afraid of intellectual inquiry. But more, through the scholarship of the New Quest we can understand how traditional interpretations of Christian faith rose out of a more fundamental encounter and are to be distinguished in their time-bound character from their matrix in the experience of a real human being with qualities that can be understood by moderns. Further, the recovery of the historical Jesus will enable us to develop models of contemporary interpretation both faithful to the primal experience of Jesus and illuminative of present experience. "If historical knowledge of Jesus is possible at all (as even Bultmann affirms; and that is now difficult to deny), then any view of Jesus held in faith . . . is only justified if this identifying interpretation also includes this historical knowledge in a consistent way."[63]

The search for the historical Jesus is more than an exercise in intellectual inquiry and contemporary apologetics. It is an invitation to faith.

[O]ur purpose is, along with his disciples, as it were, to follow the way of Jesus from Nazareth right up to his death so as in that way (and again "as it were") to trace for ourselves how the faith-inspired interpretation of Jesus as the Christ came into being. Secondly, we are looking for traces in the life of Jesus that, for us as for the disciples, could constitute an invitation to assent in faith to what is indeed God's great work of salvation in Jesus of Nazareth. . . . So someone who examines the Jesus event and his self-understanding from a critical standpoint, yet "in faith," can still see in the exegetically rather vague and meager result something more than that Jesus had perhaps not yet arrived at the clear articulations of the primitive Christian communities.[64]

Encountering Jesus in the companionship with the disciples in a way that is facilitated by historical reconstruction, the believer today must then do what the disciples did. Historical scholarship, therefore, serves a "pastoral" function.

62. *Christ,* p. 48.
63. *Interim Report,* p. 27.
64. *Jesus,* pp. 258, 318-19; see also *Interim Report,* pp. 31, 33-34.

[L]ike the first Christians from out of their background, he may himself reflect as a Christian, out of his own background, on the data provided by this historical reconstruction. The pro-existence or loving service which Jesus' entire life was and (as historical and exegetical analysis would indicate) which manifestly came to a climax in his death, may then have to be expressed for us in an articulation containing different emphases and distinctions from the interpretations in the New Testament, conditioned as they were by already given cultural and religious concepts.[65]

For these converging reasons Schillebeeckx launches upon the meticulous work of piecing together the admittedly "rather vague and meager" results of historical-critical studies to form a historical reconstruction of Jesus. It takes form as a fresh and intriguing picture of "the eschatological prophet," the final envoy of God in a tradition of Judaism that looked for a new Moses who would interpret the law and bring the Good News of salvation. Jesus' preaching of the Reign of God, his proffer of salvation, and his relationship with sinners and outcasts expressed in his parables, healings, and table fellowship, and grounded in his Abba experience fit the profile of this expected one who comes to offer a last chance before the culminating divine act. Within the particular time-bound model of eschatological prophet, Schillebeeckx finds an enduring figure whose relationship to and vision of God and solidarity with suffering humanity constitute the source of authentic Christian experience, then and now, and the reference point for true christological confession, then and now.

Prominent in our analysis of Schillebeeckx's use of historical scholarship is its function of providing a plausible reconstruction of Jesus "as he was" that can serve as a guide and test for christological assertions. But from time to time Schillebeeckx appears to deny that this is his intention.

I am not, however, saying in any way that the picture of Jesus as reconstructed by historians becomes the norm and criterion of Christian faith. This would be absurd; the first Christians, at any rate, were never confronted with this "historical abstract," which is what a historical-critical picture of Jesus amounts to (*Jesus*, 34f.). In this sense there is a difference between the "Jesus of history," i.e., Jesus himself living in Palestine in contact with his contemporaries, and

65. *Jesus*, p. 319.

"the historical Jesus," in the sense of the abstract result of a historical-critical investigation. The historical argumentative approach represents a qualitative change from the spontaneous, living story of Jesus down the ages (1, 34f.). It is not the historical picture of Jesus but the living Jesus of history who stands at the beginning and is the source, norm and criterion of the interpretive experience that the first Christians had of him. However, precisely when we consider this structure of early Christian belief, a historical-critical investigation can clarify for us how the specific content of earliest Christian belief is "made up" by the Jesus of history, and has a corrective function with regard to the inadequacy of some later formulae. Thus a historical reconstruction can be an invitation to join the first disciples of Jesus in their *itinerarium mentis,* following Jesus from his baptism in the Jordan until his death. In that case, in the course of this history modern readers too can arrive at the discovery, "Did not our hearts burn within us while he talked to us on the road, while he opened to us the scriptures?" (Luke 24.32): It is therefore a question of a *fides quaerens intellectum historicum* and at the same time of an *intellectus historicus quaerens fidem.* To call all this nineteenth-century liberal Christology, or a Christology for philanthropists, is to be blind to what is going on.[66]

Does this response to some critics who apparently want to link Schillebeeckx with an earlier Jesusology in fact set aside the use of historical reconstruction as a christological criterion? This does not appear to me to be the case. The first half of the response makes the point that a real person, not an abstraction, evoked the disciples' commitment and interpretation. It is doubtful that even the guilt-by-liberal-association critics would deny this or accuse Schillebeeckx of confusing the two. On the heels of this disquisition there is a statement of the refrain that critical apparatus can show the relation of "the Jesus of history" to the evolving christological confessions. But with it goes acknowledgment of the very point in question, namely the "corrective function," and thus the criteriological function, of historical reconstruction. Next comes a reference to yet another rationale for the historical enterprise, the fifth in our earlier delineation, the pastoral intention, *intellectus historicus quaerens fidem* (with the citation of the same text used years earlier for the sacramental encounter). This pas-

---

66. *Interim Report,* pp. 33-34.

sage is illustrative of the difficulty of following the argument of a brilliant theologian who not only writes but "writes it down," as an illustrious Dutch colleague describes it. The cascade of comments on a given topic, done time and again, but sometimes in less than logical order, makes for diverse interpretation of Schillebeeckx's intentions and the need for a careful dissection of his argument, one that may have to take issue with random inconsistent expressions of it.

Related to the disclaimers about too-ready reliance on the historical Jesus norm is the struggle in which Schillebeeckx is engaged throughout his work with the question of historical relativity. As is nicely put by Leo O'Donovan in a review of *Christ:* "The unnoticed guest at this feast of wisdom and erudition is Ernst Troeltsch, whose name is mentioned only once, in a late note, but whose central concern emerges here in a newly vital form."[67] The determination to engage in the theological task with full awareness of Troeltsch's challenge will prompt one to draw back from any apparent claim to have found normative trans-cultural assertions. At the same time, his uneasiness with the premise of historical relativity brings Schillebeeckx back repeatedly to the search for stable points to carry on his theological work. As he refines his christological position, therefore, we hear about "anthropological constants,"[68] a "structural history" along with "conjunctural" and "ephemeral" ones,[69] and "structural principles" which both abide in the New Testament and are normative for our own "thinking, living and acting."[70] These latter "four formative principles" (theological and anthropological, christological, ecclesial, and eschatological) look very much like the "bones" we have here identified. They constitute an appeal to the historical Jesus against the background of a contrast Easter experience with the foreground challenge of ever-fresh ecclesial interpretation.

Assessment

No justice can be done to the richness and subtlety of Schillebeeckx's Christology, or even of the four elements here identified, in a few pages of

---

67. Leo O'Donovan in a review of *Christ* in *Interpretation* 36 (1982): 192.
68. *Christ,* pp. 731-43.
69. *Jesus,* pp. 577-82.
70. *Christ,* pp. 631-44; *Interim Report,* pp. 51-55.

evaluation. Comments will be restricted, therefore, to two motifs, the contrast experience and the relation of experience to interpretation. But these subjects will become entry points for more wide-ranging assessment of his christological proposals, since they open out into his view of the Easter experience and the historical Jesus and, beyond that, point toward the larger soteriological question of the Work of Christ. We shall stop at that line, recognizing, however, its own continuity with the whole orb of Christian doctrine.

The Contrast Experience and Its Environs

The encounter with the datum of evil poses a fundamental human quandary. The fragments of real life and love we experience are under regular assault by the powers of death and hate. Further, the contrast between what we know of each is exacerbated by the sense that there is a basic wrongness to this juxtaposition: we are made for better things, but where is the Maker? There rises within us the ancient *cri de coeur:*

> Let the day perish wherein I was born. . . . I am allotted months of emptiness, and nights of misery are apportioned to me. . . . Why do the wicked live, reach old age, and grow mighty in power? Their children are established in their presence, and their offspring before their eyes. Their houses are safe from fear, and no rod of God is upon them. . . . What is the Almighty, that we should serve him? (Job 3:3; 7:3; 21:7-9, 15)

The problem of suffering and finally "Job's problem," the stark and unjust discrepancy between the experiences of good — the confidence in Good — and the fact of evil, is a universal anguish. Schillebeeckx has put his finger on it.

More than that, he has brought this sensibility into his christological work out of a generation whose social experience has pressed home Job's problem with acuteness. A decade of visionary experience and expectation — the human rights movements, the peace movement, Vatican II renewal aspirations, "socialism with a human face," the ecological momentum — was followed by an era of shattered hopes and murdered visionaries. It is no accident that a Moltmann wrote about "the crucified God" in sequel to a "theology of hope," and that this christological experiment uses "the contrast experience" as its horizon. For many sobered hopers the encounters of vision and reality in the cultural problematic is personal theodicy writ large.[71] Once again Schillebeeckx strikes a responsive chord.

While not identified as such, there is another dimension to the contrast experience presupposed in the disciples' Easter encounter. As a conversion vision it entails repentance. The contrast problem in this dimension is neither evil (suffering) inflicted by other persons nor events colliding with good experienced or expected, but the sin done by oneself over against the good experienced from and expected by Another. Schillebeeckx believes that the Easter experience of the disciples was related to the awareness of sin as well as the consciousness of evil. His use of Paul's Damascus road encounter as suggestive of the Easter experience behind "the appearance tradition" fortifies this attention to the problem of sin. The same note of infidelity to Christ, albeit in a persecution context, is found there as a contrast embedded in the conversion experience. This is a very fruitful line of inquiry.

In the overall setting and direction of Schillebeeckx's anthropology and Christology, however, this second aspect of the contrast experience exists as a foreign body. The contrast experience in the *structure* of his thought is focused on the "problem of evil." From beginning to end, the contrast question as we have described it in its six features is not "given our guilt how are we to find forgiveness?" but, rather, "given our suffering, how are we to find assurance?" so "that we may not grieve as others who have no hope." The Easter experience is the trust of a hope that overcomes the datum of evil, not the trust of a faith that overcomes the datum of sin.

What gives further support to the focus on the datum of evil/suffering is the assumption that a christological confession should be able to trace its origins and find its warrants in Jesus' own career and experience. The Easter experience has its correlate in Jesus' Abba experience. This experience as defined by Schillebeeckx is a response to the contrast problematic of evil. Given the doctrinal assumption about the sinlessness of Jesus, a Roman Catholic theologian would not find it speculatively fruitful to talk about some "datum of sin" for which Jesus sought forgiveness. More than that, what seems to be at work here is the conjoint influence of two of

71. The clash of vision with reality and of liberation and reconciliation with bondage and alienation provides interpretive motif-metaphor for Fackre, *The Christian Story*, vol. 1.

Schillebeeckx's basic working principles: the universal contrast experience of evil at the foreground of contemporary sensibility, setting the terms for today's articulation of faith, and the rootage of all christological confession in critically recoverable aspects of Jesus' career.

Additional evidence of the marginality of the sin-forgiveness theme is the fact that references to our own Easter experience are consistently made in terms of the framework of hopelessness and hope. It is the threat of meaninglessness and its resolution, not the peril of guilt and its reconciliation, by which our faith in Jesus Christ is to be understood and interpreted.

The themes of meaninglessness and meaning and of despair and hope are, of course, familiar ones in modern theology, traceable to an earlier existentialist influence and more recent restatements by theologies of hope, the future, promise, etc. But does the question a culture asks determine the answer which that faith gives? While it is true that the Christian community cannot be content to give answers to questions that are not asked, it is equally true that profound questions may never be asked by a culture because they are too threatening to it. This means that the faith community must not only answer questions but also question questions. It may have to speak to the culture's quandaries in a manner that the culture is led also to ask the unasked question.

The reinterpretation of Christology essentially in terms of a universal contrast experience is too narrow a view of the human problematic. Yet, reformulation in an era fraught with peril to the whole human prospect itself can (and should) *begin* with these anguished issues, but it cannot end there. To each must finally come the unasked question of our own complicity in the cause of suffering, human and divine. How do we stand *coram Deo?* The way we perceive the anthropological issues will shape our christological interpretations.

The source and norm of christological confession for Schillebeeckx is to be found in the Jesus-of-history cum historical Jesus. That includes the understanding by Jesus of his death, as well as the experiences, relationships, and teachings of his life. Only after the full drama has been lived out can it be viewed as a whole and the career of Jesus seen for what it is. Just as considerable weight is given within the New Testament to the significance of Jesus' death, so it is important for subsequent interpretation to incorporate it into the meaning of finding salvation in Jesus. But to do it aright, according to Schillebeeckx's goal of recovering what we can of the Jesus of history, is to search for clues in Jesus' own self-understanding of his approaching death. In this connection he examines three traditions of inter-pretation: The "contrast" view, which records the shock of encounter be-tween the offer of salvation by the eschatological prophet and its rejection by the people of Israel; the divine "must" view, which sets the untoward events against the background of the purpose of God, but leaves unspoken what that intent might be; and a soteriological view, which holds Jesus' death to be itself instrumental to salvation, a theme that came to predomi-nate in more elaborate forms in much of the *post hoc* New Testament inter-pretation.[72] He then reviews what evidence there is for Jesus' own self-understanding and finds lines that go out toward all three of the early in-terpretations.

In making this inquiry, the effects of the contrast experience presuppo-sition are visible. In all three scenarios the fact of death is read in the light of the frustration of the promise of well-being. For example, the meaning of the soteriological strand in Jesus' self-understanding centers on a dis-cussion of whether the faith of Jesus in the future of God derived from his Abba experience is to be held "in spite of his death or whether it is a faith grounded in that event, but one that reaches out to include death as a means of realizing its promises."[73] Schillebeeckx's conclusion is that the significance of the death of Jesus for subsequent interpretation is its func-tion as a model of pro-existence of the One who chose to give his life for the rest of us. The background that renders meaningful this determined self-giving is the Abba experience: an assurance "even unto death." As Jesus had faith in the warrants of the Abba experience that persisted through crucifixion, so should we.[74]

72. *Jesus*, pp. 273-94.

73. *Jesus*, pp. 298-331.

74. *Jesus*, pp. 636-43. In his exegetical work on the Pauline letters, Hebrews, etc., in *Christ*, Schillebeeckx must, of course, deal with the themes of sin and guilt, justification by faith, and vicarious atonement. He refers critics of *Jesus* who raise questions about the rela-tive absence of the sin-guilt issue to the explorations in his second volume, *Christ* (*Interim Report*, p. 100). But the questions remain, for three reasons: (1) The context for the treatment of *sin* is an analysis of the variety of issues that confront one or another New Testament community. Those whose historically shaped problem was that of the role of law and salva-tion by works would, of course, be prompted to think about grace in terms of the forgive-ness of sin. Thus, the problem of sin does not have the force of a *universal* contrast experi-ence, as does the problem of evil. Even in the discussion of sin as a particular issue of *some* of the New Testament writings, the subject undergoes a transformation from guilt to suffering. A discourse on Job appears as a key interpretation of Romans (*Christ*, pp. 134, 137-39); Ephe-

There is something fundamental missing in this investigation and its conclusions. The prominence given to the death of Jesus within the gospel accounts and in the metaphors and motifs that seek to interpret this event suggests a much deeper measure of both the negative and the positive import of Golgotha. Only after Jesus' death can we understand the meaning of his life, but that death deals with the datum of sin as well as the datum of evil. As such, a question mark is placed over the perpetrators as well as over what is perpetrated. How stands a humanity capable of murdering its premier manifestation? How can we have "crucified God"?

This kind of contrast cannot be overlooked when we try to understand what constitutes the Easter experience of disciples then and now. Schillebeeckx's treatment of the conversion vision indeed gives a clue. The association of an act of repentance and faith with the disciples' role in the birth of the Christian community is a genuine insight, for it demonstrates how integral an about-face is to all discipleship, including the very first. But the seriousness of the bondage from which the captive is wrenched

---

sians (read in conjunction with Paul's soul-searching remarks of his captivity to self-serving impulse, *Christ*, p. 198) is interpreted as a response to current fatalism-cum-contrast experience (*Christ*, pp. 198-201); and suffering rather than sin is viewed as the refrain of Hebrews with the corresponding relativization of the priestly work as sacrifice for sin (*Christ*, pp. 282-92). (2) The analysis of grace in Paul is viewed in relationship to the belief in the grace of the Tanach. The two are treated, therefore, as two different ultimate commitments: some find salvation in Jesus and others in the Tanach. Missing here is the *substantive* issue of whether Law can be grace in the same sense as it is in the free gift of God's pardon in the initiative taken on Golgotha (*Christ*, pp. 122-24, 143-44). A similar failure to probe the sin-guilt issue appears in the treatment of Hebrews (in other respects, a searching inquiry). Attention is drawn to the way of Jewish sacrifice and the way of Jesus' sacrifice as two ultimate commitments, but the further questions of their meaning vis-à-vis the resolution of the fact and results of human defiance of God are not adequately dealt with (*Christ*, pp. 243-46, 251-58, 263-65, 288). (3) The two-and-a-half-page section, "Liberation from guilty failure: guilt and the forgiveness of sins," appears near the end of *Christ* (pp. 832-35). In it is declared, "Justification through grace in faith is therefore the nucleus of salvation from God in Christ, in the light of which all other aspects of liberation become comprehensible" (pp. 833-34). How convincing is this assertion, given its location as an addendum to the structure of Schillebeeckx's christological proposal as well as to this particular volume? We have attempted to show how a contrast experience based on the negativity of suffering is decisive for the structure of his thought. A closing declaration that presupposes another and larger framework does not change that. Furthermore, the characterization of guilt before God as "failure" obscures the titanic quality of human self-assertion as it is identified in the biblical narrative.

loose is conveyed far better by the *hubris* to which Paul testifies in his "conversion vision" — "Saul, Saul, why do you persecute me?" — than in the defection theme about which Schillebeeckx speculates. When our assault on the purposes of God — on God — is measured in these terms, more is required than the sense of forgiveness brought to being from memory of how Jesus related to "sinners and tax-gatherers." The juxtaposition of this compassion and the world's utter hatefulness toward it on the cross aggravates rather than answers the contrast question. How could that kind of forgiveness be, given our knowledge after the crucifixion of what we are capable of doing as humans to the holy love of God embodied in this Jesus? We are face to face here with a sin whose wage is death, a thrust that goes deep into the center of God's being and doing — the God *of holy* love whose righteousness holds us accountable even as the divine vulnerability receives the wound — and must be dealt with by a commensurate act. The *disclosure* of the divine love in Galilee makes us look for *a deed* in which that love is vindicated, and the alienation disclosed and enacted on Golgotha is overcome.

When the contrast experience is viewed from this angle — a "Good Friday experience" inseparable from an Easter experience — the positive as well as the negative significance given in the New Testament witness to Golgotha comes clear. A flood of metaphors and meanings — juridical, ritual, commercial, interpersonal — pours out to try to articulate the positive deed done on the cross (expressive of anterior intent) that somehow cancels out the negative one done at that very point (also expressive of anterior fact). Yes, these cultural borrowings are time-bound. And, when they are imported in pre-packaged fashion from their cultural setting, without christological modification and transformation, they portray a transaction in which an angry deity is mollified by another's sacrifice; a Judge "up there" exacts a sentence on an innocent "down here," etc. These caricatures tear asunder the Person from the Work, the love of God disclosed in the eschatological prophet from the deed done by the eschatological priest (2 Cor. 5:19 and John 3:16 from Eph. 2:13 and 1 Pet. 3:18). They do not know that it is the pain of God with which we have to do on Calvary when the Blessing takes into itself the Curse (Luther), when the Judge is judged — indeed not in a transaction "over our heads" but as the blood of God spilled in the blood of Jesus. The culture-relativity of ancient models and the confusions of countless pious exponents who falsely polarize the wrathful Father and the gentle Son are no excuse for abandoning the second-level ontological affirmations at their heart merely because modernity knows nothing against itself: in the death of Christ judgment is rendered on our sin, and mercy covers our guilt.

The question we have been asking in various ways is whether Schillebeeckx's christological approach can do justice to the contrast problematic when it is measured in its fullest dimensions, a Good Friday and Easter that deal with sin as well as suffering. Faith must address not only the misery that is and might well be, but also the "me generation" whose sins of omission and commission lie behind the prospect of a nuclear holocaust and/or the further degradation of God's poor.

We must ask the same question about the adequacy of the christological formulations as they address the datum of evil itself. Has the contrast experience in the Schillebeeckxian sense itself been gauged deeply enough? And, if it has not, what are the effects of this on the view of Christ developed by Schillebeeckx?

The sheer number of times that Schillebeeckx alludes to the experience of negativity and the poignancy of his descriptions argue for the seriousness with which he takes the factuality of evil. Yet, as with the datum of sin, so with the datum of evil, the crucifixion must raise for us (as it surely raised for the disciples) the sense of unspeakable agony. In making the case for a mid-career awareness by Jesus of the resistance to his program and possible historical frustration of it, some of the edge is taken off the sharpness of the cut made by his death. The attention given to Jesus' passion and death in the gospel narratives as well as in the metaphors and motifs of interpretation (especially those in the conflict and victory tradition) suggests that it was not only the appalling fact of human sin but also the peril to the very purposes of God that was being measured in the apostolic testimony. The cry of dereliction, whatever its critical status, is certainly evidence of this. The wages of evil as well as sin are death, the death of the very dream of God, or "death *in* God" as Moltmann expresses it. The destruction of this Nazarene whom the disciples believed lived in singular unity with God meant the defeat in some way of the One to whom he was mysteriously conjoined.

If evil was conceived to be as terminal in its consequences as this interpretation suggests, can the recovery from it have been an "assurance" grounded in recollections of Jesus' historical experiences and actions? Or could ascent from this pit be by way of a post-crucifixion "vision," albeit a veridical vision? As with Schillebeeckx's case for the disciples' sense of forgiveness, so here with their confidence in the vindication of Jesus and his cause, a turn is made to a "disclosure experience," either past or present. But sin taken in its full measure led to apostolic focus on a *deed* done, and one done in the same history in which our crime against God was committed. It would seem by analogy, and within another dimension of the universal contrast experience, that only a *deed* could contest the death done — and a deed also unambiguously of a piece with the history where death took place. The disclosure of God's faithful love in Jesus' Abba experience could not help but be remembered by the disciples as background to their Easter experience. But standing alone in the light of Jesus' subsequent death it would appear to create a problem rather than provide an answer to a Mary Magdalene wondering if it was all a grand illusion. A deed of such violent magnitude is incommensurate with the reports of disclosure, ours or another's. Only *another deed will do,* one in which a work is done on the same terrain in which defeat was administered, by the One who in solidarity with that death brings life.

We are, of course, speculating here, but doing it in the framework of Schillebeeckx's appeal for reasonable faith. That is, when all the facts of human experience, the depths of sin, and the depths of evil whose issue is death are taken into account, and when the texts are read with the help of the most careful scholarship, what is the more reasonable explanation of the birth of the disciples' Easter faith? And what are the warrants for the character of our own Easter faith? Indeed, that faith comes by grace, not by warrants, but it cannot fly in the face of them as "mystification." Our route into those issues has been by way of the contrast experience, and the response to it is from within our faith community. We turn finally to the allied issue of the relation of our "faith-motivated experiences" to their interpretations.

Experience and Interpretation: Possibilities and Problems

Already noted are what appear to be two conflicting theories on the relation of experience to interpretation in Schillebeeckx's christological experiment. We will try to make the case here that Schillebeeckx's use of the first eliminates features of the norm for christological proposals, and that a consistent application of the second undercuts his effort to establish a standard for adjudicating claims of christological interpretations.

Theory One

One of Schillebeeckx's significant contributions to systematic theology today is the attention he gives to exegesis. His intense struggle with the texts and his meticulous review of the work of biblical scholarship will surely have an effect on the way theology is done in the years ahead. In particular, his presentation of materials from the New Quest, as they are supportive of his thesis about the importance of the figure of Jesus both in understanding early christological confession and in reformulating it for our own time, is an impressive one.

Touching the question of experience-interpretation, Schillebeeckx's "Jesus work" comes to this: The memory of the historical Jesus — his preaching of the Reign of God, the reality and effects of his Abba experience, his relationships to the outcast and marginalized — is enshrined in the varied christological confessions of the primitive communities, and the same must be true of any confessions we make of Jesus today in the context of our own peculiar issues and models. Using the framework of his earlier eucharistic analysis, there are "second-level" beliefs that are inseparable from an authentic Jesus encounter which must be preserved in any third-level interpretations. This means that, as Schillebeeckx goes about the task of restating the claim that "salvation comes through Jesus from God" (the formal norm), he takes meaningful contemporary visions and idiom — "emancipation" — and fashions them according to the historical Jesus reference points (the material norm). Therefore, the latter function as the "real presence" motifs do in the eucharistic exploration. ("*Conversio*" in the latter parallels the "conversion vision" in the former.)

The recovery of the place of the historical Jesus in Christology and objective soteriology and its support by methodical scholarship are a healthy corrective to kerygmatic and existentialist understandings and traditional formulations that either ignored or obscured the role of the ministry of Jesus. We are in Schillebeeckx's debt for his massive experiment in retrieval. However, the recovery as it is argued theologically by Schillebeeckx is an invitation to another kind of reductionism. By lifting up the career of Jesus as determinative of christological confession, descriptively and normatively, and by shifting to the position of third-level interpretation the explicit apostolic testimony to the death and resurrection of Jesus — apt for its time but not normative for ours — a dubious move has been made. Indeed, it has been made in order to correct earlier excisions of the historical reality of

Jesus, to connect with contemporary human-oriented sensibilities, to speak to the contrast problematic as perceived by this culture and in response to the historicist premises of modernity. But the price paid is both an obscuring of the importance of the cross and resurrection in the apostolic testimony to Christ as it related to the deeper aspects of the contrast problematic just discussed, and the elimination of fundamental refrains about the meaning of the cross and resurrection in the apostolic testimony that are themselves constitutive of any subsequent christological reformulation. The New Testament witnesses to a deed and disclosure of God in the *life and ministry* of Jesus normative for Christian belief, a deed and disclosure of God in *the death* of Jesus normative for Christian belief, and a deed and disclosure of God in the *resurrection* of Jesus normative for Christian belief. Together they constitute the point of adjudication for christological and soteriological proposals and are not collapsible into one or another of their components. All these configurations as events and their "second-level" premises are reference points for third-level interpretations.

There are two important assumptions behind this criticism of Schillebeeckx's reduction of the christological norm to the career of Jesus. First is a conception of revelation that includes the apostolic testimony to the cross and resurrection as well as the life and ministry of Jesus as authoritative for theological formulation. Second is a way into the motifs that form this structure through the threefold-office formula given extensive articulation in the Reformation churches but present also functionally in Roman Catholic and Eastern Orthodox traditions. By this standard, Schillebeeckx's brilliant detective work on the eschatological prophet gives empirical force to the prophetic office, while his mesmerism by this theme weakens his ability to give proper attention to the priestly and royal offices. In passing, it should be said that the use of the *munus triplex* as an instrument for discerning soteriological motifs integral to Scripture and tradition is not wed to its culturally contingent language and lore: what a prophet, priest, and king were and did can be captured today in our own figures of visionary, vicarious sufferer, and liberator.

Theory Two

If the inseparability of experience and interpretation means that our confrontation of testimony from the past is so shaped by interpretative concepts that the claims of another age are not accessible to us in the way they were intended, then there are serious consequences for any New Quest and any christological program based upon it. It is true that Schillebeeckx makes provision for the presumed chasm of interpretation between our time and another's experientially: by existential encounter within our own context of issues and idiom we meet the same Jesus who addressed the early communities through their particularities. Jesus comes to us only in the mode of engagement. However, we are talking here not about how the Spirit *attests to* faith, but how theologians *test* interpretations. If our historically contingent understanding cannot get out of its interpretive framework to view the Jesus affair as it was, how can we use the results of scholarship that make claims, albeit modest, about the lineaments of Jesus' message, relationships, and Abba experience to test our proposals?

Our historical conditioning is regularly visible when systematicians and New Testament scholars make New Quest as well as Old Quest assertions about Jesus. The Jesus of Hans Küng often looks like a reformer taking on the local ecclesiastical establishment. But the fact that we succumb regularly to acculturation is different from making historical relativity a plank in one's hermeneutical platform. This is what Schillebeeckx seems to be saying in many passages on the subject of the relationship of experience to interpretation. However, the fact that there is another theory alongside of it, one that functions in his efforts at Jesus' reconstruction, suggests the impossibility of this program and even the incoherence of the idea. A passage from Marx and Engels should put us on notice to this. In the *Manifesto* these astute observers of the ideological character of bourgeois thought — and thus an inseparability of interpretation from experience (social-economic existence) that would prevent any detached universal truth claims — tell us:

> When the class struggle nears the decisive hour . . . a small section of the ruling class cuts itself adrift, and joins the revolutionary class. . . . a portion of the bourgeoisie go over to the proletariat, and in particular, a portion of the bourgeois ideologists, who have raised themselves to the level of comprehending theoretically the historical movement as a whole.[75]

75. Karl Marx and Friedrich Engels, "Manifesto of the Communist Party," in *Marx and Engels: Basic Writings on Politics and Philosophy,* ed. Lewis S. Feuer (Garden City, N.Y.: Doubleday/Anchor Books, 1959), p. 17.

Certain interesting exemptions such as this are always made to "the hermeneutics of suspicion" by its exponents. The most familiar examples are the relativists who confidently set forth their thesis, the presupposition of which denies what is asserted. Sauce for the goose is sauce for the gander. Let Schillebeeckx pursue his inquiry after stable points for christological confession as in theory one. And let others who believe that the perennials encompass priestly and royal as well as prophetic reference points seek to make their case. The veto of such efforts by the absolutists of interpretive relativity cannot be heard very well over the laughter. Finally, it is the way one's firm commitments are held, with openness to development, enrichment, and correction, with the capacity to speak the truth in love, that counts in the forum of ideas and the arena of competing values. An ardent loyalty to the absolute of historical relativity — the transiency of interpretive schemes in our context here — is no guarantee of that, as the history of its own orthodoxies shows. Teachability and vulnerability are gifts of grace, ones that have something to do also with what can be learned from the Work of Jesus in Galilee, at Calvary, and on Easter morning.

CHAPTER 11

The Crucified Christ[1]

We return to Bonhoeffer's question. What is the meaning of the cross
for us today? The answer will require attention to both Christian
tradition and our contemporary experience. Varying historical circumstances drew from the Christian community different metaphors to interpret the cross. These figures in turn became elaborated into theories of the
Work of Christ. Thus a time of feudal structures with honor accorded by
vassal to lord, and an accompanying penitential system, evoked the satisfaction imagery and formulations of Anselm; a period of widespread anxiety about demons and the debilitations of finitude elicited patristic descriptions of the sword of the cross that felled evil spirits, and a death on
Calvary (supported by a Bethlehem evening and an Easter morning) that
brought life and immortality; the rising nationalisms of the sixteenth and
seventeenth centuries with their patterns of law and justice, and an allied
individualism with its pangs of personal culpability, brought into prominence the law-court metaphor and penal theory. The biblical imagery on
which these interpretations drew remains for us the source and corrective

1. As at the beginning of this volume a start-up essay on Christology appeared (Chapter
2), showing signs of an earlier "today," so in this final section is included a stage on the journey of Christ from that earlier era with its liberation/oppression and vision/reality motifs,
their discontinuities but also continuities with the idiom and issues of the early twenty-first
century.

for any subsequent attempts at communication. But we must do our own listening for, and speaking in, the idiom of this day, as other metaphor-makers did in theirs.

We return to our earlier characterization of our late twentieth and early twenty-first century "today" as a time of *vision and reality,* light and darkness. An array of movements for freedom and peace, economic plenty, ecological sanity, and even biological utopia have stirred long-dormant hopes. The formative *visual* media have combined with these *visionary* impulses to give power to the image of "vision." But each forward thrust meets formidable resistance, every hope seems to be imperiled. Our culture has dreamed great dreams, yet has seen them shattered by the imperial self in which it places such confidence, and by demonic powers it had believed to be long since exorcized. Society strains to keep its visions alive, yet intractable realities threaten it with despair. This perception of a chiaroscuro world is our metaphor. It is rooted deeply in the Christian tradition as well as in cultural sensibility. We shall attempt to interpret the meaning of Golgotha in terms of it.

Liberation and Reconciliation

The cross is the nodal point of a Work of Christ that stretches out in two directions, back through the life and career of Jesus and forward into the resurrection and "kingly rule." A full treatment of the Work would have to give careful attention to all the deeds and words of Jesus. Yet in this climacteric is intensified and summarized all that went before and came after. In examining the meaning of the cross we shall be traveling constantly on the boundaries of past and future, and drawing out their implications and influence.

The Work of Christ in the theological tradition is the "Atonement." We understand this to mean, "the state of being or becoming 'at one,' reconciled with someone else."[2] The reconciling act on the cross is an at-one-ment of the alienated. As has been traditionally asserted, the basic rift to be overcome is that between God and the creature with the human face who has savaged the divine purposes. But Atonement also includes "making

2. Robert Paul, *The Atonement and the Sacraments* (Nashville: Abingdon Press, 1960), p. 20.

peace" within the human community, the breaking down of "the dividing wall of hostility" between estranged brothers and sisters (Eph. 2:13, 16).[3] And in the eschatological framework to be developed in conjunction with the theme of vision, we view Atonement on a larger canvas as the coming together of *all* things formerly alienated: powers as well as persons, nature as well as history, the cosmos as well as humanity. Here is the work of a "cosmic Christ" who brings a "shalom" in which God is all, and in all.[4]

A reconciliation that is authentic is not the uneasy peace of insurgents now rendered docile by superior firepower. It is the opposite — slaves emancipated and prisoners released, captives liberated from oppression, who are now *free* to be together. Reconciliation, therefore, includes liberation. This note has been muted in too many traditional interpretations of Atonement. The consequence has been the emergence of christological correctives that rightly stress liberation, but tend in turn to polarize it with reconciliation. Reconciliation without liberation is crippled. Liberation without reconciliation is aborted.

The final coming together of all things in freedom and peace is the Goal toward which history moves in the Christian drama. The Atonement is that point in the pilgrimage at which the Not Yet of the vision intersects reality, announcing the ultimate convergence of vision and reality.

Incarnation and Atonement

What takes place in the Atonement can only be understood from the perspective of the Incarnation; the Person is inseparable from the Work. While both the status and role of Christ can be explored independently, the assumptions of each are buried so deeply in the other that the pursuit of the meaning of the cross cannot be carried on without understanding

3. All biblical references for this chapter are from the New English Bible unless otherwise indicated.

4. For a treatment of the New Testament data see George Caird, *Principalities and Powers* (Oxford: Clarendon, 1956), and R. Leivestad, *Christ the Conqueror* (London: SPCK, 1954). For translation and application of these themes in contemporary terms, see William Stringfellow, *An Ethic for Christians and Other Aliens in a Strange Land* (Waco, Tex.: Word Books, 1973); Hendrikus Berkhof, *Christ with Powers* (Scottdale, Pa.: Judson Press, 1962); Albert van den Heuvel, *These Rebellious Powers* (New York: Friendship Press, 1965); and Allan Galloway, *The Cosmic Christ* (London: Nisbet, 1951).

its incarnational presuppositions. Hence this brief preliminary comment on the Person of Christ.

The Logos, the cosmological organizing principle in a variety of ancient philosophies (middle Platonic, Stoic, Gnostic, Philonic) and the Wisdom motif in one strand of Hebrew tradition, became an important factor in early Christian apologetic, as the Word of God.[5] We interpret it here, in terms of the visionary and visual media motifs of our own epoch, as the Vision of God (not our vision of God, but God's vision of us). Consonant with the psychological analogies of Augustine, the Trinity can be portrayed as Envisioner, Vision, and Power.[6] "In the beginning was the Vision, and the Vision was with God, and the Vision was God. . . ."

The Vision of God is the eternal purpose and divine resolve of Shalom. It is the will for communion with a partner, Love expressive in mutuality. The context of Shalom is sketched by the seers of the Vision, the prophets who pointed toward the liberation and reconciliation of all things: the wolf together with the lamb, swords beaten into plowshares, the child with its hand over the asp's nest, each under his or her own vine and fig tree, the coming of justice and peace among humanity, nature, and God.[7]

The definition of Shalom comes in the history of Israel in the midst of peril to that Vision. While a full understanding of the scale of the assault by human sin and the powers of Evil awaits the cross itself, the struggle and suffering of Shalom is pointed to in the despairs and hopes of the prophetic tradition, and finally by the Messianic expectations. How shall the resolve of God ultimately deal with the rebellion of the creature? The Christian response to this dilemma begins with the incarnation. "The Vision became flesh and lived among us." The Presence is in our midst to accomplish its purposes. In the words of the creed: "Who for us and our salvation came down from heaven and was incarnate by the Virgin Mary. . . ." The Person of Christ, as the hypostatic union of the Logos with the real

---

5. A careful examination of the Greek and Hebrew strands is found in C. H. Dodd, *The Interpretation of the Fourth Gospel* (Cambridge: Cambridge University Press, 1963), pp. 263-85.

6. Cf. Augustine, *De Trinitate,* VII, 10; IX, 2, 12; XV, 7, 21-23.

7. The metaphor of vision so interpreted is an embracing one covering the natural, institutional, personal, and theological spheres. For an important discussion of the typology of religious metaphor — "macrocosmic, mesocosmic, and microcosmic" — see James Luther Adams, "Root Metaphors in Religious Social Thought," Presidential Address, American Theological Society, April 1973.

humanity of Jesus, is the organ for the Work of liberation and reconciliation. The stage is set in the Incarnation for the Atonement and its central act, the cross. To this final encounter we now turn, seeking to do justice to its dimensions in the categories of vision and reality, light and darkness.

Disclosure

The most popular image for interpreting the Atonement in the late patristic period was that of fishhook and bait.[8] Today it is the traditional figure on which most scorn is heaped. While there are different versions of the imagery, there are recurring accents within them. They provide us with a framework for understanding what we shall call the Work of Disclosure. Included are: 1) The purity of the human Jesus which entices the prey, the Devil, from its undersea haunts. 2) The Adversary devouring Jesus, the "bait." 3) The contact made by the Devil with God by virtue of the divine nature hidden in the human nature of Jesus' innocent humanity. 4) The divinity concealed in the humanity conquers the Devil. We shall use the first three of these points as a structure for explicating the Work of Disclosure, and the fourth as an introduction to the subsequent Work of Eclipse, attempting a "collation of images" (Jaroslav Pelikan).

The Purity of the Human Jesus: A Model of Shalom

The man Jesus was what we are called to be. While the race turned away from the beckoning of God toward the vision of Shalom, this human being oriented his life toward the Light. In both word and deed he pointed to and embodied the divine intention of liberation and reconciliation. While we, Adam, bend inward in stubborn self-serving, the Second Adam turns outward in love to his Father and neighbor. Where we are creatures of insurrection, he trusted God and pursued the divine purposes. This sturdiness of intent and conduct is the "active obedience" of Christ. Such faithfulness

---

8. Important expositions include John of Damascus, Gregory of Nyssa, Rufinus, and Gregory the Great. A key passage is found in Gregory of Nyssa's "An Address on Religious Instruction" (also known as the "Catechetical Oration"), chapters 22-26, in *Christology of the Later Fathers*, ed. Edward R. Hardy and Cyril C. Richardson (London: Westminster Press, 1968), pp. 298-304.

marks Jesus as truly human, in the normative sense of fulfilling the hope of God for the covenant partner (as well as being truly human in the descriptive sense of sharing our common lot).

In describing the fulfilled humanity of Jesus, we have, by implication, traced its history well back behind the cross into the Galilean life and ministry. The foundation is laid in the career of Jesus for the culminating act of self-sacrifice on Calvary. A full treatment of the Work of Disclosure as a manifestation of our intended true humanity would take us into an exploration of the life of Christ and his message about the Kingdom of God. Here, however, our focus is on the cross. But there is no discontinuity, for it merges with a life of obedience to the Vision and brings it to its highest expression. Golgotha reveals a faithfulness to Shalom that is ready to "humble itself" and be "obedient to death."

The Devouring of the Bait: The Assault on Shalom

There are intertwined themes in the patristic descriptions of the approach of the Devil to this "choice morsel." First, the Adversary seeks to destroy the perfection set down in front of him. Second, Behemoth is drawn from his underwater hiding place to execute this intention. Third, he is emboldened to do so because the helpless flesh of Jesus' humanity poses no apparent threat. These are suggestive motifs that invite restatement in contemporary terms. The Fathers grasped the biblical truth that the authenticity of Jesus' life calls into radical question our own inauthenticity. Hate cannot bear the sight of selflessness. It must strike out at it. Love heaps "live coals" on its enemies (Rom. 12:20). Shalom is an embarrassment to humanity, prompting it to destroy what stands in judgment upon it.

The oldest tradition interpreting the death of Jesus sounds this note.[9] Sometimes it was put in terms of the world's hostility to the prophet. "O Jerusalem, Jerusalem, you kill the prophets, you stone the messengers God has sent you!" (Luke 13:34). Those who had seen the Vision and call the people to Shalom are an unwelcome presence that must be put away. And when the Vision is not only announced but embodied, the angriest attack of all is evoked. Hence the response of the vinedressers to the final emissary. "The

9. Wolfhart Pannenberg, *Jesus — God and Man*, trans. L. Wilkins and D. Priebe (Philadelphia: Westminster Press, 1968), pp. 246-47.

only one left to send was the man's own dear son. . . ." And the sequel, "Come let us kill him and the vineyard will be ours!" (Mark 12:7 TEV).

While the wrath of the people against the prophet is stressed in these passages, the patristic authors emphasize the role of "the Devil" as antagonist. This accent is related to the cultural climate of demon-consciousness and an attempt to exegete the ransom passages in the New Testament. It is also a perception of the reality of that surd of evil in the universe which cannot be neatly traced to the perversity of the human will. Following Pauline thought on the *exousiai,* and a strand of contemporary interpretation, we view the demonic as corrupted "principalities and powers." They express themselves in nature and history, in the depths of the self in the structure of society. At the crucifixion they are at work in the institutions of political, military, and ecclesiastical power, and in the captivity of the people to the idols and passions of the hour. The powers and principalities are created by God as good, capable of playing a role in the divine economy. But like humanity they have fallen and now exist as enemies of Shalom. The obedience of Jesus stands as their accuser. Thus both human-being-in-sin and the powers-in-evil (which we shall describe as Evil) share complicity in Golgotha.

An era like ours, characterized by both great visions and powerful forces seeking to thwart them, can grasp something of the realism of the cross. Moreover, the ravages of the twentieth century have taught us to look for attack from two quarters: the perennial malevolence in the human heart, and structures and processes of evil. The ferocity of the assailants seems to be in direct proportion to the nobility of the visions. Those that "have a dream" and lead movements of liberation and reconciliation draw the most intense fire.[10] Against this background the outline of the cross on which shalom itself dies can be seen with clarity.

In the lunge toward the bait the Fathers asserted that the Enemy was brought out of his lair. We take this to mean that the full strength of the forces inimical to the divine intention came into view. This aspect of the Work of Disclosure is an exposure of the depths of sin and Evil that could not heretofore have been known. But this unveiling is more than noetic. It brings into actuality what before existed only in potentiality. The cross shows us of what the human heart is capable. Our "malignant nature never appeared so much in its proper colors, as it did in the act of murdering the

---

10. As in the murder of Martin Luther King Jr.

Son of God."[11] Here the ultimate arrogance is unmasked. "We are exposed and made known and have to acknowledge ourselves as the proud creatures who ourselves want to be god and lord. . . ."[12] The Calvinist strain in theology has sought vigorously to sensitize the Christian conscience to this aspect of the crucifixion. "Only at the Cross of Christ does man see fully what it is that separates him from God. . . . Nowhere else does the inviolable holiness of God, the impossibility of overlooking the guilt of man stand out more plainly."[13]

The cross that exposes our lethal capabilities performs more than the function of consciousness-raising about personal guilt. A new fact has appeared in human history and a new relationship entered upon. Human willfulness and the authorities of this world never before had the truly human within their reach. There had never been such a prize to garner, nor a prey that so enraged its hunter. In the encounter on Calvary, new resources of cunning and animosity were brought into play. The full reality of sin and Evil came both into action and into view.

The ancient Church believed that the Devil was emboldened to act because of the helplessness of the humanity of Christ. In this imagery is the recognition that the organ of human nature is integral to the Work of liberation and reconciliation. The Incarnation is basic to the Atonement. And in this case it seems that the battle with the powers of Darkness was entered upon by an enfleshed Love truly of a piece with this world. Further, as Gregory of Nyssa argues, Evil would not be drawn into engagement unless it felt secure in its reach, the naked power of God being hidden in a seemingly harmless human nature.

Taken together, these two points comprise an Atonement insight of continuing validity: it is on the plane of history that God must meet and deal with the foe, for here is where the center of resistance to the divine purposes is to be found. The Work of liberation and reconciliation takes place in the arena from which the attack is launched against the Divine vision. It was the radical obedience of the historical Jesus that provoked the radical disobedience of human-beings-in-sin and the powers-in-evil, thus

11. Jonathan Edwards, *The Works of President Edwards,* vol. 8 (London: James Black & Sons, 1817), p. 482.

12. Karl Barth, *Church Dogmatics,* IV/1, trans. G. W. Bromiley (Edinburgh: T. & T. Clark, 1965), p. 515.

13. Emil Brunner, *The Mediator,* trans. Olive Wyon (Philadelphia: Westminster Press, 1947), p. 453.

exposing the depths of alienation. Here in our world of time and space the Enemy took up its position and showed its colors. On this terrain the battle is to be undertaken.

The Divine in the Human: Contact

Consonant with a full doctrine of the Incarnation, the patristic thinkers declared that Leviathan's grasp at the humanity of Jesus brought it unknowingly into contact with the divine nature as well. While the Fathers described this impact without further ado as the disastrous end of a surprised Adversary, we pause to explore an implication that did not bulk large in patristic commentary but does touch upon an important aspect of the reinterpretation here pursued. The Fathers' reticence on this point can be traced in large part to philosophical notions of divine impassibility drawn from Greek culture that stood in the way of developing a crucial Atonement theme.[14]

The scope of the assault that takes place on the cross is grasped only when we understand that it drives to the core of the divine being itself. With characteristically bold paradox Luther declares, "In his nature God cannot die. But now that God and man are united in one person, when the man dies, that is rightly called the death of God, for he is in one thing or person with God."[15] In *The Crucified God*, Moltmann wrestles with this divine vulnerability, drawing on trinitarian motifs. It is God the Son in unity with the historical Jesus who sustains the shock waves of the powers of Darkness. This is not the death *of* God but rather "death *in* God."

> If this divine nature in the person of the eternal Son of God is the center which creates a person in Christ, then it too suffered and died.[16]

---

14. The survey of J. K. Mozley is a good introduction: *The Impassibility of God* (Cambridge: Cambridge University Press, 1926). See also Berkouwer's discussion of the same in *The Work of Christ*, trans. Cornelius Lambregtse (Grand Rapids: Eerdmans, 1965), pp. 264-88.

15. Luther, WA 50:590, 10, cited in Jürgen Moltmann, *The Crucified God*, trans. R. A. Wilson and John Bowden (London: SCM Press, 1974).

16. Moltmann, *The Crucified God*, p. 234. See also Barth, *Church Dogmatics*, IV/1, pp. 215, 216, 277.

On Calvary the divine heart was broken.

An understanding of the second Person of the Trinity as the Vision of God puts this aspect of the Work of Disclosure on the cross in its starkest terms. The effect of the attack on Jesus is the destruction in the Godhead of the Vision itself. On the cross the Hope of God is crushed. The Dream of Shalom in which humanity and the powers of the cosmos freely join their Creator in a liberated and reconciled creation is shattered. The invitation of Deity to this Homeland is rejected. The Son of God is killed and with this death there passes away the hope of the coming together of all things on the basis of the primal overture. This is the profoundest horror of the cross, that the hate of the world reaches into the depths of God. The Enemy penetrates the inner recesses of the Deity as these have been rendered vulnerable by the entry of God into history. Thus Golgotha stretches from a lonely hill outside Jerusalem to "the cross in the heart of God."

The cross tells us how far antagonists are prepared to go to destroy the Vision and its Envisioner, thus exposing the depths of the world's enmity. At the same time, this event reveals undisclosed depths in the divine life and how far God is willing to go to meet the assailants. How the hurt of the cross itself becomes the way of healing takes us from the Work of Disclosure to the companion themes of the Atonement.

Eclipse

The climax of the book and bait analogy is "catching the fish." The divinity concealed in the humanity conquers the Devil. At the very moment that death seems to have overwhelmed Christ, the enemy is met and defeated.

This imagery conveys a fundamental meaning of the cross: the forces inimical to the divine will are here met by God who brings victory out of defeat. In Pauline thought, and in other strands of the New Testament interpretation, human-beings-in-sin and the powers of Evil are annihilated on Calvary. On the one hand, the old Adam was put away: "I have been crucified with Christ . . ." (Gal. 2:19); "one man died for all and therefore all mankind has died" (2 Cor. 5:14).[17] On the other hand, "On that cross he discarded the cosmic powers and authorities like a garment; he made a

17. See also Col. 3:3; Gal. 2:20; 6:14; Rom. 6:5-6.

public spectacle of them and led them as captives in his triumphal procession" (Col. 2:15).[18]

The "negative" work of God on the cross has been given special attention by Karl Barth. He forcefully describes the "No" that God says to humanity-in-sin.

> In His person He has delivered up us sinners and sin itself to destruction. He has removed us sinners and sin, negated us, canceled us out. . . . Order is created not by any setting aside of sins, but by that of the sinner himself . . . if the faithfulness of God and the love of God towards him in Jesus Christ is to attain its goal, it had in fact to have the form of the consuming fire of his wrath. Burning down to the very foundation, consuming and destroying the man himself who had become the enemy of God.[19]

While Barth has concentrated on the death of a corrupt humanity, a clear word has to be spoken as well about the fate of the principalities and powers, those structures and processes of history and nature that imperil Shalom. Scandinavian theology has brooded over the powers of Evil and their relationship to the cross.[20] Gustaf Aulen brought the "classic view" of Atonement into the foreground of theological discussion at a time when demonic structures of political powers were casting their shadow over Europe.[21] And Leivestad has skillfully explored the biblical basis of the Atonement:

> It is not of great importance whether we imagine a humiliating degradation of the powers, whereby their mantles and other insignia are taken from them, or a military conquest at which they are deprived of their weapons by the conquerors. The important thing is that the crucifixion of Jesus is, in one way or the other, depicted as a divine triumph over the cosmic powers.[22]

---

18. See also Heb. 2:14 and Eph. 2:16.

19. Barth, *Church Dogmatics*, IV/1, pp. 253, 296.

20. Barth also deals with the defeat of "the powers" in IV/1, p. 254, for example, and in his *Letter to Great Britain from Switzerland* (London: Sheldon Press, 1941), but takes issue with Wingren and others on the emphasis upon them. See Karl Barth's *Table Talk*, recorded and edited by John Godsey (Richmond: John Knox, 1962), pp. 16-17.

21. Gustaf Aulen, *Christus Victor*, trans. A. G. Hebert (New York: Macmillan, 1951).

22. Leivestad, *Christ the Conqueror*, p. 104.

Can the biblical declarations of the end of human-beings-in-sin and the powers of Evil be meaningfully translated into the framework of vision and reality? We have spoken of the assault of Jesus that was ultimately felt in the depths of the divine being. This death in God of the Vision now means that there is no future for the invited covenant partners. The passing of the divine Hope spells an end for its participants. When this scenario was rejected there went with it the original players. While the fallen world empirically continues, it has been displaced from the Not Yet that was to have been its intended fulfillment. It no longer exists in the purposes of God, having died to the Future. Its successful attack on the Hope of God was, therefore, also an act of self-destruction.

While the enemy dies, it is the gibbet of Jesus Christ on which this obituary is written. Our Adamic future went into oblivion, but the experience of this death fell upon Another. "He who was just suffered for the unjust" (1 Pet. 3:18).[23] We who are still alive were separated from our destiny, but it is the Son of God who took the consequences of our rebellion into himself. We lost our future, but the execution of that loss was carried out on the cross of Christ. Here is the vicarious act that was so central to the New Testament reading of the cross. And this is the theme pursued determinedly by sacrificial, penal, and satisfaction theories of the Atonement. Yet the traditional renderings of the theme in these theories not infrequently distort it or do an injustice to some other aspect of Christian faith. And the metaphors from which the theories are developed — ritual sacrifice, punitive forensic codes, and feudal practice — no longer have clear cultural resonance. We shall attempt to capture the theme of exchange described in a variety of ways in the New Testament, and elaborated by subsequent theories, in the idiom of vision and reality, and also make active use of the incarnational presuppositions of this aspect of the Atonement.[24]

The passing away of the future of sin and Evil takes place not only on a hill outside an ancient city, but also in a cross set in God's heart. Here is where the Vision fades. Thus the final cost of our judgment is borne within

23. See also Rom. 4:25; 5:6; 8:3; John 10:15; 1 Cor. 15:13; 2 Cor. 5:21; Col. 1:21-22; 2:14; Gal. 3:13; Eph. 1:7; 5:2; Heb. 2:9; 9:28; 1 Pet. 1:19; 2:22-24; Titus 2:14.

24. Assumed here are several levels of theological discourse about the cross: (1) the event interpreted in an elemental way as a chapter in the Christian story — thus "Jesus died for our sins . . ." and "God so loved the world that he gave . . ."; (2) the event as translated into a metaphor that connects with our experience; (3) the metaphor elaborated into a theory. Metaphors are illuminated by, and theories are tested by, the Storyline.

the divine being. The work of the Atonement is through and through God's own work, as in the *locus classicus* of this incarnational premise. "God was in Christ reconciling . . ." (2 Cor. 5:19). It was the "love of God in Jesus Christ" (Rom. 8:39) that initiated and underwent the atoning action.[25] Earlier we spoke about this pain as the measure of the malignancy of the world. Now we view the same event from another perspective as a measure of the lengths God is willing to go to in pursuit of Shalom. In the one case, the cross demonstrates what is done *to* God, in the other what is done *by* God. The "passive" aspect discloses the grief caused by the titanic assault of sin and Evil; the "active" aspect is the agony in God that takes the death we deserve. The darkness at the center of Deity is the vicarious suffering that absorbs the consequences of our guilt. As Donald Baillie expresses it,

> The Lamb of God that taketh away the sins of the world is none other than the eternal Word, the eternal God by whom all things were made. . . . The expiation is made in the heart and life of God Himself.[26]

Or again in the words of J. S. Whale, "God vindicates his own law by accepting and bearing the penalty in his own heart."[27] Moltmann's searching reflection on the suffering of God returns time and again to the trinitarian setting in which it must be understood.

> The Father who abandons him and delivers him up suffers the death of the Son in the infinite grief of love. We cannot say here in patripassian terms that the Father also suffered and died. The suffering and dying of the Son forsaken by the Father, is a different kind of suffering from the suffering of the Father in the death of the Son. The grief of the Father is as important as the death of the son. . . . If God has constituted himself as the Father of Jesus Christ, then he also suffers the death of his Fatherhood in the death of the Son.[28]

25. See also Rom. 3:24-26; 8:31-32; Gal. 1:4.

26. Donald M. Baillie, *God Was in Christ* (New York: Scribner, 1980), p. 178.

27. J. S. Whale, *Victor and Victim* (Cambridge: Cambridge University Press, 1960), p. 75. See also Brunner, *The Mediator*, pp. 483f., and Carl Braaten, *The Future of God* (New York: Harper & Row, 1969), pp. 82-108. On the contrast between a "fiat" deity and the divine self-oblation, see Aulen, *Christus Victor*, p. 53.

28. Moltmann, *The Crucified God*, p. 243.

In all these ruminations there is a common note: a death in God means the suffering of God. This passage signifies that it is God who ultimately pays the price for our grievous act. The cost of it, the death of the future of the old foes, is experienced as an eclipse in God of the primordial Light.

The development of this crucial dimension of the Atonement as an act of God on the cross has led some interpreters to a fatal misstep. As they underscore the Divine action on Calvary, the human action becomes lost from view. This is yet another failure to take seriously the incarnational presuppositions of Atonement. As Berkouwer has argued, the cross is a "historical act" and to treat it otherwise is to succumb to Docetism. Thus many interpretations of divine suffering locate the passion so exclusively within the Godhead that Golgotha becomes superfluous except as a sign of a movement within Deity. "The Church objected to 'theopaschitism' because it kept speaking of 'God himself' whereas Scripture speaks of Jesus Christ, the Word incarnate."[29] The crucifixion happens in, and is chosen by, the Person of Christ in its fullness, humanity as well as divinity (1 Tim. 2:5).

The objective theories of the Atonement have stressed the role of the humanity of Jesus in the atoning work. Thus sacrificial metaphors have been used portraying a blood offering integral to securing the divine mercy; forensic images have been interpreted to mean that Jesus suffered in our place the retribution exacted by a court of law; and the satisfaction theory views Christ's supererogatory action toward an offended divine honor as enabling release from the just recompense of the Sovereign. While in each case there is a corollary declaration that the process of sacrifice, substitution, or satisfaction was initiated by God, the drift of the theories emerging historically from the metaphors has been toward both the understatement of this theme and the virtual absence of its crucial companion affirmation that "God was in Christ." This discontinuity between the humanity of Christ and the incarnate God gives rise to both a theology and piety the logic of which is finally expressed in the exclamation of the convert won by fervent but foreshortened penal preaching: "I love Jesus, but I hate God."[30] While the action of Jesus is fundamental to the meaning of the cross, his "obedience unto death" was not an upsurge within the human arena whose good deed won the mercy of God (a works-righteousness view). As the Incarnation took place out of the divine pre-

---

29. Berkouwer, *The Work of Christ*, p. 280.
30. William Wolf, *No Cross, No Crown* (Garden City, N.Y.: Doubleday, 1957), p. 112.

venience and with the divine presence, so the Atonement is a drama of the God at work in, with, and under the real human choices that brought Jesus to Golgotha. As the initiative was God's at the beginning, so at the end the nails driven into Jesus reached into God. A view of the Atonement grounded in the christological paradox will neither fall prey to the *"Umstimmung"* that obscures the source in and cost to God,[31] nor will it ignore the crucial reality of the humanity of Jesus by treating it simply as a window through which we look at supernatural mysteries. Instead there are integrity and simultaneity of actions that correspond to the antinomies of Bethlehem, and are reflected as well in the unity-in-duality of other Christian doctrines (church, sacraments, faith, etc.). While this mystery cannot be finally penetrated, its dimensions can be explored. And concepts of Atonement that fail to honor the full presence of either the divine or human in the vicarious work must be called to account.

In all that has been said so far about the destruction of the future of a fallen creation, and the pain undergone in that rejection by the God who was in Christ, there is implicit an assumption about the divine holiness. The mercy of a holy God toward treacherous partners is not an amiable indulgence. Light does not tolerate Darkness. Those who weaken the understanding of the Atonement by ignoring the accountability of the marauder must fall under the famous stricture of Anselm, "you have not as yet estimated the great burden of sin."[32] One of the contributions of P. T. Forsyth to a contemporary interpretation of the Atonement is his insistence on this point. It is related to his commitment to the "moralizing of dogma" and the communication of the Christian faith to a society becoming sensitized to the mandates of social justice. God

> could will nothing against his holy nature, and he could not abolish the judgment bound up with it. Nothing in the compass of the divine nature could enable him to abolish a moral law, the law of holiness. That would be tampering with his own soul. It has to be dealt with. Is the law of God more loose than the law of society? Can it be taken liberties with, played with, and put aside even at the impulse of love? How little we should come to think of God's love if that were possible![33]

31. Berkouwer, *The Work of Christ*, pp. 258ff.

32. Anselm, *Cur Deus Homo*, XXI.

33. P. T. Forsyth, *The Work of Christ* (London: Collins, 1965), p. 107. Also *The Cruciality of the Cross* (London: Independent Press, 1948), passim.

Or in the terse comment of Whale, "Forgiveness is neither intelligible nor credible unless justice is vindicated and guilt confirmed."[34] God's mercy is not cheap grace. It is paid for dearly by suffering and death. The future is really ended for sin and Evil. And that closure comes in the darkness that descends on God. The cost is paid through Jesus on the cross and by the Dream that died in the Father's depths.

How judgment is executed, as well as where it falls, must be stated in a fashion more faithful to the New Testament reports of the event than is the case in much popular interpretation. Too often it is conceived in terms of a vindictive wrath that must exact retribution for the breach of its honor or codes. Yet the actual New Testament picture has more the character of a sad withdrawal than the punitive fall of an axe. God's judgment appears as a retiring Presence, a Light departed. How powerful is this portrayed in the cry of the abandoned Christ, "My God, my God, why have you forsaken me?" Once again Forsyth has captured an aspect of the cross that eludes many traditional formulations.

> Did God not lay on him the iniquity of us all, and inflict the veiling
> of his face which darkened to dereliction even the Redeemer's soul? It
> is not desert that is the worst thing in judgment, but desertion . . . the
> forsakenness is the worst judgment.[35]

When this event is viewed in its trinitarian context, the abandonment of Jesus is "God-forsakenness" in the sense of being of, as well as by, God.[36] In the eclipse of the Vision a void appears in Deity. The death of the Son is a dark night in the Soul of God.

The eclipse of God on the cross is a drama to be reported to a generation torn between illusions about the brightness of the future and despair over the shadows it does perceive. The Dark Work of God is the death of the powers that harass us. The swaggering Principalities that seem to control the future have themselves had their future taken away. The social, political, and economic monoliths that dominate our horizon and tyrannize over those struggling for liberation and reconciliation are dust and ashes. Empowerment to act toward the future comes when the wretched of the earth perceive that it is open to them. This mobilizing hope is announced

34. Whale, *Victor and Victim*, p. 190.
35. Forsyth, *The Work of Christ*, p. 190.
36. Moltmann, *The Crucified God*, p. 152.

from the cross where the powers of Evil that pretend to bar the path to the future received a mortal wound. This is a vision that the eyes of faith see and share with a dispirited age. And for those overwhelmed by a sense of abandonment before the power structures, or burdened by the ills of the flesh or the cares of the world, there is also a word that the One who was fully human and fully God experienced the agony known in those depths and participates now in forsakenness.

The dark Word of God bears away sin as well as defeats Evil. That too comes as a good word to those here and there whose naïveté about human nature is shattered by the storms of the times. As they ask "Whatever became of sin?"[37] they may be led to wonder about grace as well. But the recognition of human culpability that can accompany broken visions does not automatically move from accusation to confession. By ourselves we do not know anything about ourselves. The Work of Disclosure enables us to peer into those depths. And the Work of Eclipse makes it possible to bear what we see in the abyss. In that darkness we discover that the tyranny of sin has been ended, taken away in the death of Another. This too is God's "act of liberation in the person of Christ Jesus" (Rom. 3:24).

Relumination

As the meaning of the cross stretches into the past of Christ's life and ministry, so it also reaches into the future and his resurrection. The final Work must deal with "the last enemy," death. As such it points toward Easter morning when the final darkness gives way. We describe the movement out of the night as "relumination." It brings new Light and therefore also new sight. The resurrection is a re-lighting and re-vision. The new envisioning in the Godhead begins at Calvary, but its confirmation and climax take place in the resurrection of Christ.

Together with the other actions of the cross, relumination is accomplished in the Person of the God-Man. The fullness and unity of divine and human reality is the presupposition of this Work of Light. It is God who grapples with the last enemy, but this struggle takes place in and through the destiny of Jesus of Nazareth.

The ending of the reign of humanity-in-sin and the powers of Evil

---

37. As in Karl Menninger, *Whatever Became of Sin?* (New York: Hawthorne, 1973).

means that a new possibility is opened up for the covenant partners of God. But this possibility can be rendered secure and ultimately become reality only if a new kind of relationship between the parties to the covenant is established. When the obstacles to the ultimate purposes of God are removed, the sought-for unity can take place. The liberation from sin and Evil prepares the way for the reconciliation of all things. It is on the boundary between cross and resurrection that the path to the final reconciliation is found. Here the last enemy to be overcome, the death of Shalom, is met and the deliverance from the powers of darkness is crowned by translation into the kingdom of Light. "He rescued us from the domain of darkness and brought us away into the kingdom of his dear Son, in whom our release is secured and our sins forgiven" (Col. 1:13-14).

It is the suffering love of God active in the Dark Work that makes possible a new relationship in a Work of Light. In the old relationship, God beckoned persons and powers toward freedom and peace, calling for a life together contingent upon a creaturely "Yes" to the divine invitation. The "No!" that was forthcoming, and its death upon the cross, ended this "covenant of works." But on the same cross is shed the "blood of the new covenant."

> This is the covenant which I make with them after those days . . . their sins and wicked deeds I will remember no more at all . . . the blood of Jesus makes us free to enter boldly into the sanctuary by the new, living way. . . . (Heb. 10:16, 17, 19-20)

Speaking of Jesus' own understanding of his passion Vincent Taylor says,

> When he described it as "my blood of the covenant," he was clearly thinking of a covenant relationship between God and men established by His death. His outpoured life would be the medium of a new fellowship with God.[38]

Thus a covenant of grace replaces a covenant of works.[39] In it the covenant of shalom is replaced by a suffering Love that establishes the future for the

---

38. Vincent Taylor, *The Atonement in New Testament Teaching* (London: Epworth Press, 1958), p. 14.

39. In this concept of covenant we are following, with some changes, the double covenant tradition as developed by Ursinus and later the federal theology of Coccejus, and formalized in the *Westminster Confession*, Chapter VII, 2-6.

covenant partners. Toward humanity there reaches a patient mercy that accepts the unacceptable, a grace that receives the sinner. God anticipates the futurelessness of human-beings-in-sin, projects an "alternative future" of human fulfillment, and acts toward us now in that Light. God takes us for what we shall be, and goes before us with a mercy that covers what we are. And this same suffering Love deals in similar fashion with the fallen principalities and powers. They are accepted for what they shall be in the new Future of broken swords, justice that shall roll down as the waters, nature healed, suffering overcome, tears wiped away. Persons and powers now exist as creatures to a new paradigm of grace and hope.

The new covenant is the raising of the Son, and, therefore, the resurrection of the Vision of God. The old covenant, the old Vision, died on Calvary, but the Envisioning Father did not pass away. Death in God is not the death of God. The act of divine envisioning is empowered by the Holy Spirit, "the assurance of things hoped for," the guarantee of the intention of God. The Spirit resurrects the Dream, transfiguring it into a covenant of grace. Liberation and reconciliation shall be, for a prevenient Agape that makes no bargains, that is turned aside by no contingencies and suffers all things, presses toward the goal. It is this gracious love that conquers the last enemy, the death that felled the original Vision, and establishes an indestructible bond with the partners of God.

The Work of Light assures us of the eschatological fulfillment of the resolve of God. But even now we live in the half-light of the resurrection dawn.[40] In the Already-Not-Yet between Easter and Eschaton, signs and portents of the Future break into view. The covenant of grace in which we now live is not only promise but power. In the life of persons, liberation from sin and reconciling mercy bring with them a sanctifying strength. Unmerited favor toward us is no empty pardon but means the possibility of growth in grace. In the life of principalities, the presence of the Future means that the structures of history and nature can be bearers, albeit broken bearers, of liberation and reconciliation. Political, social, and economic institutions and instruments of power witness to the Not Yet. And nature too is not bereft of earnests of a redeemed cosmos as these manifest themselves in possibilities of healing, from ecological to biomedical. The

40. I have developed this imagery as a way of telling the Christian story in "Dawn People," preparatory material for Section I, *Jesus Christ Frees and Unites,* 5th Assembly, World Council of Churches, pp. 22-23.

risen Lord moves with sovereign power in a historical future that belongs to him.

While the Easter relumination announces the Meridian, at dawn there are still shadows on the land. Sin and Evil are futureless and tomorrow belongs to Shalom, but today is marked by chiaroscuro patterns. The doomed powers of Darkness continue to range across it, contesting the coming Light. In the depths of the self, sin parasites on every moral and spiritual growth, threatening to turn it into a demonic self-righteousness. And in its collective expression, it imperils every social advance with megalomania and consequent new tyranny. Suffering persists in nature and history as Evil harnesses processes and institutions to its purposes. For the natural eye it is not hard to believe that hope has perished and death has conquered. And the eye of faith has no illusions about the shadow side. What makes that perception bearable, and in fact empowering, is the vision of another horizon. But the risen Christ it sees there is the crucified Jesus who still carries the mark of nail and spear. A long-suffering Lord bears history towards its completion. "Christ reigns from the cross."

Our discussion of this Work centered upon the new covenant of grace rising within the Godhead. Re-envisioning could be falsely interpreted, however, if the incarnational premises so basic to the Atonement were not drawn out to the fullest. The coming of a triumphant Vision is not just a happening in the inner-trinitarian life, subsequently exhibited to us in the light of Easter morning. The historical events of crucifixion and resurrection are integral to the saga itself. They enact as well as reveal the new covenant.[41] It was the person of the God-Man, fully human as well as fully divine, on the cross and in the resurrection, through whom the new covenant was achieved. The indestructible Vision of humanity reconciled and a world redeemed was effected, as well as exhibited, by these findings.

The paralysis of will that afflicts both frustrated visionaries and self-styled realists is not unrelated to their perception of a closed future. For them the dreams are dead, so why bother about futile gestures toward tomorrow? The news that Christ is risen and the future is open is a disturbing note to those comfortable with the accommodations they have made to "the way things are." Yet it carries with it a releasing power. To believe that the future is penetrable empowers one to thrust toward it. Especially so when a word comes that not only have the old impossibilities that

---

41. Pannenberg, *Jesus — God and Man*, pp. 66-114.

barred the way been done away with, but new possibilities are now visible. The perception of the Not Yet yielded by the cross and resurrection opens up vistas unseen by those whose gaze is fixed upon the abyss. The latter mesmerism expects no release from the bondage of our self-serving, no justice for the oppressed, no healing for our hurts, no tears wiped away. And the result is a self-fulfilling forecast. The Work of New Light was done to pierce that gloom and break that trance.

The Search for Wholeness

In the reconstruction of the doctrine of Atonement attempted here, we have made use of many kinds of building blocks. The deepest foundations have been laid in the biblical accounts and affirmations, with their supports in patristic thought. The superstructure has drawn materials from medieval, Reformation, and contemporary theology. A special concern has been to bring together traditions in Atonement teaching that have customarily been considered alien to one another.

In an era whose survival depends on putting behind it the insularities of another day, theology must also venture out of old bastions. How could it be otherwise for a perspective whose reference point is the wholeness of Shalom? This means the risk of unusual mosaics, ones that incorporate the brilliant colors of liberation with the more somber hues of a Niebuhrian realism. It requires both the honoring of the triumph of grace in a Karl Barth and the melancholy rumination of "Northern" theologies on the demonic. It involves listening to and learning from the sober orthodoxy of a Berkouwer as well as a willingness to hear out the affirmations of the theologies of hope. It also means getting past the polarities of piety and action, self and society, the historical and the cosmic, that have prevented us from seeing the biblical unities and totalities.

Consonant with this quest for a synoptic vision, the three aspects of the cross explored in these pages correspond to a familiar symbol of the comprehensive Work of Christ, the *munus triplex:* Jesus Christ as Prophet, Priest, and King. This figure represents the whole work, spanning the pre- and post-Easter life of Christ, but it is fitting as well for the cross, the quintessential expression of that larger arena of atoning action. While the conception of the threefold office has never been without its critics, it has had a venerable history, and continues to be actively used as a framework.[42] In this interpretation, the work of disclosure, when filled out by the life and teachings of Jesus, constitutes the Office of Prophet. The Work of Eclipse is a formulation of the office of Priest. And the Work of Relumination, developed further by the Lordship themes of resurrection and ascension, is a statement of the office of King. While the threefold understanding of the cross here must stand on its own merits, the continuity with the ancient typology reflects its efforts to deal with the accents that recur in the long struggle with the meaning of the Atonement, and it also makes available to the interpretation an important pedagogical tool.

One of the serious problems in the use of devices such as the threefold office, and in the kind of comprehensive schematization attempted here, is the impression given of having a profound mystery encapsulated too easily in human formularies. Indeed there is a very important place for "scientific theology" that must be defended against the current anti-intellectualism in both church and culture. But the closer we approach the center of the cross the more the carefully interpreted theological construct must yield to the stammering of faith. The recognition that the metaphors and motifs we find meaningful are creatures of transient historical experience will serve further to demythologize any lingering pretension. Restatements are critical to the ongoing communication of Christian faith. Yet the dim sight of the theological eye makes necessary a large measure of modesty in any claims made by the theological mouth.

Participation in the Cross

All talk about the cross, bashful or bold, must at last be tested in the carrying of it. The deep things of Golgotha are plumbed by those who have been there. The "one suffering made once" cannot, of course, be duplicated by the disciple. But the risen Lord is engaged in a "continuous work" in our midst, coming to us wherever suffering Shalom makes its way in the world, and inviting us to keep company with him there.[43] To "participate in the sufferings of God in the world" (Bonhoeffer) is to be where faith is born

42. Calvin gave it a special prominence in the *Institutes* (Book II, Chapter XV), one that was built upon in subsequent Reformation thought. However, its roots go back as far as Eusebius, and it appears in Thomas Aquinas as well.

43. Developed in Gabriel Fackre, *Humiliation and Celebration* (New York: Sheed & Ward, 1969), pp. 268-74.

and tested. The wretched of the earth come to understand something of the wounds of Christ, as the pieties and mysticisms of the cross[44] have demonstrated. Yet, in the final analysis, Kierkegaard's point is a telling one: our involuntary suffering is closer to Paul's thorn in the flesh than to the voluntary suffering of the cross. The cross is offered to us, not inflicted on us. Those who take it up and follow its first Bearer, risking with him engagement with the powers of Darkness, will not earn their salvation by some sort of works-righteousness. But they will put themselves where the suffering Christ is to be met, and where Word and Spirit can bring faith alive.[45]

If the suffering of Christ is at the hands of human sin as well as the Powers that be, then the place of engagement with him now is one that gives us a clear view also of what we did and are doing to Shalom. Our complicity in Christ's crucifixion is also what it means to participate in the sufferings of God. That sobering self-recognition is the beginning of the deepest wisdom about the cross. It is the moment of exposure when we understand just who we are, and can know as well who God is, and what God does to bring a new covenant of grace and mercy.

To bear it, to stand judged before it — these are understandings of the cross that put Christian faith in touch with the culture's own pain, and can lead it to even deeper perception of reality. And for the eyes of that same culture there is to be seen in this suffering on Golgotha, and in the passion of God, a glimpse of hope that cannot be shattered, and of a vision that will not fade.

Addendum on "The Passion of the Christ"

The 2004 release of the Mel Gibson film, *The Passion of the Christ,* produced an outpouring of public commentary on the subject at hand. A Christology in context will take up the question of the pastoral interpretation of what has become a cultural phenomenon.

"Awesome!" "Awful!" "Compassionate and Compelling!" "Sadistic and

---

44. Moltmann, *The Crucified God,* pp. 45-53.

45. On this theme see Reuben Alves, *A Theology of Human Hope* (Washington: Corpus Books, 1969), pp. 114-22, and Hendrikus Berkhof, *Christ the Meaning of History,* trans. Lambertus Buurman (London: SCM Press, 1962), pp. 101-21.

Anti-Semitic!" "It is as it was." "It is as it was not." How, in the midst of the furor, can *The Passion of the Christ* be a "teaching moment" for our congregations? And one that sheds light on the meaning of "atonement," the very premise of the film?

For those who are assigned lections and give homilies on the subject, an amateur movie review will not do. More is needed than a rehash of what can be read in a *Newsweek* cover story or a *New York Times* column. Better a movie meditation from the depths of both the heart of faith and the mind of the church, a *lectio divina* on these selective scenes and the symbol at the center of our sanctuaries.

Where we stand shapes what we see on the Gibson screen. And where we fall also affects the angle of vision. Both of these realisms are tributaries to the doctrine of reconciliation. They have to do with creation and fall, the first two chapters of the Christian story. Given our creatureliness — bodies and spirits in social matrices (Gen. 2:7, 18) — Gibson's *Passion,* and also the many fervent ruminations about it, pro and con, rise out of particular histories. And more, given the Story's tale of our state — sin as well as finitude (Ps. 14:3), they are not disconnected from self-serving agendas in the cinematography and also in the reportage, whether it be fierce warnings or teary testimonies, this commentary not excluded.[46] Vigilance is especially in order, when our partial perspectives make claims of a God's-eye view, the first chapter sliding into the second.

Regarding these matters we cannot but ask about the lens through which the producer views Jesus. For that the critics have not hesitated to go, literally, to his father, Hutton. "Don't go there," says Mel. He is right if it means the attribution to him of his father's horrific views on the Holocaust, the use, ironically, of a guilt-by-association argument by the same folk who find McCarthyism unthinkable. But the son has a finite history too, and his father's faith is part of it. The film's atonement themes cannot be understood without taking into account their common Tridentine Catholicism.

The structure of the film follows "the five sorrowful mysteries" of the rosary, treasured by traditionalist believers: "the agony of our Lord in the garden, his scourging, his crowning with thorns, the carrying of his cross

---

46. Examples of such perspectival interpretations from within the Christian community are the affirming articles in *Christianity Today* 48, no. 3 (March 2004), and the attacking ones in Chicago Theological Seminary's *In Such a Time As This* 5 (Winter/Spring 2004).

to Calvary, and the crucifixion"[47] (Matt. 26:36-46; Matt. 27:26; Matt. 27:29; Matt. 27:31-32; Matt. 27:33-50 and parallels), with backdrop in the stations of the cross. Gibson beads, and the medieval and also seventeenth-century Italian piety and paintings associated with them, can be felt and seen in the flow of the events and the underlying version of penal blood atonement.

For the particulars of the latter, the viewer must turn to the visions of the Venerables Mary of Agreda (1620-1665) and Anne Catherine Emmerich (1774-1824), the latter etched with the stigmata. A bit of what Anne sees of the scourging sounds like the script of the cinematic lacerations:

> They struck our Lord with their fists, and dragged him by the cords with which he was pinioned, although he followed them without offering the least resistance, and, finally, they barbarously knocked him down against the pillar. . . . The two fresh executioners . . . made use of a different kind of rod, — a species of thorny stick, covered with knots and splinters. The blows from these sticks tore his flesh to pieces; his blood spouted out so as to stain their arms, and he groaned, prayed, and shuddered. . . . Two fresh executioners took the places of the last mentioned, who were beginning to flag; their scourges were composed of small chains, or straps covered with iron hooks, which penetrated to the bone, and tore off large pieces of flesh at every blow. . . . The body of our Lord was perfectly torn to shreds, — it was but one wound. . . .[48]

Is the teaching point here that Gibson takes Tridentine-informed liberties with Scripture's spare reports? Yes, if we are doing a movie review. And many more departures might be added. So too the filmic interpretation of selected texts themselves, as for example the Braveheart-level violence throughout. (A case could be made that the nauseating brutalities will drive one to the ways of peace, though these scenes are not for children, remembering the ancient tradition of separating the catechumens from the liturgy of the faithful.) What of the charge of fueling hatred for the Jewish people in both the Sanhedrin and mob scenes? Yes, again. Would that Gibson had weighed the unintended consequences of following the stigmatist's accounts, especially so their pre–Vatican 2 anti-Judaism. But to

47. Donald Attwater, ed., *A Catholic Dictionary* (New York: Macmillan, 1961), p. 470.
48. *The Dolorous Passion of Our Lord Jesus Christ,* Internet accessible.

settle for what can be read about this in a Safire newspaper piece is to miss the meditative potential on the meaning of the atonement. For who, finally, drove the stake? In an interview Mel said it was his own hand. Just right: our universal culpability. But he could have made it clearer by showing his own face as well.

To return to the relation of the Jewish people to the Christian cross, so much part of the public discussion, pastors should help parishioners see it in its wider setting, that of the third chapter in the biblical story, God's covenant with a chosen people.[49] The film has its take on it. On the one hand, in Jesus the Aramaic-speaking Jew, a grieving mother, disciples both faithful and fickle, protestors of his abuse in the crowd and Simon of Cyrene the cross-bearer ("Jew!" spat out by a Roman soldier). On the other and more prominently, the accusatory temple priesthood and screaming mob. In the latter case, along with Roman authority and brutality, a portion of this people of God play their role in what theologians call the "efficient cause" (the events on the ground) of God's redemptive "final cause" (the hidden divine purposes).

Let the pastor do a canonical reading of these things and struggle with the paradoxes of Paul in Romans 9-11. How could those who do not accept this Jesus as Messiah yet be called "beloved" with their "gifts and calling . . . irrevocable," and Christians be told that "all Israel will be saved" (Rom. 11:29, 26)? Can one be a Pauline anti-supersessionist (I am), and still not censor the passages in all four gospels that portray the complicity of the religious establishment of the day with the political establishment of the day? The latter is what these scenes are all about: not the ethnicity of Jewish (or Italian) peoples but human *hubris* as such, and the corruptibility of power. The cry of "Christ-killers!" is the most devious of evasions of our own hand on the lash and the hammer, denying thereby the need for a universal atonement for our universal sin.

What then is the bearing of all the foregoing on the central chapter of the Story? Who is this figure so filmicly beset? A heroic sufferer, bloodied but unbowed? Yes, surely a human being in extremity. And, as Calvin reminded a medieval piety preoccupied with the gore, tortured more in soul than body. Whether it comes clear or not in the film, this decimated body is also God in the flesh, a Person, not only a person, "in two natures, divine

---

49. The chapters designated are from Fackre, *The Christian Story,* vol. 1, 3rd ed. (Grand Rapids: Eerdmans, 1996).

and human" as the ecumenical consensus has it. The Incarnation is inseparable from the Atonement. At the pillar and on the crossbeam we find "the
crucified God." From Bernard of Clairvaux through Johann Rist to G. A.
Studdert-Kennedy and Georgia Harkness, a thread of hymnody is not
afraid to dwell on this writhing Deity. The agony is in the heart of God as
well as on a hill. Luther sees this in his theology of cross when he speaks of
the divine Mercy there taking into itself the divine Wrath. And we might
add, with the hand of Gibson in mind, the divine Love absorbing human
wrath. Indeed, the film's flashbacks to mountain preaching, to the washing
of the disciples' feet and the table eucharist, are hints of the same.

The Atonement is not about God beating up on Jesus — the theory too
often found in pop piety, now adopted, ironically, by those who dismiss the
cross as child abuse — but the God who was *in* Christ reconciling . . . (2 Cor.
5:19). The Person does the painful Work of receiving the judgment due our
sin. Can any visualization of the passion capture this point? Is the tear of
God that falls near the close of the film an effort to suggest the divine participation in the event on Golgotha? An interpretive Word is needed as well
as a sight seen, hence the cruciality of preaching and teaching: on the path
and at the cross our sin is exposed and God's love is disclosed.

While meditating on the at-one-ment of God and the world, we need
to be reminded by patristics of the "classic" view" of these things: reconciliation has to do with conflict between the vulnerable God and the powers
of evil, and the divine victory over them through persuasion and not force.
Is that what the fleeting images of an androgynous and seductive Satan are
all about, and Jesus' refusal to meet the arrogance of power with measures
in kind? Yes, if we're clear that we have here the one-time sacrifice of God
that "takes away the sin of the world," and not a rule of thumb that coun-
sels victims to accept their lot. Or a too-quick segue from that transcendent encounter to a Manichaean dualism in which us good guys are set
against them bad guys, with little awareness of the sin that persists in the
"righteous" as well as the "unrighteous."

In sum, let the encompassing view of the atonement expressed as the
"threefold office of Christ" illumine the scene.[50] The reconciliation that
happened was brought to be by the triple ministry of Jesus: prophetic in
Galilee, priestly on Golgotha, royal on Easter morning (and each in all, as

---

50. Developed most by John Calvin, it now has ecumenical usage, as, for example, in the
Decree on the Apostolate of the Laity, Vatican II.

well), a full-orbed Work done by the one Person of Bethlehem. Look through this lens at all portrayals of Christ. Mel Gibson had his producer eye on Golgotha and the path to it. Others fix on the Galilean Jesus, yet others on the resurrection. When the stature of Jesus is reduced to one or the other, an ecumenical formulation is apt: "affirmation and admonition." Affirm the ministry the portrait celebrates. Admonish the artist about the absences. Meditate on the fullness of Christ's reconciling Person and Work. And when watching this film, pay attention to the spiritual's query: "Were you there when they crucified my Lord?"

CHAPTER 12

The Risen Christ

"Why Not Stop Here?" James Dunn poses that question after prob-
ing the meaning of the cross in his magisterial study of New Testament scholarship, *Jesus Remembered*. His answer is that it can't be done.
The reason is in the title of his chapter taken from the Apostles Creed and
the allegro of Bach's B Minor Mass, *Et Resurrexit,*

> what Christians have always (from the first) believed was the most
> remarkable thing about Jesus — his resurrection from the dead. That
> belief seems to have been not only fundamental for Christianity as
> far back as we can trace, but also presuppositional and foundational.[1]

The resurrection *is* "presuppositional and foundational" for the Christian
faith. Pannenberg puts it in the strongest of terms in his objection to views
that trace the singularity of Jesus to his teaching and its sequel, the cross:

> . . . without the Easter event, this interpretation of the crucifixion is
> absurd. . . . the biblical testimony presents the Easter event as the ba-
> sis of the faith of the disciples.[2]

---

1. James D. G. Dunn, *Jesus Remembered* (Grand Rapids: Eerdmans, 2003), p. 826.
2. Wolfhart Pannenberg, *Systematic Theology*, vol. 2, trans. Geoffrey Bromiley (Grand
Rapids: Eerdmans, 1991), p. 286. So too a myriad of commentators, as in A. M. Ramsay's

In what did this "Easter event" consist? The New Testament describes it as encounter with an embodied Christ. "Reach out your hand and put it in my side . . ." (John 20:27). The bold physicality makes us wince. "My Lord and my God!" (John 20:28). . . . But, but. . . . The accounts of the risen Jesus are strange indeed: a body that dines but "vanishes" (Luke 24:30-31); one that can be touched, but not "held on to" (John 20:17). . . . He rose again, fully but differently, "the first born from the dead" (Col. 1:18). And, so shall we.[3]

These assertions are vigorously disputed by not a few in both academia and the church who urge us to "stop here." Or, better: go way back to the Galilean Jesus. So the vocal "Jesus Seminar" whose leader wants us to be *Honest to Jesus*,[4] and the indefatigable bishop, John Spong, eager to have us know that he does "not see God as a being" and that the resurrection of Jesus' body is "not just naïve but eminently rejectable."[5]

While a corps of critics of this sort may act like a new magisterium, prompting us to smile at their pontifications, there is a place for tough academic inquiry into this matter. Indeed, James Dunn, in his study, has reviewed the range of scholarly dismissals of the New Testament witness to the resurrection of Jesus, and found them suspect on their own grounds. He argues that historical investigation must grant that the only evidence with which it can work is "the impact made by Jesus as it has impressed itself into the tradition."[6] That tradition has two foci, the empty tomb and the resurrection appearances. A careful examination of all the New Testa-

---

small classic, *The Resurrection of Christ* (London: Collins, Fontana Books, rev. ed., 1961), 9: "For them [the first disciples] the Gospel without the Resurrection was not merely the Gospel without its final chapter: it was no Gospel at all." And in another landmark work, Oscar Cullmann's *Immortality of the Soul or Resurrection of the Body* (New York: Macmillan, 1953), p. 43: "Is *Easter* the starting point of the Christian Church, of its existence, life, and thought? If so, we are living in an interim time. In that case, the faith in resurrection of the New Testament becomes the cardinal point of Christian belief. Accordingly, the fact that there is a resurrection body — Christ's body — defines the first Christians' whole interpretation of time."

3. Gabriel Fackre, "I Believe in the Resurrection of the Body," *Interpretation* 46, no. 1 (January 1992): 44, 45.

4. Robert E. Funk, *Honest to Jesus* (New York: HarperCollins, 1996).

5. John Shelby Spong, *A New Christianity for a New World: Why Traditional Faith Is Dying and How New Faith Is Being Born* (New York: HarperCollins, 2002), pp. 2, 4. On the details of his criticism of the New Testament teaching about resurrection, see *Resurrection: Myth or Reality?* (New York: HarperCollins, 1995).

6. Dunn, *Jesus Remembered*, p. 876.

ment data on these subjects discloses the physical resurrection of Jesus to be a "core belief" from the beginning, one that did not correspond to any then-current paradigm — from hallucination through apocalyptic vision to resuscitation.[7] Even given the diversity of reports of the risen Jesus,

> it is in the end of the day the tradition itself which pushes us to the conclusion that it was something perceived as having happened to *Jesus* (resurrection evidenced in empty tomb and resurrection appearances) and not just something which happened to the *disciples* (Easter faith) which provides the more plausible explanation for the origin and core content of the tradition itself.[8]

While it is interesting to learn that plausibility now seems to lie with historical investigations that make room for, if not support, classical Christian teaching, Hans Schwarz rightly observes that "the resurrection of Jesus cannot be fathomed by purely historical research."[9] It has to do with trust in the Word that speaks to us through Scripture as it is read christologically in the church immersed in the world.[10] That final authority is the premise of this chapter. As Carl Braaten, after a comparable review of alternative construals of the resurrection that look to extra-biblical norms, rightly asserts: "There can be no authentic Christianity without belief in the resurrection of Jesus," adding, as it relates to our subject of the uniqueness of Christ,

> If Jesus is the risen Lord, that makes him different from all other putative messiahs, prophets and religious founders. There is no need to be mission-minded if we do not believe that Jesus' resurrection is

---

7. Dunn, *Jesus Remembered*, pp. 870-76.

8. Dunn, *Jesus Remembered*, p. 876. Contra Edward Schillebeeckx, the theologian whose massive works, *Jesus* and *Christ*, have been the most ambitious modern effort in systematic theology to relate Christology to historical-critical studies, thereby giving pride of place to Easter experiences rather than to the New Testament witness to the resurrection of Jesus from the dead. See my detailed examination of Schillebeeckx's writings on the subject, "Bones Strong and Weak in the Skeletal Structure of Schillebeeckx's Christology," *Journal of Ecumenical Studies* 21, no. 2 (Spring 1984): 248-77.

9. Hans Schwarz, *Christology* (Grand Rapids: Eerdmans, 1998), p. 268. See also in this work Schwarz's critical review of current feminist and pluralist Christologies, pp. 277-336.

10. So argued in Gabriel Fackre, *The Christian Story*, vol. 2, *Scripture in the Church for the World* (Grand Rapids: Eerdmans, 1987), passim.

God's unique way of reclaiming the whole world for himself, and that he is the one and only way of salvation for Christians and people of other religions and no religion alike.[11]

Thus, the resurrection as foundation and basis of the Christian faith includes its role in establishing the uniqueness of Jesus Christ vis-à-vis world religions. What follows is a commentary on that affirmation.

A Three-Dimensional Singularity

The Christian faith makes three claims about the uniqueness of Jesus Christ. They are summarized tersely in John 14:6: Jesus Christ is "the way," "the truth," and "the life." To translate these biblical assertions into historic theological terms: Jesus Christ is the "way" (path/*hodos*) God makes into the world to effect *reconciliation* with the world, the "truth" of *revelation* about God and the world, the "life" of *redemption* from the death consequent upon alienation between God and the world.[12] The resurrection is the validation, the announcement, and the application of these Christian assertions about the uniqueness of Jesus Christ.

In John 14:6 "truth" and "life" are epexegetical of the primary predicate "way."[13] When God in Jesus Christ makes the one reconciling way into the world to overcome sin, attendant are revealing truth and redeeming life. Easter is more than mortality overcome, a near universal hope in the world's religions. In the Christian story, the triumph over physical death is the sign of the conquest of *eternal* death as estrangement from God and thus reconciliation accomplished, the bringing of "eternal life." Paul puts it this way in a letter to Timothy as he distinguishes "life" so understood from "immortality" and gathers up all three of the Johannine threads in describing how reconciliation

> has now been revealed through the appearing of our Savior Christ Jesus, who abolished death and brought life and immortality to light through the gospel. (2 Tim. 1:10)

11. Carl Braaten, "The Reality of the Resurrection," *Nicene Christianity: The Future for a New Ecumenism*, ed. Christopher Seitz (Grand Rapids: Brazos Press, 2001), pp. 116, 118.

12. See my development of this trinity in "Claiming Jesus as Savior in a Pluralist World," *Alister McGrath and Evangelical Theology* (London: Paternoster Press, 2003), pp. 213-34.

13. Explored in Fackre, *The Christian Story,* vol. 2, pp. 254-340.

To grasp the interrelationships of way, truth, and life, we shall explore their uniqueness in the framework of the overarching biblical story.

The Grand Narrative

The Christian account of the world differs from all others, religious or secular.[14] The difference is based on its premise about the seriousness of the world's plight. Not ignorance, not suffering, not physical death, the issues that come to the fore in alternative religions and philosophies. These problematics are also within the Christian judgment about the world's present state, but are situated in a deeper context. That abyss is the alienation of "the made" from its Maker because of *sin*. Christians measure the full meaning of sin by our response to the coming of the Son among us: hanging him on a cross, and thus "crucifying God." The state of the world is disclosed in all its horror on Golgotha. Our exposure there as the enemy of God is the framework for the Christian reading of the Old Testament report of a tree's enticements. Our radical estrangement requires a deed of God in kind, and thus the singularity of the primary Johannine predicate of Jesus Christ, "the way" of radical reconciliation with its accompanying gifts of truth and life. There's a story here. We move to it.

Prologue

The doing of God rises from the being of God. And who is God? As with the state of the world, so with the nature of deity, we look to the center of the Story for an understanding of its origins. To anticipate again, the only Son came from the Father by the Holy Spirit disclosing thereby the Author, as well as the chief Actor of this drama. As such, the authorial prologue is about a triune Life Together.

The unique source of this unique story is the one tri-personal God. Father, Son, and Holy Spirit are Persons that indwell one another in such a manner that "They" are, in fact, a "Thou." While other religions may profess that God is loving, the Scriptures of this faith declare God *is* Love, the triune Life Together.

---

14. The history and faith of the Hebrew people as interpreted in the Christian Bible being the exception to be investigated in Chapter 3 of the Story.

Chapter 1

"God calls the worlds into being. . . ." So says one Church's narrative State-ment of Faith.[15] To what end? By our trinitarian reckoning, the call is into the temporal "being" of a life together with the eternal triune Being. God's purpose for creation, and the covenant with creation to pursue that end to the End, mirrors the divine Life Together. The *perichoresis* of Father, Son, and Holy Spirit is willed for the world, but only in derivative pointer form as there is no parallel in our sphere to the divine coinherence.

Who and what are called into this derived mutuality? In the canon, three candidates emerge: ourselves, our habitat, and the mysterious realm of "principalities and powers."[16] (As triplicity recurs in our account, do we have to do with Augustine's *vestigiae trinitatis,* the traces of the Trinity found ev-erywhere?) We can describe these invited partners of God as nature, human nature, and supernature. They are made for a life together, within their arena, among one another, and each and all with God, so portrayed in Reve-lation's vision of the goal toward which God moves the world (Rev. 21).

Special steward of God's creative bounty is the one made in the divine image. Within the call to, and covenant with, creation is the call to, and covenant with, the creature with the human face. In the Genesis account, our representative figures, Adam and Eve, are gifted and charged to image the divine mutuality (Gen. 1:26-27) in their response to God, their care for one another and for the earth. As such, the future of creation is inextrica-ble from their call and response.

Chapter 2

What response did and do we make to the divine beckoning? Not a Yes re-turned to God's Yes, but a stark No! The made seeks to usurp the place of the Maker, playing God (Gen. 3:5), turning away from the role chosen for us in the divine drama. Such idolatry — ourselves at center stage in the place of the chief Author and Actor — our Story names "sin." We have been in bondage to it since our beginnings.

15. The United Church of Christ Statement of Faith.

16. For an exploration of the latter see Gabriel Fackre, "Angels Heard and Demons Seen," *Theology Today* 51, no. 3 (October 1994): 345-58.

"The wages of sin is death" (Rom. 6:23). Death, in this narrative, is the "life apart" juxtaposed to life together, the stumble and fall away from the reaching hand of God. This killing "fall" is the consequence of sin, and thus the alienation of humanity from deity, "eternal death." All creation is impacted by this posture, the interrelationships of fallen humanity, fallen nature and fallen angels, asserted but never explained in our story.

How the fallen are raised up, how alienation can become reconciliation, how death can be overcome by life are varied ways in which creation's conundrum is posed by the unfolding Christian narrative. Chapter 3 tells of God's next move.

Chapter 3, Part I

"God gave Noah the rainbow sign. . . ." So it is sung in an African American spiritual. The implacable quest of the God of Scripture will not let us go our own way. Comes yet another promise: "I have set my bow in the clouds, and it shall be a sign of covenant between me and the earth" (Gen. 9:13). The covenant-making Creator moves back toward creation with the pledge to continue the story. Our No will not deter the divine Yes.

The Noachic covenant brings with it visible signs of God's patience. The multi-colored rainbow indicates the multiple mercies scattered across creation that sustain us in our journey toward another end than the death we have brought upon ourselves. They are glimpses of "truth, beauty, and goodness" still discernible by our *imago Dei,* an image broken by the fall but not destroyed. To the extent that it is intact, its preservation is by a "common grace." Commonality is an everywhere-ness of the divine generosity that makes possible intimations of truth and life and "orders of preservation" — family, nation, economy — that institutionally both set boundaries to our rampaging sin and reflect something of our intended life together. However identified, all of these are signs and supports of God's faithfulness.

Enter at this point in the story one interpretation of the place of the world's religions in the purposes of God, a view yet to be explored more fully. To follow the rainbow imagery and the promises of Noah's covenant: wherever "holiness" keeps company with truth, goodness, and beauty, making human life livable in a fallen world, we have the work of a common grace. All such gifts have their source in the triune God, hence what is common is also christological, the blessings of the Spirit of the Son of the Father. The varied colors of the bow in the sky suggest the manifold ways in which common grace is present in the world's high religions.[17]

As with every evidence of sustaining grace in a fallen world, so too that discernible in a world religion is measured by the gold standard of the gospel.[18] The source and norm of common grace can be discerned and measured only by "Jesus Christ, as attested by Scripture . . . the one Word of God."[19] To that Word we listen in our Christian encounter with world religions. More to follow on this as we probe more deeply into the Work of the Word enfleshed.

Chapter 3, Part II

There is one "world religion" different in kind from all the others. The covenant promise to keep the Story moving forward moves from the universal to the particular. The rainbow ends at a point in time and settles at a point in space, resting on a chosen community: "I will take you as my people, and I will be your God" (Exod. 6:7).

In a broken world the promise of an unbreakable bond comes to a small Mediterranean tribe. The mystery of its election is an integral part of this epic. The importance of this special covenant is demonstrated by the two-thirds of the Christian Bible devoted to the chosen people's history.

Through all its ups and downs the story unfolds. The covenantal pledge and call to Abraham and his response in faith set the stage. Times of testing come, and generations of heroes and villains pass before our eyes. Living in a land bridge between marching armies North and South, turmoil is a constant, finally turning to captivity. But then another turn in the tale: a baby rises from the reeds, grows to lead an escape from tyranny, a pilgrimage to a promised land, the reception of "the law" on the way, but a leader left at the boundary with others to take up the trail. Kings arise —

---

17. With a question raised to Gerald R. McDermott, who in an otherwise splendid book assumes that common grace is monochromatic. See *Can Evangelicals Learn from World Religions? Jesus, Revelation and Religious Traditions* (Downers Grove, Ill.: InterVarsity, 2000), pp. 52-53, 113, passim.

18. See, interestingly, Karl Barth, *Church Dogmatics*, IV/3, first half (Edinburgh: T. & T. Clark, 1961), pp. 114-37.

19. The Barmen Declaration, II, 1.

David, Solomon; a temple is built and priests appear. Wars rage, injustice is rife, nations rampage, prophets speak their words of protest and peace; exile intrudes and with it lamentations. But more — hope for redemption ahead, even apocalyptic assurances thereof, all grounded in the covenant promise of the faithful God.

Yes, there will be things to come in this story, chapters yet to be, hopes fulfilled. But after-the-fall covenants with Noah, Abraham, Moses, and their heirs are not over and done with. Just as God never abandons his original covenant with creation itself, as manifest in this very story we are tracing, so the rainbow promise of a preserving grace can be counted on to the End, and God's promises to Israel will be kept. Paul reminds us of the first in his speech at Lystra, asserting that God "has not left himself without a witness in doing good . . ." (Acts 14:17), and of the second in his letter to the Romans, the "gifts and the calling of God are irrevocable" (Rom. 11:29). The book of the people in this chapter is about the covenant faithfulness of God, and without it we would not have evidence of the divine patience and persistence that have brought us to this point.

And beyond this point? So many indicators in the chapter itself — the expectation of a "man of sorrows acquainted with grief" (Isa. 53:3 KJV) who will be "wounded for our transgressions, crushed for our iniquities" (Isa. 53:5). The establishment of offices — prophetic, priestly, and royal — necessary for any exposure, expiation, and triumph over what separates creation from its Creator. And on the boundary of this chapter and the next, one Jew who points to another and says, "Here is the Lamb of God who takes away the sin of the world!" (John 1:29).

Chapter 4

Now we are at the center of the story, its symbol, appropriately, a cross, the intersecting of vertical and horizontal lines. So God comes into our midst, as the visible One who all along has been the invisible Logos source of light and life in earlier anticipatory covenants. If the Noachic rainbow arced over the whole of the world, with an end reached in Israel, then it penetrated earth itself at Bethlehem.

How could "the sin of the world" that makes for a life sundered from God otherwise meet its match than by the presence of a Life Together in its midst?

And the Word became flesh and lived among us, and we have seen his
glory, the glory of a father's only son. . . . (John 1:14)

The Son is the perfect image of the Father, and so the second Person of the
triune life together arrives among us to do battle against estrangement.
Source of all the preserving and promising traces of the Trinity to date,
here is now One

full of grace and truth. . . . From his fullness we have all received,
grace upon grace. (John 1:14c, 16)

With Word among us, what does it take to rescue the world from alienation? Trajectories from Israel's irrevocable "gifts and calling" come now to
their place in the central chapter, Jesus Christ in his prophetic, priestly, and
royal acts. Incarnation makes atonement possible, the at-one-ing Work of
the divine-human Person.

Jesus Christ is the Prophet who discloses the purposes of God. In his
life, preaching, teaching, praying, healing and miracle-working, he forth-
tells who God is and does and what we are to be and do. These are signs of
the kingdom of God coming now here among us. But Christ is the Prophet
who exposes as well as discloses, lighting up the dark places in the human
heart and history, foretelling as well as forth-telling the accountability to
be, the tough as well as the tender love of God.

The supreme act of prophecy is at one and the same time the center of
Christ's priestly work. On the cross, his death exposes the depths of human
sin, so profound that it is willing to crucify God. Yet at the very bottom is
to be found as well the love of God's broken heart that takes into itself the
wrath we deserve. Here is fulfilled the other prophet's words that anticipate the one who will be

wounded for our transgressions, crushed for our iniquities. (Isa. 53:5)

Christ our Priest makes the supreme sacrifice. On Good Friday God
proved his love for us that "while we were still sinners Christ died for us"
(Rom. 5:8). Because of Bethlehem, the work of Christ transpired within
the divine heart as well as on Calvary's hill. It was not just the human nature of Jesus that took away the sin of the world, for

. . . in Christ, *God* was reconciling the world to himself. (2 Cor. 5:19)

How do we know these things are so? Enter Easter. In this unfolding drama the resurrection of Jesus Christ confirms the work done in Galilee and on Golgotha, and declares it to all who have ears to hear. Easter is the *demonstration* of the victory of life over death and its *proclamation*. Thus the royal office assures and announces the validity of the prophetic and priestly offices. Death, the consequence of the sin that separates, has been undone, and the life-in-communion that God is and wills for us is secured!

On the matter of confirmation, Robert Jenson puts it this way:

> The message which Jesus' followers brought into the world was, in briefest statement, "Jesus is risen." The import of this statement depends of course on what "risen" means, and we can see in Luke's account of Paul's visit to Athens that this could be problematic. But precisely when "risen" is explained, whether the message is then good news or bad news or no news depends on who Jesus is, i.e. on how we should identify him. . . . the message "Stalin is risen" would be no gospel. Replace the proper names with identifying descriptions, "The unconditional friend of sinners and publicans is risen" is good news to anyone willing to be a sinner or publican; "The chief keeper of the gulag is risen" would be good news to very few.[20]

The identity of Jesus is associated with what Jesus does: proclaims and manifests the coming of the realm of God in his Galilean ministry, and suffers and dies on Golgotha in our place for what we have done to thwart its arrival. The work of this Prophet and this Priest has been vindicated by this victorious King, the one and the same Person who thereby brings good news to us "sinners and publicans."

The good news is that the life apart that has marked this fallen world is now a life together that mirrors the divine Life Together. Whereas before, death was our destiny — estrangement from God — now its opposite is ours. The resurrection as the life that overcomes death removes the wages of sin. And the physical sign of that deeper death of estrangement — mortality — is also replaced by the One who brings *both* "life and immortality."

How could such good news not have breath-taking consequences? Those who saw the risen Lord could not still this story! This event "was ba-

20. Robert Jenson, "Jesus' Identity as a Theological Problem," unpublished paper, Center of Theological Inquiry, 2003, p. 3.

sic to the faith of the disciples," and is "presuppositional and foundational" for the church's being ever since. Without the resurrection as announcement to those able to hear it, there is no continuation of the narrative in a community called to proclaim the gospel. More about that when we move to the next chapter. For now, attention is given to this second side of the empty tomb, its publication as well as its confirmation of the good news.

How then are the "three Rs" related to the fourth one focal to this chapter of the Great Story — and the Christian claim of uniqueness inseparable from John 14:6? If the prophetic office is the disclosure of who God definitely is, obscured from the world as a consequence of the fall, then here definitive *revelation* is given. If the priestly office delivers us from the sin that estranges us from God, then on the cross *reconciliation* is accomplished. If the royal office delivers us from death in all its dimensions, then *redemption* is ours to have and hold. The life that resurrection brings is the confirmation of the revealed truth and the reconciled way. The singularity of Jesus Christ among the religions of the world is the reconciliation achieved, the revelation granted, and the redemption sealed.

All these things have to do with revelation, reconciliation, and redemption accomplished at the *center* of the Story. But the narrative goes on. So too do the scandalous Christian claims of uniqueness. Revelation, reconciliation, and redemption having been "accomplished," have yet to be "applied." Here, as well, the resurrection is key to this claim. The risen Jesus is a living Lord. His prophetic, priestly, and royal ministries by the person and power of the Holy Spirit continue until the end of time.

Chapter 5

From the right hand of the Father, Jesus the Prophet discloses to us *now* who God is and what God does and wills. The prophetic office of Christ is exercised where Christ lives among us in his body, the church. Here the Word — written, studied, preached, taught, and shared — is his organ of communication, an office exercised in the ministries of both pastor and people.[21] From that same locale, Jesus the Priest sprinkles the waters of baptism on those brought to the temple, nourishes them with his own body and blood received by a faith that ascends to his throne of grace, and

---

21. See Chapter 4.

lights the incense of worship directed to those heights.[22] Jesus the King rules from that same throne. Wherever death is defeated through the Word proclaimed and life triumphs through worship, water, bread, and wine, there the King rules. The Work of the Spirit of the Son thus calls, gathers, enlightens, and sanctifies the church of Christ.

The church as the "ark of salvation," the steward of the means of saving grace deserves a chapter in itself. To it, the chapter on salvation, we shall presently turn. But, first, associated with this ecclesial chapter is the question, "What of the world beyond the church?"

In one sense, there is no "beyond" in the universal realm of Christ, for all are under the rule of the risen Lord. As such, there is prophetic, priestly, and royal work in the wider world as well in the church. We have met it before in another chapter of the story, the covenant with Noah. Yet now in retrospect, after the resurrection, it is impossible to read any chapter without taking account of the resurrection of Christ and his rule, universal in time as well as space. As he reigns everywhere through his threefold office, whatever things are found that are "true . . . honorable . . . just . . . pure . . . commendable" (Phil. 4:8), there his universal grace is present. Thus the Prophet speaks sustainingly in every truth, as that is discerned by the measure of the one Word spoken in Jesus then, and in the Word heard in the church now. And the Priest acts preservingly wherever egoity is acknowledged and suffering assuaged by the measure of Calvary's sacrifice. And the King acts with power to keep the story moving to its Center by life triumphing over death as it is measured by resurrection morning.[23]

---

22. See Chapter 3 and John Nevin, *The Mystical Presence: A Vindication of the Reformed or Calvinistic Doctrine of the Holy Eucharist,* ed. Augustine Thompson, O.P. (Eugene, Ore.: Wipf and Stock, 2000).

23. The various interpretations of the weight of Christ's work outside the range of Christ-church-salvation are taken up in the section on "A Range of Current Views" in Chapter 1 of this volume, viz. as in Rahner's anonymous particularity, Barth's christological particularity, etc. Currently receiving much attention is the "parallel particularity" developed in most detail by S. Mark Heim. He makes a case for describing these extra-ecclesial graces as "salvations" in *Salvations: Truth and Difference in Religion* (Maryknoll, N.Y.: Orbis Books, 1995), and later, declining to impose Christian categories on others, speaks of them as "religious ends" in *The Depths of the Riches: A Trinitarian Theology of Religious Ends* (Grand Rapids: Eerdmans, 2001). While not reaching the fulfillment God intends in Christian faith, they can be seen as lesser realizations of the purposes of the triune God, made possible by the objective Work of Christ, with the hope that exposure to the gospel, here or hereafter, and the truth that is in them will lead their believers to confess Jesus Christ. In these works, Heim makes an admira-

As noted, the singularly enfleshed Word of 4 A.D. who lives on as the Head of the Body of Christ also rules the wider world and gives it the sustaining common grace. The Word we are granted in the church remains to the end of time always received under the conditions of finitude (Chapter 1) and sin (Chapter 2). As such, the definitive revelation given to us is "in a mirror, dimly" and only then "face to face" (1 Cor. 13:12). Yet the promise is for growth in understanding of the truth, even as there is the sanctifying growth in the Christian life, "more light and truth" to break forth from the Word (John Robinson). Our Teacher in that learning can use any of his avenues of grace, and has. Could that universal range even include the wisdom of the world given to us to better understand Jesus Christ? And, by the same logic, could the wisdom of a world religion be a means of better grasping the Person and Work of Jesus Christ? Why not? asks evangelical Gerald McDermott.[24] Of course, only if such were measured by "the one Word as attested by Holy Scripture." But the freedom of the risen Christ is such that he can exercise his prophetic office in Christian encounter with a world religion, drawing out as a fruit of such a meeting, aspects of truth, latent but not to that point patent in Christian faith itself.

Chapter 6

The intention of the tri-personal God is for a life together with persons. At the heart of the story is their sin that separates them from that communion with their Maker. As Christ has removed that barrier in his life, death, and resurrection, a grateful faith is the response commensurate with such saving grace. Such justifying faith brings a person into union with

---

ble attempt to affirm, unambiguously, the scandal of particularity, even the urgency of evangelism, while at the same time seeking to honor the universal reach of the triune God. The case for the role of other religions as gifts of the grace of preserving the world on its movement toward the Center is here strong. When a further step is taken to project their ends into the eternal purposes of God, and hence into forms of "eternal life," the biblical evidence is missing. Then can these eternal ends be viewed as "hell" rather than "heaven"? Heim chooses to leave the question open. But it must be asked: Would God so order world religions as agents of damnation? The Dantean alternative to this would be a multi-tiered heaven, a view that is intimated in Heim's cordial exposition of Dante. However, again, the biblical warrants for such are not there. Understandably so, as the singularity of eternal life in and with the risen Christ is the clear New Testament vision of personal fulfillment.

24. McDermott, *Can Evangelicals Learn from World Religions?* passim.

Christ.[25] As a Person within the Life Together that God is, such an engrafting into Christ brings the believer into the divine Communion, a participation that some traditions name as "deification."[26]

Salvation by grace though faith that brings persons into the Community that God is means the gift of a special kind of life. Though originating at a point in time and therefore unlike the everlastingness of God, it is denominated by Scripture as "eternal life." The Father loved us so much

> that he gave his only Son so that everyone who believes in him may not perish but have eternal life. (John 3:16)

To enter into union with Christ by faith is to begin in time participation in the eternity God always was and will be. Here is "life" in its meaning as "immortality." Physical death is not the last word for the believer. Nor is mortality the end for the unbeliever. But in this case immortality is conjoined to life-as-the-end-of-estrangement-from-God, and thus never-ending fellowship with the triune God.

This eternal life does not wait upon the moment of death. It begins now. So the letter of John:

> I write these things to you who believe in the name of the Son of God, so that you may know that you have eternal life. (1 John 5:13)

For the believer the estrangement of God has ended and the promise of life with God is forever assured.

The victory over death in the eternal life of the faithful is the continuing work of the royal office. With it is the continuing work of the Prophet whose Word draws the believer into a "knowing" like no other. And the continuing work of Priest renders personal through saving faith the sacrifice made once and for all on Calvary.

The beneficence of the triune God wills mutuality not alone for persons in communion with deity, but also in human-to-human relationships. In this story there is no God without the kingdom of God, the hope

25. P. Mark Achtemeier has shown the importance of the *Unio cum Christo* teaching in the Reformed tradition, beginning with Calvin, in "The Union with Christ Doctrine in Renewal Movements in the Presbyterian Church (USA)," *Reformed Theology: Identity and Ecumenicity* (Grand Rapids: Eerdmans, 2003), pp. 336-45.

26. Carl E. Braaten and Robert E. Jenson, eds., *Union with Christ: The New Finnish Interpretation of Luther* (Grand Rapids: Eerdmans, 1998).

for its final coming being at the center of Jesus' own message and its earnest in his very being among us. The ultimate community is one in which

> the nations will walk by its light and the kings of the earth will bring their glory into it. (Rev. 21:24)

Salvation is from suffering, misery, war, injustice, and error in and among human beings as well as rescue from the sin that lies behind all the inglories of our fallen world. Believers look for that kind of ultimate life together. Indeed they participate in its fragmentary life together here and now, as members of the body of Christ that exists as a sign and portent of the kingdom to come, albeit in the broken form of a community, like their own eternal life, *simul iustus et peccator*. And more, they can share in, and are called to be in solidarity with, yet other signs of the divine intention for the world walking together: the struggle for bread, justice, and peace, the witness to God's will for our harmony with nature as well as neighbor. All these things will finally be in the realm that has no end, and as such, are a lure and mandate for our participation in those dimensions of life together right now.

How are not these penultimate signs of what is to come also the portion of others who know no "union with Christ"? The generosity of the triune God is such that these penultimate portents of what is to be in and among persons, among nations, and with nature are everywhere to be seen. Indeed, without them the story would close before its center and end. Thus we return to the rainbow light and life of God, the multiple gifts of a universal grace that preserves the fallen world. Here is Christ's general revelation spread in many and diverse ways across creation, in worlds religious and secular, wherever "human life is made and kept human,"[27] suffering and physical death assuaged, ignorance challenged, justice done, peace made in hearts, homes, and on the battlefields of nations and nature. There the extra-ecclesial work of Prophet, Priest, and King is done by the power of the Spirit according to the will of the Father. While not "life eternal," it is the good "life earthly," a broken mirror in a fallen world of the kingdom yet to come.

In this chapter we meet once again the uniqueness of Jesus Christ. The "foolishness" to the Greeks (1 Cor. 1:23) is unambiguously affirmed in the

---

27. A formula widespread in the "secular mission" accents of the 1960s, as in Colin Williams, *Where in the World?* (New York: National Council of Churches, 1963).

accent on *sola fide*. Only by faith in Jesus Christ does a person enter eternal life, being so brought into the divine Community. Graced faith saves from the ultimate estrangement.

At the same time, a generous universality is asserted in conjunction with the scandalous particularity. Christ does not abandon in this world those who do not hear and receive the Word. Temporal life — as the relief from suffering, release from the fears and pains of physical death, lightening the darkness of ignorance — is made possible through the many and varied streams of common grace, not the least being those at work in the world's religions. Such is also a work of worldly rescue done by the hidden Christ.[28]

Chapter 7

The final chapter in the Christian story has to do with "last things." In creedal summary they are: the return of Christ, the resurrection of the dead, final judgment, and everlasting life.[29] "Christ will come again," as we confess in the liturgy, the dead will join the "quick" before Christ in the Great Assize, and for the faithful, life with God in the eternal realm will climax the purposes of the Creator for creation.

"What about those who have not heard?" asks a recent book.[30] So is raised the ultimate personal question about the relation of the uniqueness of Christ to the world religions. And more, to the billions of persons who have not heard the saving Word before Christ and beyond the church. And yet more, how the purposes of the all-loving and almighty God can be fulfilled while there are yet those who are consigned to eternal death rather than granted eternal life. To answer these questions, we must go first through a doorway into the last things, the "next-to-last things" — "the intermediate state" — the interim between our death and the fourfold End.

28. Note the two means of "salvation" in *Cruden's* famous 1737 *Concordance*, salvation as "deliverance from sin and its consequences" and also "preservation from trouble or danger" (561).

29. For their exploration see Fackre, *The Christian Story*, vol. 1, pp. 210-34.

30. John Sanders, Ronald Nash, and Gabriel Fackre, eds., *What about Those Who Have Never Heard? Three Views on the Destiny of the Unevangelized* (Downers Grove, Ill.: InterVarsity Press, 1995).

The resurrection means that Christ ranges over all creation, including the realm of the dead. Read christologically, the Psalmist says

... where can I flee from your presence? If I ascend to heaven you are there. If I make my bed in Sheol you are there. . . . (Ps. 139:8)

With that in mind, the Apostles Creed has us declare that Christ "descended to the dead." Earlier generations of theologians took that to mean that believing Jews before Christ heard on Holy Saturday from the lips of the descended Christ about the triune Source of their own justifying faith, and hearing so confessed. Later Christian thinkers, who, from the missionary movements of their day, had their consciousness raised about the vast numbers unreached by the gospel, took yet another step. We take it with them.

Nineteenth-century missionaries to the Pacific's Sandwich Islands (now Hawaii) were asked by converts shaped by a deep reverence for their forebears, "What of my ancestors? Will they go to hell because they have not heard the gospel?" The question was passed on to the faculty of Andover Seminary in Massachusetts that had spawned the era's North American outreach overseas. To the creed they turned and to the New Testament texts behind it (eminently 1 Peter 3:18-20; 4:6) and concluded that the divine perseverance could not be stopped by the gates of death. The Hound of Heaven breached them and pursued the last and the least. Thus Christ spoke the Word to those who had not heard, for

the gospel was proclaimed even to the dead. (1 Peter 4:6)

When so understood, this passage opened one's eyes to the similar import of others (Matt. 8:11; 12:40; Luke 13:28-30; John 5:25-29; Acts 3:21, 25; Rom. 10:7; Eph. 1:9ff.; 4:8-9, Col. 1:20; Phil. 2:10f.; Heb. 9:15; 1 John 2:2; Rev. 1:18; 5:13; 21:25). Although it was articulated by earlier European nineteenth-century theologians,[31] it came to be called in America "the Andover theory," or "postmortem evangelism" as it is sometimes described.[32] This view

31. As for example Isaac Dorner. See *Dorner on the Future State,* trans. with introduction and notes by Newman Smyth (New York: Charles Scribner's Sons, 1883), pp. 91-112. For a review of the literature, see John Sanders, *No Other Name: An Investigation into the Destiny of the Unevangelized* (Grand Rapids: Eerdmans, 1992), pp. 177-214.

32. See Thomas P. Field, "The 'Andover Theory' of Future Probation," *The Andover Review* 7 (May 1887): 461-75.

is now espoused by evangelical thinkers of the stature of Donald Bloesch and George Lindbeck.[33] Its strength has to do with an unswerving commitment to the uniqueness of Christ with special reference to Chapter 6 of the story — the New Testament association of salvation with the confession of Christ in numerous New Testament references,[34] along with the Christian story's overall trajectory that purposes the Good News for all people. At the heart of this double accent is the resurrection of Jesus Christ. Only as a risen Lord carrying forth his threefold ministry can the prophetic Word be spoken to all, the priestly sacrifice be made available to all, and the royal power to breach the gates of death make possible the universal prophetic and priestly work.

If there is no one excluded from the good Word, why would not its power convict and convert every hearer? Isn't the persevering love of God that universally seeks out the last and the least of a piece with the persevering love of God that would seek as well "universal salvation"? The homecoming of all by the grace of God appears to be a logical partner to the pursuit of all by the grace of a God who will not stop short of the total life together intended for creation. Such has been argued by great minds of the church from yesterday's Origen to a company of today's ardent evangelicals.[35]

As Scripture is the source for our Story, does it speak of a universal homecoming? One reference to "all" does appear in Paul's searching inquiry into the destiny of the Jewish people. So the assertion that "all Israel will be saved" in his letter to the church at Rome (Rom. 11:26).[36] While, together with the affirmation that "the gifts and call" of the chosen are "irrevocable," an anti-supersessionist case can be made,[37] the exegetical complexities of that "all" are too many to build a case for the salvation of every Jewish believer on a single verse. And as for the whole of the human race,

---

33. George Lindbeck, *The Nature of Doctrine: Religion and Theology in a Postliberal Age* (Philadelphia: Westminster Press, 1984), pp. 57-63, and Donald Bloesch, *The Last Things: Resurrection, Judgment, Glory* (Downers Grove, Ill.: InterVarsity Press, 2004), pp. 44-47, 277-78.

34. See Fackre, *The Christian Story,* vol. 1, pp. 219-20.

35. See the evangelical pros and cons in Robin Parry and Christopher Partridge, eds., *Universal Salvation? The Current Debate* (Carlisle, UK: Paternoster Press, 2003).

36. Of course, 1 Tim. 2:4 speaks of God "who desires everyone to be saved . . . ," short, however, of the unambiguous assertion of universal salvation.

37. Investigated in Chapter 7.

the New Testament message is clear that a double destination for the sheep and the wolves is integral to the End. And it is no less than Jesus Christ himself, the judge of the living and the dead, who will send each on their respective paths (Matt. 25:31-46).

Yet, it is fair to ask: how long the path? If the fires of hell are the fires of love — how can they be other than so purposed if their source is in the Christ of the divine Life Together? Then is the burning road lasting, or everlasting? Can fires be cleansing, and punishment rehabilitating? We put these as questions that do not lend themselves to clear biblical answers. *Apokatastasis* is not a teaching of Scripture and cannot be a doctrine of the church. Yet the trajectory of the story we have been following is toward the fulfillment of God's purposes. And about a Lord persisting and a love persevering beyond the grave. But that all-seeking God as the all-loving One that will not let us go is by nature invitatory, working not by despotic force but by persuasion, as the Fathers asserted ever and again. An eternal No is our option then as well as now.[38] Or if this C. S. Lewis–like judgment seems to grant too much to human choice, then let the modesty fall on the Calvinist side, and say, it is God's decision, not ours that will determine just how the divine intention for life together will be achieved. But surely we have to do, here in eternity as in time, with the paradox of grace, "I . . . yet not I . . ." (1 Cor. 15:10).[39] On no basis, our choice or God's, or the more profound paradoxical both/and, can we forecast a universal homecoming. At best, as with Barth, it is an article of hope, not an article of faith.[40]

---

38. C. S. Lewis, *The Great Divorce* (New York: Macmillan, 1946).

39. For wise words of struggle on this perennial question, see Paul Jewett, *Election and Predestination* (Grand Rapids: Eerdmans, 1985), pp. 106-15.

40. See Barth: "If we are certainly forbidden to count on this as though we had a claim to it, as though it were not supremely a work of God to which man can have no possible claim, we are surely commanded the more definitely to hope and pray for it as we may do already on this side of this final possibility. I.e., to hope and pray cautiously and yet distinctly that, in spite of everything which may seem quite conclusively to proclaim the opposite, His compassion should not fail, and that in accordance with His mercy which is 'new every morning' He 'will not cast off forever' (Lam. 3:22f., 31)." Barth, *Church Dogmatics,* IV/3, first part, p. 478.

Conclusion

Our survey of the path God has taken to fulfill the divine purposes has been from its peak point in the resurrection of Jesus Christ. From this site, we see second-hand what the disciples first viewed in the flesh. Discernment of the turn in the trail, yes. But more, for the risen Christ there defeated eternal death as well as disclosed its end. Thus a fourth "R" made possible the "3 Rs" that define the uniqueness of Jesus Christ. Resurrection is the guarantor of reconciliation, revelation, and redemption. We have traversed in this narrative the journey of the One who is and wills communion with and for the world from creation through the fall, to the covenant with Noah and its multi-colored preserving grace from which the world's religions are not excluded to the irrevocable special covenant with Israel, one that leads to the singular deed done in Christ, the birth of the church, the flow of salvation and the consummation of the divine plan. At its center, we find the only *way* God made into our midst to bring reconciliation out of alienation, and with it the definitive *truth* of revelation and the derivative *life* of our redemption. Both the pilgrimage over time, and its decisive center, are the Work of the second Person of the triune God, in response to the Father's will and by the power of the Holy Spirit. All along the storyline it has been, is, and will be, in church and world, the Prophet, Priest, and King who brings the light and life of rainbow, pillar of fire, Easter sunrise, and the meridian yet to come.

Conclusion

Our premise in this work has been that classical Christology must be interpreted, ever and again, in the context of our varied todays. Yet context is ecclesial as well as cultural, especially so for an attempt at pastoral systematics. What then is the state of the church in which today's pastors preach and teach about the Person and Work of Christ? That conjunction of Sunday text (or Monday textbook) and social context will be the burden of Volume 5 of this *Christian Story* series, the doctrine of the church. For now, however, a footnote on the state of the church as it bears on Christology.

According to some current commentary, our ecclesial context is not a hospitable one. R. R. Reno speaks of his own effort to steward the gospel as one carried on, as his title says, *In the Ruins of the Church.*[1] Chronicling cultural captivity in doctrine and practice, worship and witness, his problem, as his subtitle states, is the question of "sustaining faith in an age of diminished Christianity."

As sharp as Reno's indictment is from within, Alan Wolfe, from outside the church, goes him one better, as noted in the Introduction. Indeed, the latter commentator holds his exposure of religious hypocrisy to be a cause for comfort. Jonathan Edwards, Wolfe's symbol of a take-charge religion

---

1. R. R. Reno, *In the Ruins of the Church: Sustaining Faith in an Age of Diminished Christianity* (Grand Rapids: Brazos Press, 2002).

inimical to the well-being of our secular society, is dead. To us in the church the word is: your Christianity is a toothless tiger.[2]

The analyses of both Reno and Wolfe have their shortcomings. Reno concentrates on his own Episcopal habitat, whose problems have a specificity that cannot be neatly transported to other locales. Wolfe's pop research lacks scholarly depth, relying often on anecdotal evidence and unidentified sources, and showing ignorance of comparable critical studies of the same phenomena.[3] However, the disparity between profession and practice in the contemporary church that both authors argue for can be seen everywhere. The point of these critiques, from both within and without the church, cannot be ignored. Pastors who preach and teach the Person and Work of Christ do so in an environment that militates against their fundamental premises.

We have been exploring in this volume the counter-Word that needs to be heard "today," one that includes the ecclesial diagnoses of Reno and Wolfe. Karl Barth speaks it well in the rest of his reminder to beleaguered British Christians of another time and place:

> The present age is the time of God's long-suffering until the day when the same Jesus Christ shall come in His glory. . . . Although at present the glory of the Kingdom of God is held out to us only as a hope, yet the Kingly rule of Christ extends not merely over the Church as the congregation of the faithful but, regardless of whether men believe it or not, over the whole of the universe in all its heights

---

2. Alan Wolfe, *The Transformation of American Religion: How We Actually Live Our Faith* (New York: Free Press, 2003).

3. I am drawing on the conclusions of a study group that spent many months working through both volumes. For example, Wolfe's argument that change in the "tradition" of a given religion, induced by the American ethos of change, demonstrates that its substance has been eroded. He is innocent of the long theological examination of the distinction between "tradition" and "traditionalism" (as in Jaroslav Pelikan's studies with their deft aphorism, "the living faith of the dead" and the "dead faith of the living"), the Vatican II affirmation of *aggiornamento* in tradition, the concept of the development of doctrine that views change along the line of a trajectory from the past as a welcome state of affairs, Karl Barth's Reformed stress on the divine sovereignty noted earlier that looks forward to the revision of tradition as a work of the Holy Spirit, and much similar affirmation of "change" as integral to rather than departure from tradition. For a more careful review of the same data see Vincent Miller, *Consuming Religion: Christian Faith and Practice in a Consumer Culture* (New York: Continuum, 2004).

and depths; and it also confronts and overrules with sovereign dignity the principalities and powers and evil spirits of this world. . . . It is only as shadows without real substance and power that they can still beset us. We Christians . . . have no right whatsoever to fear and respect them or to resign ourselves to the fact that they are spreading throughout the world as though they know neither bounds nor lord. We should be slighting the resurrection of Jesus Christ and denying His reign on the right hand of the Father, if we forgot that the world in which we live is already consecrated, and if we did not, for Christ's sake, come to grips spiritedly and resolutely with these evil spirits.[4]

Yes, given this Work of Christ, we "have no right to fear and respect" the "powers and principalities" that wreak havoc on our world and in our churches. No right to be servile before fact.

What Barth does not say, at least not here, when the evidence of the natural eye did show that the "evil spirits" were "spreading throughout the world as though they know neither bounds nor lord," is that the resurrection of Christ from the dead and his rule over both church and world are not without *signs* of that sovereignty even short of the kingdom's full and final coming.[5] So the dramatic growth of Christianity in the world beyond the West testifies to a vitality not found in the "diminished Christianity" that Reno and Wolfe chronicle.[6] And within the West, indeed in this nation, we take heart at the evidence of resistance to the acculturation of the church that is visible to the eye of sight as well as the eye of faith.[7] The Work of Christ done in prophetic, priestly, and royal ministries, both then and now, examined in the preceding pages, is the counter-message that is ours to steward as we "come to grips spiritedly" with our own demons.

What Christ has done, does, and will do is made possible by who Christ is. As affirmed throughout this investigation, the Work is inseparable from

---

4. Karl Barth, *Letter to Great Britain from Switzerland* (London: Sheldon Press, 1941), pp. 9, 10.

5. He says it elsewhere, as in *Church Dogmatics* IV/3, first part.

6. Philip Jenkins, *The Next Christendom: The Growth of Global Christianity* (New York: Oxford University Press, 2002).

7. I document such in my own small corner of the church universal, itself too often a showcase of the cultural accommodation to which Reno and Wolfe point. See Gabriel Fackre, *Believing, Caring and Doing in the United Church of Christ* (Cleveland: Pilgrim Press, 2005).

the Person. So John Milton will have the final say on that Bethlehem, and sum up, as well, the burden of this book.

> Ring out ye Crystall spheares. . . .
> speckl'd vanity
> Will sicken soon and die,
> And leprous sin will melt from earthly mould . . .
> And sullen Moloch fled . . .
> He feels from Juda's Land
> The dreaded Infant's hand . . .
> Nor all the gods beside
> Longer dare abide . . .
> Our Babe to shew his Godhead true
> Can in his swaddling bands controul the damned crew.[8]

8. "Hymn on the Morning of Christ's Nativity," *The Oxford Book of English Verse*, ed. Arthur Quiller-Couch (Oxford, 1919).

Index

Index